POLITICAL ENGLISH

POLITICAL ENGLISH

Language and the Decay of Politics

Thomas Docherty

BLOOMSBURY ACADEMIC
LONDON • NEW YORK • OXFORD • NEW DELHI • SYDNEY

Bloomsbury Academic
Bloomsbury Publishing Plc
50 Bedford Square, London, WC1B 3DP, UK
1385 Broadway, New York, NY 10018, USA

BLOOMSBURY, BLOOMSBURY ACADEMIC and the Diana logo are trademarks
of Bloomsbury Publishing Plc

First published in Great Britain 2019

Copyright © Thomas Docherty, 2019

Thomas Docherty has asserted his right under the Copyright, Designs and Patents Act,
1988, to be identified as Author of this work.

Cover design: Eleanor Rose
Cover image © Getty Images

All rights reserved. No part of this publication may be reproduced or transmitted
in any form or by any means, electronic or mechanical, including photocopying,
recording, or any information storage or retrieval system, without prior permission
in writing from the publishers.

Bloomsbury Publishing Plc does not have any control over, or responsibility for,
any third-party websites referred to or in this book. All internet addresses given in this
book were correct at the time of going to press. The author and publisher regret any
inconvenience caused if addresses have changed or sites have ceased to exist, but
can accept no responsibility for any such changes.

A catalogue record for this book is available from the British Library.

Library of Congress Cataloging-in-Publication Data
Names: Docherty, Thomas, 1955- author.
Title: Political English: Language and the Decay of Politics / Thomas Docherty.
Description: New York, NY: Bloomsbury Academic, [2019] | Includes bibliographical
references and index.
Identifiers: LCCN 2018055637 | ISBN 9781350101395 (hb) | ISBN 9781350101388 (pb)
Subjects: LCSH: Language and languages–Political aspects. | English language–
Political aspects. | Communication in politics.
Classification: LCC P119.3.D63 2019 | DDC 320.01/4–dc23
LC record available at https://lccn.loc.gov/2018055637

ISBN: HB: 978-1-3501-0139-5
PB: 978-1-3501-0138-8
ePDF: 978-1-3501-0141-8
eBook: 978-1-3501-0140-1

Typeset by Deanta Global Publishing Services, Chennai, India

To find out more about our authors and books visit www.bloomsbury.com
and sign up for our newsletters.

For Bridie May Sullivan and Hamish Docherty

CONTENTS

Introduction 1

1 On pluck: English and money 13

2 English nativism and linguistic xenophobia 33

3 Fundamentalist English: The stiff upper lip 67

4 On truth and lying in a political sense 95

5 Words, deeds and democracy 137

6 Profanity and free speech 165

7 Remnants of dissent: Free speech, political silence and guilt 191

Select bibliography 229
Index 234

INTRODUCTION

> *Prospero: I pitied thee,*
> *Took pains to make thee speak, taught thee each hour*
> *One thing or other: when thou didst not, savage,*
> *Know thine own meaning, but wouldst gabble like*
> *A thing most brutish, I endow'd thy purposes*
> *With words that made them known.*
> *Caliban: You taught me language; and my profit on't*
> *Is, I know how to curse. The red plague rid you*
> *For learning me your language!*
> **(SHAKESPEARE, *THE TEMPEST*, ACT 1; SCENE 2)**

'To write poetry after Auschwitz is barbaric'. Adorno made this claim first in 1949, in an essay on 'Cultural Criticism and Society'.[1] The statement invites at least two ostensibly mutually incompatible questions. Can there be a language that is adequate to atrocity? And, even if there is, how dare we minimize atrocity by finding a language that adequately respects the extent of a political atrocity such as Auschwitz? The question posed in the book you are about to read is related to this. What happens when political language itself becomes so vicious and degraded that it itself becomes an occasion of atrocity? What happens when the condition of our political debates is such that the language itself damages the lives of those citizens who are subjected to it, and even subjected by it?

When Adorno reiterated his argument again, in 1968, he wrote that 'I do not want to soften my statement that it is barbaric to continue

---

[1] Theodor Adorno, *Prisms* (trans. Samuel and Shierry Weber; MIT Press, Cambridge, MA, 1983), 34.

to write poetry after Auschwitz'. However, he also added that literature 'must ... be such that it does not surrender to cynicism' because 'the abundance of real suffering permits no forgetting'.[2] There can be little doubt, obviously, that poetry continues to exist even after the most extreme atrocities. Equally, there can be little doubt that much of this poetry is edifying. In 1949, the essential burden of Adorno's question was whether there can ever be a language that is not only adequate to but also respectful of atrocity. In this book, I am wondering about a related issue. What if the real issue since 1945 is that Adorno's concern has been answered by the normalization of a language that is atrocious in and of itself? What if atrocities, committed in and through our political discourses, might occasion the decay of an entire cultural and personal life?

More recently, Seamus Heaney pondered similar issues. He pointed out, in a lecture entitled 'The Government of the Tongue', that, 'faced with the brutality of the historical onslaught', poems and the imaginative arts in general 'are practically useless'. While it is true that 'the efficacy of poetry is nil – no lyric has ever stopped a tank', nonetheless poems 'verify our singularity' and confirm our individuated existence. They do this provided their language is 'mannerly', and such a mannerly poetry 'does not trace the given map of a better reality but improvises an inspired sketch of it'.[3] Poetry, in the face of historical atrocity, can earn its keep by becoming a custodian of the language as such, with a view to offering us a route away from the repetition of atrocity, or the potential legitimation of atrocity through a stultifying reduction of it to a silencing cliché. If this is so, then – and this is the case especially after Auschwitz – we need such poetry more than ever before.

In less extreme mode, but in terms that are increasingly pertinent to the contemporary moment, Heaney was once asked what he felt about Joseph Brodsky's suggestion that poetry 'should, like the Gideon Bible, be available in hotel rooms and should be distributed like handouts at supermarket checkouts'. His reply was that, although there is no doubt a playfulness involved in Brodsky's idea, nonetheless it might be taken more seriously. His response was that 'a populace that is chloroformed day and night by TV stations like Fox News could do with inoculation by

---

[2]Theodor Adorno, *Notes to Literature*, vol. 2, ed. Rolf Tiedemann (trans. Shierry Weber Nicholsen; Columbia University Press, New York, 1992), 87–8.
[3]Seamus Heaney, *The Government of the Tongue* (Faber and Faber, 1988), 94, 107.

poetry. Obviously, poetry can't be administered like an injection, but it does constitute a boost to the capacity for discrimination and resistance'.[4]

The political rhetoric of our contemporary moment – conditioned partly by a voice that is utterly 'informed' by Fox News, such as the voice and battered lexicon of Donald Trump – is anything other than mannerly. It is conditioned by boastful egocentricity, insult, diatribe and violence; in its display of resentment and anger, it is often barely coherent; it prefers coercion to charm; it demands thoughtless affirmation based on tribal affiliation; it determinedly reduces the range of thought as it infantilizes its vocabulary. Such degraded language, emanating as it does from the office of political authority, engenders the decay of daily and living politics. With this, there is no map of a better reality; rather, there is the ravaging of our political landscape. The paradox, obviously, is that even in describing this Trumpian language accurately, one is in danger of falling into exactly the same lexicon that one wishes to excoriate. Thus it is that the possibility of an edifying democratic discourse is menaced. Part of my point in this book will be to note that Trump's language is no longer utterly exceptional; rather, his linguistic tactics and strategies are increasingly deployed by so-called 'respectable' politicians as well as by the more obvious demagogues who patrol our political realms today.

In what follows here, I will explore the relation of political language to political realities. It is important to note here that this book is not simply a jeremiad about the imperilled state of our democracies; rather, I try to understand the ways in which our social, cultural and political lives are shaped by our modes of address, by the ways in which we relate to each other in our differing views and beliefs. At its most fundamental, the book holds the view that politics is that institution that seeks to circumvent the damage inherent in what, without the political compass, would be the resolution of differences through violence. We might agree, more or less cynically, with Clausewitz's famous proposition that 'war is a continuation of political commerce … by other means', but, in this book, what will be at issue is the precise nature of those 'other means', especially in terms of political rhetoric.

* * *

---

[4]Dennis O'Driscoll, *Stepping Stones: Interviews with Seamus Heaney* (Faber and Faber, 2008), 381.

But first, an actual war. On 28 October 1914, a young Austrian concert pianist found himself in the trenches of the Great War, fighting against the Russian forces. He was shot in the elbow, and the injury was so severe that his right arm had to be amputated. His name was Paul Wittgenstein. When his younger brother, Ludwig, heard the news, he wrote 'How terrible! What philosophy will ever assist one to overcome a fact of this sort?'[5] The question of philosophy was much on Ludwig's mind, for this was the period when he was abandoning a potential career as an aviation engineer and becoming instead the philosopher whose work would centre so much on questions of language. At the moment of Paul's disaster – and while he himself was also facing mortal dangers on the battlefield front lines – he was making his notes towards the *Tractatus Logico-Philosophicus*, which would eventually be published in 1922.

That book closes with a famous formulation that, in some ways, prefigures the thinking behind Adorno's later famous claim. Ludwig Wittgenstein survived the 'June Advance' of 1916, when the Russians (led by General Aleksei Brusilov) launched one of their few extremely successful attacks on this particular battlefield front, and during which his fellow soldiers suffered massive injuries. It was really from this moment, two years after hearing of Paul's injury and now witnessing directly the concrete and material effects of war, that he started to develop a new philosophical attitude. In notes made in 1916, he recorded that 'there are, indeed, things that cannot be put into words. They *make themselves manifest*.'[6]

It is clear that Wittgenstein's philosophy of language comes up against the fundamental facts of empirical and physical violence in the face of the political realities of war. War is no longer a mere abstract concept but a set of material realities. The war forces him to raise a philosophical question that asks about the adequacy or otherwise of a language to respond to material and historical sensations, such as the body in pain. There can be no doubt that this informs that famous final proposition of the *Tractatus*, the proposition that prefigures Adorno on Auschwitz: 'Whereof one

---

[5] Ray Monk, *Wittgenstein: The Duty of Genius* (Vintage, 1991), 141. Monk is citing from MS 101. See also Brian McGuinness, *Wittgenstein: A Life* (Duckworth, 1988), 223.
[6] Monk, *Wittgenstein*, 142. (This eventually reappears in the *Tractatus* as proposition 6.522.) Emphasis in original.

cannot speak, thereof one must be silent.'[7] In fact, however, while Wittgenstein himself thought this, his brother, Paul, was anything but silent. He determinedly overcame his personal physical injury, returning from war to arrange and adapt many existing piano compositions, and even eventually commissioning some pieces by celebrated composers such as Hindemith, Korngold and – most famously – Ravel's 'Piano Concerto for the Left Hand, in D Major'.

So, while Ludwig was thinking that the only response to the situation could be suicide – or, in philosophy, silence – Paul was answering Ludwig's despairing question of how philosophy responds to political realities differently. Paul – no doubt with great personal qualities of stoicism and a profound resilience – called upon art, specifically on the *poiesis* or making of music as the key to survival and a good life. A half-century later, when Adorno himself came to write about the music of Schoenberg, and especially the 1947 piece *Survivor from Warsaw*, he argued that here, at least and at last, was some kind of adequate response to atrocity. 'Horror', Adorno wrote, 'has never rung as true in music, and by articulating it music regains its redeeming power.'[8] Perhaps art – poetry or music – can indeed redeem atrocity; and perhaps, therefore, an adequate language can be found that will address political realities. The question is whether this language can actually *inform* or shape such political realities.

It is noteworthy too that Adorno begins his essay on Schoenberg with an epigraph from the poetry of Keats, who, having described his Grecian Urn as an 'unravish'd bride of quietness' and 'foster-child of silence and slow time', says that 'Heard melodies are sweet, but those unheard / Are sweeter; therefore, ye soft pipes, play on'.[9] The importance of finding a language adequate to all that is unspeakable has, indeed, a long history. For Wittgenstein, it became a central preoccupation. In his outstanding biography of Wittgenstein, Ray Monk argues that the 'central message' of the *Tractatus* is concerned above all 'to preserve the purity of language by exposing to ridicule the confused thought that stems from its misuse',

---

[7] Ludwig Wittgenstein, *Tractatus Logico-Philosophicus* (trans. C.K. Ogden; bilingual edn; Routledge, 1992), 188–9.
[8] Adorno, *Prisms*, 172.
[9] John Keats, 'Ode on a Grecian Urn', in *Poetical Works*, ed. H.W. Garrod (Oxford University Press, 1976), 209.

adding that 'the nonsense that results from trying to say what can only be shown is not only logically untenable, but ethically undesirable'.[10]

* * *

All of this is a world away from the simplistic language of today's populist political rhetoric. What music or poetry is there in the execrable outbursts and twitter-fed banalities of Donald Trump, say, or, indeed, in the equally vituperative responses to his Calibanesque language? Trump is, however, simply the most recent and most egregious example of a general tendency to degraded language among our major politicians. Did it dignify the quality of debate when Conservative MP Boris Johnson referred to Nick Clegg, the then (Liberal Democrat) deputy Prime Minister in the Coalition administration of 2010, as a 'prophylactic protection device' – a condom – for Conservative Prime Minister David Cameron, or that the liberal satirical cartoonist Steve Bell depicted Cameron with a condom always covering his head (and thus as 'a dickhead')? How edifying was it, for example, to hear Nicholas Sarkozy describe, in deliberately inflammatory terms, the disenfranchised people living in the banlieues of Paris as 'bandes de racaille' (broadly translatable as 'rabble' or 'scum')? Did it help when Sarkozy's ultra-leftist opponent, the philosopher Alain Badiou, called Sarkozy 'Rat-Man' in response? Was Silvio Berlusconi's description of Angela Merkel as 'an unfuckable lard-arse' a positive contribution to international relations?[11] Is the excremental savagery of Putin's attacks on his many perceived enemies usefully enlightening or uplifting?

These are but a very small sample – not even the worst – of a contemporary degraded political language, and some of this will be explored in detail in this book. Some will believe that we have come a long way from the seemingly much gentler or discreet political insults of even a recent generation, as when Labour's Denis Healey described Margaret Thatcher as 'La Pasionaria of middle-class privilege', or when he said that debating with his Conservative opponent Geoffrey Howe

---

[10]Monk, *Wittgenstein*, 156. Monk cites Wittgenstein's letter of 9 April 1917 to Paul Engelmann: 'this is how it is: if only you do not try to utter what is unutterable then *nothing* gets lost. But the unutterable will be – unutterably – *contained* in what has been uttered' (ibid., 151).

[11]Questioned directly about this, Berlusconi was evasive: he did not actually deny saying it, noting only that it was a political opponent who reported it.

was 'like being savaged by a dead sheep'. Yet it would be a simplistic falsification to suggest that the current position represents a significant new turn in political rhetoric. As early as 1946, for example, Orwell wrote 'Politics and the English Language', arguing that there is an intimate link between the decline of a language and decay in the political and economic sphere in which the language is spoken. He asserts that most people at the time 'would admit that the English language is in a bad way', and he suggests that, for most, 'Our civilization is decadent and our language – so the argument runs – must inevitably share in the general collapse'.[12] For Orwell, the dynamics are clear: degeneracy in economic and political actuality produces degenerate language as a new norm. It is as if the language seeks the appropriate vocabulary for a malevolent social condition and finds that the only vocabulary or lexicon is one that itself falls into decay.

However, what if the dynamics were different from this? What if linguistic decadence produces new political norms that are as crude as the dominant modes of a society's speech? Is there not at least a dialectic at work, or a mutually reinforcing structure in which both language and political realities can enter a spiral of horror, mutually reinforcing a gravitational pull downwards into the gross brutalities of hand-to-hand fighting in the muddier trenches of a war-zone: a narrowed vocabulary, as in Orwellian Newspeak, narrowing the range of human possibilities, possibilities that we would usually describe as the extension of our freedoms? This book explores that question. Behind it lies the serious implication of Clausewitz: is a degraded and degrading political language the first skirmish in the provocations towards actual violence, even war?

* * *

Something is rotten in the state of English.

If this is so, would it follow that something is also rotten in the state of England? The English language has a peculiar and particular standing in relation to these issues. While I will also briefly consider some examples of political discourse in other languages and jurisdictions (French, Italian, German and Russian, primarily), the focus will primarily be on English and its intrinsic political muscle. English claims a standing as

---

[12]George Orwell, 'Politics and the English Language' (1946), repr. in Orwell, *Inside the Whale* (Penguin, 1972), 143.

one of the world's most important languages. It is often the language of international commerce and communication and is a dominant medium for most contemporary technological platforms. To explore the political structure of how this language works is also to explore the political structure of world governance in our time.

When the character of Marcellus, in Shakespeare's *Hamlet*, says that 'something is rotten in the state of Denmark', he is addressing a very specific situation. His concern is primarily about political decadence. Prior to the play's action, we are told, Old Hamlet (now the Ghost) had wagered and won a significant tract of land from Norway. Now, young Fortinbras of Norway is mounting an insurrection and planning to attack Denmark to get the land back. This is common knowledge among the Danish. The rot that Marcellus detects derives from the fact that the new Danish king, Claudius, carouses carelessly in the face of this insurgent violence.

The rot lies in two things: an inadequate response to the political reality of impending war and the deviation from political realities into the luxuriousness of the sexual self-indulgence of Claudius and Gertrude. This represents something that has its contemporary counterpart in a sense that establishment politicians live in a world apart from the citizens over whom they exert power, and that these politicians indulge their own selfish desires for power while the rest of society is engaged in a daily struggle for a good life. Contemporary serious media increasingly also follows the populist newspapers in diverting attention from serious political issues in order to attend voyeuristically and salaciously to the sexual activities of our politicians. With the resulting shrivelling of consciousness into pious hypocrisy, the lexicon of political debate shrinks from the public sphere into the private: a focus on activities in the boardroom gives way to an interest in the bedroom. This is one of the factors that, in Shakespeare, produced the political hesitations that stem from Hamlet's fevered imagination, and that provokes the eventual tragedy in which too many people die completely unnecessarily, while Fortinbras enters to assume political control.

Shakespeare was more than usually aware of the power of political rhetoric, and he was also engaged deeply in the question of how our use of language shapes a polity. I cited the celebrated exchange between Prospero and Caliban from *The Tempest* as my epigraph above, and that exchange is fundamentally about the ways in which language and politics are utterly intertwined. The standard reading of the relation between these characters situates them in a colonial and burgeoning imperialist power-struggle. Prospero establishes what will be the accepted lexicon of communication, and has a mastery of it, which leaves Caliban in the perennial position of the subservient. Yet Caliban can strike back, by using that very lexicon in an abusive fashion: the curse of empire is intrinsic to its own linguistic formulation.

This is of special importance in relation to the status of English, at least since the period in which Shakespeare is writing. The events that initiate the process by which English begins its global ascent to the position of a dominant world language is exactly coterminous with the moment when Shakespeare is making his plays, in fact. It is in 1603 that James, the monarch in a newly emergent 'United Kingdom', calls for 'a Bible well translated into English', a book that would yield 'a uniform translation ... done by the best learned in both universities, then reviewed by the bishops, presented to the privy council, lastly ratified by royal authority'.[13] One of the key things about the Authorized Version is that it is, among many other things, a commercial business enterprise. Robert Carroll and Stephen Prickett point out that all Bibles are 'partisan ... the product of a particular interest group – whether religious, commercial, or, increasingly nowadays, both'.[14] The political conditions informing the production of the Authorized Version are of great importance for a consideration of the contemporary standing of English as a global force.

The translators were bringing what were essentially the languages of the Middle East into an acceptable and comprehensible English form. This, however, was not something that stands above commerce and trade, and the consequence is that this Bible is itself a political engagement with what is the emergence of a world trading enterprise. Within this, there is the corollary that the very ideas that had constituted Middle Eastern life and that had informed their peoples were now essentially given a very specific form of legitimization, and that legitimization was encoded in the book that is written in English. This places England and English at the core of world communication and commerce. It is from this that Milton will essentially derive the observation that 'when God speaks, he speaks first of all to his Englishmen'. Even more extravagantly, just before the Authorized Version came into production, John Aylmer, Bishop of

---

[13] As cited in Robert Carroll and Stephen Prickett, eds, *The Bible: Authorized King James Version* (Oxford University Press, 1997), xxxvi.
[14] Carroll and Prickett, eds, *The Bible*, v.

London, had already made the claim that 'God is English', a claim that he would have felt to be justified by the very fact of the material existence of the King James Authorized Version.[15] This has its counterpart in the twentieth century, when Enoch Powell repeatedly claimed that English is 'the tongue made for telling the truth in'.[16]

It is from this history, through which the English language assumes a kind of absolutist and fundamentalist status, that it rises to become a dominant world language. The politics of that dynamic growth and power, once analysed, will help us to see more clearly the status not just of the English language but also of the political construction of 'the English' as a people. It is this that sits at the cornerstone of Churchill's belief in the status of 'the English-speaking peoples', a construction that has its contemporary political counterpart in the so-called Anglosphere that sits at the centre of Anglo-Atlanticism, and that sees England's desire to ally itself, politically and culturally, with America. If there is indeed a world-English, it is now, of course, a world-American-English, thanks not just to technology but also to brute economics and political standing. In all of this, deriving from 1603 and the status of the Authorized Version, there arises a particular confusion in which the *medium* of the English language is identified with the *message* of a putative divine authority. The modern account of this is found, of course, in Marshall McLuhan's famous formulation in 1964 that 'the medium is the message'.[17] Obviously, however, this American-English as an absolutist or fundamentalist site of intrinsic truth, guaranteed by the medium of the language itself, has come under extreme pressure in the age of a 'post-truth' presidency and world politics.

* * *

Politics has always had an uneasy relation to truth. It is, indeed, a truth universally acknowledged that politicians do not tell the truth. In recent times, however, this has taken a troubling new turn. In the days of so-called post-truth politics, we have some politicians whose language is designed to make us call into question the very possibility that truth itself might exist. We may have thought that we had the classic formulation

---

[15]Christopher Hill, *Milton and the English Revolution* (Faber and Faber, 1979), 279–80.
[16]Enoch Powell, *Freedom and Reality*, ed. John Wood (B.T. Batsford, 1969), 256.
[17]Marshall McLuhan, *Understanding Media* (Routledge and Kegan Paul, 1964), 7ff.

of this when Kellyanne Conway denied the empirically verifiable facts regarding the size of the crowds at Trump's presidential inauguration. When she endorsed Sean Spicer's obviously fallacious claim that the crowds at the inauguration were the greatest number ever, Chuck Todd, the CNN reporter, challenged her. At this point, she invented the concept of 'alternative facts'. Instead of simply suggesting that there were different ways of looking at a fact, she here claims that the facts themselves do not have empirical substance or reality. The effect of this is to call the realm of fact itself into question.

However, this takes a yet further and more sinisterly menacing twist when Rudy Giuliani, Trump's lawyer, advised Trump against testifying in Special Prosecutor Robert Mueller's investigation into Russian meddling in the presidential election. Giuliani stated that Trump should not testify lest he should perjure himself. As a lawyer, Giuliani knows that perjury, in law, means 'something very precise': it is 'the act of willfully telling an untruth when on oath'. That definition presupposes that first of all, a witness knows that her or his statement is, if truthful, verifiable by validation against empirical facts, and second, that it is, in principle, possible to lie or 'willfully tell an untruth' regarding what the witness knows to be the factual case. Giuliani, however, now essentially denies the very possibility of any such validation of a statement at all. There is just 'the classic "he said she said" puzzle', he claimed, and it follows from this that 'Truth isn't truth'.[18] At a stroke, Giuliani here discards the entire concept of truth while, paradoxically, also claiming that anything that President Trump says is and must be true simply because it is President Trump who says it. This is a further advance not just on Spicer and Conway but on Trump's Republican nearly impeached precursor President Nixon, who asserted that 'when the President does it, that means it is not illegal'.[19]

Although Giuliani defended himself by stating that 'My statement was not meant as a pontification on moral theology', he was, in fact, making what is essentially a theocratic statement regarding the fundamentalist

---

[18]See transcript and video-recording at https://edition.cnn.com/2018/08/20/politics/rudy-giuliani-truth-isnt-truth-response/index.html (accessed 6 September 2018).

[19]See the transcript of the celebrated interview between David Frost and Richard Nixon, available at: https://www.theguardian.com/theguardian/2007/sep/07/greatinterviews1 (accessed 6 September 2018), and the report in the *New York Times*, available at: https://www.nytimes.com/1977/05/19/archives/nixon-says-a-president-can-order-illegal-actions-against-dissidents.html (accessed 6 September 2018).

veracity of Trump, as if Trump's word were equal in status to the biblical word of a god. Here, the word becomes equivalent to the deed, and deeds replace facts. At the extreme, this translates as 'violence replaces politics'.

* * *

This book looks at how we might understand the significance of political rhetoric, especially that conducted in English as a world language, in our time. That entails a consideration of the effectiveness of language, not just to make policy (word becoming deed) but also to critique policy (word modifying deed). Its closing section investigates the status of free speech and the power of dissent, especially in a period when free speech is often determined by money and economic considerations and when dissent is so effectively silenced by various political regimes. In the end, what is at stake in all of this is the condition of democracy, and the book makes a determined effort to revitalize the very idea of political democracy in an age where it is under threat in ways that are increasingly extreme and ideologically extremist.

1 ON PLUCK: ENGLISH AND MONEY

In October 2009, just nine months after taking office, President Barack Obama was awarded the Nobel Peace Prize. The citation commended 'his extraordinary efforts to strengthen international diplomacy and cooperation between peoples'. The award was controversial, and not just because, as Obama himself noted, he was 'at the beginning, and not the end, of my labors on the world stage'. Coming so early in his tenure, some might have reasonably thought that he was awarded the Prize 'for not being George W. Bush', whose presidency had led the United States and various allies into an ill-judged and quite possibly illegal war in Iraq. The Nobel press release stated explicitly that 'Obama has created a new climate in international politics' and noted his prioritization of language over force in matters of statecraft: 'Dialogue and negotiations are preferred as instruments for resolving even the most difficult international conflicts,' it noted.[1] Obama would be different from Bush. Indeed, Obama's presidential campaign had been characterized by a linguistic fluency and rhetorical persuasiveness that Bush had clearly lacked, and that John McCain, Obama's Republican opponent in 2008, could not hope to match.

Famously, Bush gave us an entire series of linguistic infelicities, telling us (for examples) how 'they misunderestimated me' or that 'the past is over'.[2] By contrast, Obama delivered an entire series of inspirational

---

[1] See 'The Nobel Peace Prize for 2009' [Press release], available at: https://www.nobelprize.org/nobel_prizes/peace/laureates/2009/press.html (accessed 9 January 2018).
[2] For an amusing series of these, see Richard Thompson, 'Make the Pie Higher', a 'poem' made up entirely of such phrases, all taken verbatim and simply listed together. See the entire text at: https://www.theguardian.com/world/2002/oct/10/usa.poetry (accessed 15 August 2018), and commentary on the text, with an evaluation of Richard Thompson's

speeches during his campaign (many of them written or co-written by Jon Favreau), with an oratorical rhythm that was often incantatory, and always literally 'charming', seductive and charismatic.

George Orwell would have been profoundly aware of a historical degradation of political language, especially in English, since the moment of those highlights in Obama's oratory. Indeed, Orwell had already explicitly lamented what he saw as the decadence of the language of politics in his own day. In his 1946 essay, 'Politics and the English Language', published in *Horizon* in April that year, he took as his opening gambit the observation that 'it is clear that the decline of a language must ultimately have political and economic causes'.[3] For Orwell, in this immediate post-war moment, there was an intimacy to be discerned between the condition of a national language and the condition of the same nation's politics.

Notwithstanding the fact that Orwell's laments show us that complaints about the degradation of political language are not new, we might nonetheless feel a need to investigate a similar phenomenon. How, exactly, did we get to the banalities of Donald Trump, say, whose vocabulary is utterly impoverished and degrading? How does the banal vacuity of much contemporary political discourse in the United States, the UK and elsewhere bring its speakers to power and into government? Part of the point of this book will be to examine that degradation and to analyse what it signifies. There is, however, another important aspect of the work that I am undertaking, and that is to look at the structural relations between politics and language. In particular, I will be examining the nature of 'political English' (though I will also examine the same phenomenon in some other languages), with a view to understanding whether dialogue and rhetoric can ever be a good – peaceful – means of avoiding martial or other expressly political forms of violent conflict and confrontation.

This was in Obama's mind during his Nobel address. He did not shy away from the controversy around his being awarded the Peace Prize, and acknowledged it openly in his acceptance speech. Indeed, that

---

cartoon-making processes, available at: http://illustrationchronicles.com/How-Richard-Thompson-Made-the-Pie-Higher (accessed 15 August 2018). Thompson died in July 2016, just months prior to Trump's election as President.
[3]George Orwell, 'Politics and the English Language' (1946), repr. in Orwell, *Inside the Whale* (Penguin, 1972), 143.

speech is itself extraordinary: in accepting the Nobel Prize for Peace, Obama talked insistently of war and of the need, in certain occasions, for war as a political reality. He had, of course, inherited a set of military predicaments and engagements when he took office, and he noted the peculiarity that 'the most profound issue surrounding my receipt of this prize is the fact that I am Commander-in-Chief of the military of a nation in the midst of two wars'. His address then – worrying away at the question of 'A Just and Lasting Peace' – becomes a meditation on the adequacy or inadequacy of words and of speech-making in the face of what he sees as the occasional necessity of violence and war. Speaking as if from the lingering rubble-strewn shadows of the Twin Towers in New York, he said that 'Negotiations cannot convince Al-Qaeda's leaders to lay down their arms'. Nonetheless, he went on to say, words are indeed important, because 'if we want a lasting peace, then the words of the international community must mean something': words must promise material action, and the speakers of those words must honour their promises.

The intrinsic contradictions or tensions here – rhetoric against force, language against politics – run all the way through the speech. For a Peace Prize speech, it is remarkable in its insistence that the route to peace is often through violence, however unsavoury it might be to contemplate or to hear that fact. Obama associates a just and lasting peace with those jurisdictions that respect human rights, especially the right to freedom of speech, freedom of religious worship and freedom of assembly. This, he claims, is essentially what gives the very idea and fact of 'America' its identity as a polity, stressing especially a respect for the right to free speech and assembly.

If the promise of respect for human rights is not respected in material fact, then 'peace is a hollow promise', Obama argues, going on to say that 'I believe the peace is unstable where citizens are denied the right to speak freely or worship as they please; choose their own leaders or assemble without fear'. Obama represents such rights as being universal, and then claims that America is the paradigmatic case of a jurisdiction that 'will always be a voice for these aspirations', precisely because they constitute a kind of truth universally acknowledged. That is to say, freedom of speech is itself *the* universal language that all people speak, and they will do so *in the medium of* and under the protection of an American voice, and perhaps even of *the* American voice. Indeed, it is worth recalling here the politically charged fact that the 'Voice of America' was established as the state's news agency in the late 1930s, expressly with the claim that it was a reliable source of news; and at least part of its propagandistic point was to unify the world around one language and one univocal account of reality.

In this last comment on freedom of speech, Obama is essentially claiming that 'America' is, by definition, that which speaks a universal – or at least unifying – language, and that, under his presiding watch, that language will speak for peace by encouraging yet more words, yet more freedoms to speak and to talk together in common assembly. This is to be a shared language, like a 'world language', and it is spoken, here, in American English. Our question – the exercise that this book engages – will be to put this to the test and to set it against the obvious historical and empirical evidence that contemporary political speech is damaged. As Mark Thompson has pointed out, 'Across the political spectrum, there is a growing acknowledgement that something has gone awry with our politics and the way in which political questions are debated and decided in America, Britain and other western countries.'[4]

The question that I wish to pose relates to the intimacy or otherwise between the state of a language and the state of a polity. To put it simply, can we judge the political difference between, say, Obama and Trump, in terms of the linguistic and rhetorical difference that separates them? For the English novelist Howard Jacobson, 'Trump is uniquely stunted', and he contends that 'A child listening to two of his speeches could reproduce a third without a dictionary'. The political link, for Jacobson, is clear. He worries that 'If his is to be ... an authoritarian presidency, his wordlessness is the means by which it has already and will in future be achieved'.[5] If there is the slightest truth and substance to this argument, then the issue of 'political English' is of central importance to the survival not just of the American polity but also of the planet itself, given the status of English as a global means of communication, or miscommunication.

* * *

We can begin by taking a look at the conditions that lay behind the award of another ostensibly surprising Nobel Prize to another important statesman and politician: Churchill's 1953 Nobel Prize, which was not (as many might have expected, given his role in the 1939–45 war) for Peace

---

[4]Mark Thompson, *Enough Said: What's Gone Wrong with the Language of Politics* (Bodley Head, 2016), 8.
[5]Howard Jacobson, 'Point of View', *The Guardian: Review*, 8 April 2017, p. 13.

but rather for Literature.⁶ Those conditions start with another American president, also in the midst of another war.

On 16 April 1953, shortly after the death of Stalin, President Eisenhower sat in the Statler Hotel in Washington and prepared to deliver a speech to the American Society of Newspaper Editors, to be broadcast simultaneously on national television and radio. The speech is usually referred to as 'The Chance for Peace', but the cornerstone on which the speech is built is – in some ways akin to the rhetoric of Obama's Nobel speech – the demand for war. Eisenhower lists a number of key tasks facing the world, in the wake of the Second World War, the death of Stalin and the emergence of a new Soviet leadership. In addition to all this, the world is now in a Cold War, due to the visible threat posed by the new and shocking potency of atomic energy. As Eisenhower warns, that energy can be so easily diverted away from peaceful economic use to the purpose instead of the mass killing of populations and the devastations of whole cities and more. He says that the now urgent tasks facing the world in this situation give a great opportunity to the world: 'the dedication of the energies, the resources, and the imaginations of all peaceful nations to a new kind of war. This would be a declared total war, not upon any human enemy but upon the brute forces of poverty and need.'

The speech was sent to Prime Minister Churchill in the UK. Churchill, at the time, had just assumed the portfolio of his Foreign Secretary, Anthony Eden, because Eden was indisposed by illness.⁷ This not only added enormously to Churchill's already heavy workload but also allowed him to assert his full prime ministerial control of UK foreign policy. Churchill had a different attitude to the Soviet Union from that of Eisenhower, and he therefore sought to take a different approach to any negotiations. Eisenhower, it should be remembered, was working in the high moment of McCarthyism, and he was working under the influential presence of his fiercely anti-communist Secretary of State, John Foster Dulles. This constrained his possibilities to a large

---

⁶The Nobel Prize for Peace in 1953 was awarded to George Marshall, architect of Marshall Aid (the 'Marshall Plan') designed to ensure the economic recovery of Europe after 1945 and thereby to prevent the potential seductions, as the United States saw it, of communism.

⁷On 12 April 1953, Eden had a cholecystectomy operation, to deal with jaundice and gallstones. A post-operative fistula developed, and he ended up travelling to Boston in the United States to be operated on by Dr Richard Cattell. For full medical details, see John W. Braasch, 'Antony Eden's (Lord Avon) Biliary Tract Saga', *Annals of Surgery*, 238:5 (November 2003), 772–5.

extent and circumscribed what it was possible for him to say, especially in any public address.

The British Prime Minister, by contrast, exuded supreme self-assurance and was working under no kinds of similar or parallel constraints on what could be said. On 17 April 1953, the day after Eisenhower's broadcast, Churchill spoke at a meeting of Scottish Conservatives in Glasgow. The death of Stalin on 5 March 1953 had left him as the 'sole survivor of the triumvirate of Allied wartime power' and had bolstered his sense of his own importance on the world stage. This was so even though his own health had started to fail significantly. The Glasgow speech, however, gave him the opportunity to present himself as the key author of a new beginning in world affairs, a quite literal breath of fresh air.[8] He revelled in his bullish self-characterization as the great and successful deal-maker.[9] He saw himself as having been the fulcrum of a total world order, sitting between and holding together the two other great world powers of the day, the United States and the Soviet Union, in the agreements that had been reached in the diplomatic negotiations in Tehran (1943), Yalta and Potsdam (both 1945). Churchill wanted to seize the moment, now, to construct and lead this new world order, and he was frustrated that Eisenhower was more cautious and that Eisenhower feared – doubtless encouraged in this fear by Dulles – that any momentous change at this moment 'would provide the new Soviet government with "another propaganda mill"'.[10]

Then, following a suggestion from the French Prime Minister René Mayer, for a meeting in Bermuda that would be attended also by Eisenhower, Churchill now envisaged the realization of a continuation of his authoritative presence on the world stage. Mayer wanted the meeting, proposed for May 1953, partly in an effort to constrain Churchill's enthusiastic eagerness to engage positively (and, Mayer feared, too

---

[8]On his standing as sole survivor of the wartime triumvirate, see Roy Jenkins, *Churchill* (Macmillan, 2001), 860. On the Glasgow speech, see Martin Gilbert, *Churchill: A Life* (Minerva, 1992), 910, where Churchill is quoted in terms of that fresh air: 'Is there a new breeze blowing in the tormented world?'

[9]Interestingly, of course, this description might also fit Donald Trump, who sees world affairs in terms of the making and breaking of deals, as if politics were simply a business. Infamously, his *The Art of the Deal* became a kind of manifesto for his political presidential campaign. Despite this superficial similarity with Churchill, it is probably a safe bet that Trump will not be awarded the Nobel Prize for Literature – or for anything else.

[10]Gilbert, *Churchill*, 910.

uncritically) the post-Stalin Soviet Union, hence, as Mayer saw it, the need for Eisenhower's presence. Churchill, however, saw an opportunity for a further exertion of British power through his own diplomatic skills, placing him and Britain yet more centrally at the fulcrum of a new and peaceful world order.[11]

Eisenhower was already dubious about Churchill's entire approach, however. The text of the 16 April speech that he sent to Churchill warned explicitly that 'We care nothing for mere rhetoric' and that 'We are only for sincerity of peaceful purpose attested by deeds'. Eisenhower, himself only recently elected to power, saw the potential disappointments, in material terms, of agreements founded in rhetoric and not in fact. He went on, 'Even a few such clear and specific acts, such as the Soviet Union's signature upon an Austrian treaty or its release of thousands of prisoners still held from World War II, would be impressive signs of sincere intent.' For Eisenhower, this was what mattered, and he was essentially warning against the potentially duplicitous and meretricious effect of the rhetoric for which Churchill would soon be rewarded by the Swedish Academy. As the President put it, such 'clear and specific acts … would carry a power of persuasion not to be matched by any amount of oratory. … The test of truth is simple. There can be no persuasion but by deeds.'[12]

This is the background of Bermuda. On the one hand, we have Eisenhower's demand for actions as testimony of truth, of intention, and of character; on the other hand, we have the power of oratory as practised by Churchill. Putting this at its simplest, we have a more or less clear opposition set up, on the international and post-war political stage, between the material power of deeds and the rhetorical power of words. This is at the core of any question concerning the relation of politics to language. In Churchill's case, this has a particular resonance, given the fact that, notwithstanding a life-long speech impediment, Churchill was renowned for his public speaking. Further, at this time, the Bermuda conference had to be postponed until 4–7 December 1953 because of

---

[11] In the end, Mayer did not attend, for his government fell after a financial crisis in France, and Joseph Laniel replaced him as French Prime Minister. For a detailed account of the Bermuda meeting and its historical background, see J.W. Young, 'Churchill, the Russians and the Western Alliance: the Three-Power Conference at Bermuda, December 1953', *The English Historical Review*, vol. 101: no. 401 (October 1986), 889–912.

[12] The text of the speech, entitled 'The Chance for Peace', is available at: https://www.eisenhower.archives.gov/all_about_ike/speeches/chance_for_peace.pdf (accessed 9 January 2018).

the stroke that Churchill suffered (and which was kept secret) on 23rd June of that year. One effect of the stroke was that his speech was further impaired for some days in the immediate aftermath, although this, unlike his lisp or stutter (the actual physiological nature of the impediment remains disputed), was not a long-lasting impairment.

* * *

It was because he was in Bermuda between 3 and 8 December 1953 that Churchill could not himself be present in Sweden on 10 December, when the Swedish poet and dramaturge Sigfrid Siwertz, a distinguished member of the Swedish Academy whose own writings were critical of some tendencies of capitalist culture, presented the Nobel Prize for Literature to him in absentia. It is something of a paradox that he was awarded this prize at a moment when, in Bermuda, his rhetoric was in fact failing to persuade. As J.W. Young has pointed out, 'In its aftermath, Bermuda was widely seen as a failure', citing a *Times* report of 9 December in which it was described as 'a spectacular meeting to exchange banalities'.[13] That is perhaps not entirely surprising, given that Churchill referred to the French delegation – at least in private – as 'bloody frogs'.[14]

The citation for his Nobel Prize commended 'his mastery of historical and biographical description as well as [his] brilliant oratory in defending exalted human values', and Siwertz opened the speech by comparing Churchill to other 'great statesmen and warriors', who have also been 'great writers'. He suggests comparisons with Julius Caesar, Marcus Aurelius and Napoleon, before settling on Disraeli as the comparator against whom Churchill's specific qualities can be highlighted. The comparison allows Churchill to shine more brightly because, according to Siwertz, Churchill differed from Disraeli in that Churchill had to deal with 'really dreadful ordeals' and – in a phrase that is troubling in its hints of anti-Semitism – 'Churchill's John Bull profile stands out effectively against the elder statesman's chalk-white, exotic mask with the black lock of hair on the forehead'.[15]

---

[13]Young, 'Churchill, the Russians and the Western Alliance', 907–8.
[14]Ibid., 906.
[15]Disraeli, of course, although born into a Jewish family and heritage, had converted from Judaism, and it was this conversion, in fact, that had made his political career possible

Churchill, as a stereotypical John Bull figure, is more fully 'English', it seems, because although Disraeli 'revered the English way of life and tradition', Churchill had these things 'in his blood'. It is as if Churchill had a profound and physical intimacy with Englishness whereas the more 'exotic' Disraeli stood at a kind of distanced angle from being fully English. It is in Churchill's body and blood that one also finds – according to Siwertz – 'steadfastness in the midst of the storm and the resolute impetus which marks both word and deed'. Unlike the supposedly masked 'exotic' outsider Disraeli, whose Englishness presumably lies under the obvious mask of the Jew, Churchill 'wears no mask, has no sign of cleavage, has no complex, enigmatic nature'. The most important thing for us at this stage of my argument, however, is the suggested intimacy between Churchill's 'blood' and his 'word': both are reputedly indications of steadfastness, certainty, honesty and truth, unlike the 'masked' Jewish Disraeli, who might mime or act out these qualities but does not essentially own them. The political character that supposedly embodies truth is at one with the English language, with those words, as spoken by a John Bull figure.

Siwertz then returns to the comparison with ancient figures, saying that Churchill's 'political and literary achievements are of such magnitude that one is tempted to resort to portray him as a Caesar who also has the gift of Cicero's pen'. In the summation of the presentation speech, it is this combination – politics and oratory – that becomes the ostensibly determining feature. Siwertz says that 'great, living, and persuasive words are also difficult and rare. And Churchill has shown that they too can take on the character of great deeds.' To sum up, 'his every word is half a deed.'[16] To speak – and to speak Churchill's English, as embodied in his English blood – is to do: word is deed; the word is made flesh.[17] This mindset, however, was precisely what did not fool Eisenhower in Bermuda.

When he was awarded the Nobel, Churchill had some major books to his name, including a biography of his predecessor, the Duke of Marlborough, and the history-cum-memoir, *The Second World War*.

---

because it allowed him to take the oath of allegiance to the Christian church, a requirement for any MP.

[16] All cited passages are from the 'Nobelprize.org' website: 'Nobelprize.org. Nobel Media AB 2014', available at: http://www.nobelprize.org/nobel_prizes/literature/laureates/1953/press.html (accessed 29 March 2017).

[17] I explore these metaphorical claims, and the political substance that they contain, in substantial detail in Chapters 3 and 5.

The latter was the most recent major publication that he had in 1953, and there is argument about how much of it he actually wrote (since a good deal of the material was put together by a group of researchers). There was, however, another large-scale history that would start to appear three years later: *The Birth of Britain*, which was the first volume of what would become the multivolume *A History of the English-Speaking Peoples* and which appeared in April 1956.

This monumental work had been initially commissioned and contracted in 1936, and although he wrote an astonishing 500,000 words quite quickly, Churchill's more obviously political duties interrupted his work on it during the war years. The very concept of the study is interesting: it is not a history of the world, not a history of England, but a history whose guiding and presiding principle is a mode of speech. It promises a history of a group of people united by an allegedly common language, but the Preface makes it clear that this language is more than just a medium of communication. 'English-speaking' is related not just to a specific idea of Englishness but also to truth itself, as if the language and its speakers had some privileged access to the natural world and to the material conditions of life itself.

Notwithstanding the twenty-year delay in producing the book, Churchill argues that the need for it in 1956, a decade after the war, is greater than ever. The war has made 'us' (by which he means 'the English-speaking people'), 'more conscious of our common duty to the human race'. He writes that 'Language, law, and the processes by which we have come into being, already afforded a unique foundation for the work' in 1936, but events since then make the work even 'more relevant' than it might have been had its production not been interrupted by war. He makes it clear that his focus on English-speaking peoples 'in no way implies any sense of restriction', nor does it indicate a disengagement from other political structures 'like United Europe or other similar groupings which may all find their place in the world organization we have set afoot'. On the contrary, those organizations will also benefit from English, because it is the English language, claims Churchill, that will rather help to 'invest them with life and truth': they will get their meaning and significance entirely from the primacy of English and of the people who speak it.[18]

---

[18] Winston Churchill, *A History of the English-Speaking Peoples, Vol. 1: The Birth of Britain* (Cassell and Company, 1956), vii.

These are somewhat extraordinary passages, underpinned by several unstated assumptions or presuppositions. First, there is that odd construction in which 'we' have a duty to 'the human race'. A 'duty' is a kind of debt owed, and, logically, one cannot owe a debt to oneself; the construction, linguistically, seems to suggest that 'we' are neither quite fully nor entirely clearly identical with others. Given that we will be investing the organizations that the world and its 'human race' makes 'with life and truth', the implication is that we are somehow above the human, a kind of *Ubermensch* and certainly an exceptional case.

Second, language itself is given a clear priority here, standing even before law and 'the processes by which we have come into being', whatever that might actually mean. Such processes presumably are not a reference to biological birth or to biological evolution but rather to 'the birth of Britain' that is to be the subject of the first volume as a whole.

Third, the logic is that, essentially by dint of the contingent fact that a certain group of people not only speak English as their first language but also do so as a condition of their being born in a particular geographical place – Britain – their language gives them a power and duty akin to that of a kind of biblical fiat, a power that is – as in biblical myth – the very power that generates a world in the first place.[19] It is as if 'English-speaking' is the *fons et origo* of all existence, as if the biblical God spoke English. Siewertz was only half-right: for Churchill, it is not the case that 'his every word is half a deed', it *is* a complete deed: it is the English-language version of a mythic, biblical and fundamentalist *fiat lux*. In the logic of Churchill's own prose, his every word is a deed simply because it is an English word spoken by an English voice in an English body carrying English blood. More than this, it is also a deed that is right and proper, unquestioningly and axiomatically the right thing to say and do, in line with the establishment of a necessary truth.

The establishment of this intimacy between the English spoken word on the one hand and, on the other hand, worldly material reality – an intimacy of rhetorical English with politics – is continued and advanced yet further, when Churchill asserts the leadership role, in and for the world, of the English-speaking people. Their status as essentially

---

[19] Very often, the slippage between 'Britain' and 'England' allows Churchill the possibility of ignoring Scotland, Wales and Ireland. That slippage, in which Britain is identified as England, persists in those ideologically committed to a supposed 'Anglosphere', about which I write more later.

coterminous and continuous with the original biblical language of the fiat means that 'There is a growing feeling that the English-speaking peoples might point a finger showing the way if things went right'.[20] This, as Churchill then makes absolutely explicit, is what underpins the appropriateness of writing his study: 'I use the term "English-speaking peoples" because there is no other that applies both to the inhabitants of the British Isles and to those independent nations who derive their beginnings, their speech, and many of their institutions from England, and who now preserve, nourish, and develop them in their own ways.'[21]

This is what Churchill means when he suggests that his terminology is not exclusivist. You might be independent now, but you are so only because of the chain that binds you to a specific mentality and character, a mentality and character that is intrinsically English and rooted in the soil of the British Isles or the blood of an English individual. Paradoxically, your 'independence' itself depends upon your intrinsic and initial dependence on the English language and its original speakers: English people who have direct access to truth, validity and legitimacy in all things, courtesy of the very physicality and bodily condition of their tongue. Churchill does indeed have England 'in his blood', as Siwertz asserted, unlike the intrinsically non-English other, as signalled by the facial profile and other bodily characteristics of the Jewish-born Disraeli.

In a sweeping overview of several hundred years of history in the prefatory remarks to his massive and extraordinarily ambitious work, Churchill explains that by the fifteenth century 'the main characteristics and institutions' of England had been shaped, and he asserts that these are related intimately and integrally to the language. Anglo-Saxon German had been smoothed out by 'the influence of Church Latin'; Norman French had been assimilated, and 'vocabularies had been extended by many words of British and Danish root'.[22] Moreover, and coterminous with the development and consolidation of the English

---

[20] This sentence surely recalls the visual image of Michelangelo's fresco of *The Birth of Adam*, on the ceiling of the Sistine chapel, in which God and Adam reach their fingers towards each other. It is a world apart from Courbet's 1866 painting of *The Origin of the World*, centring on the visual image of female genitalia. The historical shift from one to the other here is itself worthy of separate analysis, but the important issue is that, for Churchill, the voice is also not shaped by woman but is expressly male. 'English-speaking' is also 'Englishman speaking'.
[21] Ibid., viii.
[22] Ibid., xvii.

language, other institutions assumed social primacy and structural form: 'Unlike the remainder of Western Europe, which still retains the imprint and tradition of Roman law and the Roman system of government', English-speaking peoples 'achieved a body of legal and what might almost be called democratic principles which survived the upheavals and onslaughts of the French and Spanish Empires', he writes.[23]

He appears to feel no compulsion to argue that what is presented here simply as coincidence between these linguistic developments and the character of the social institutions is in any way causal: that seems to be taken for granted. The claim is substantial, given the institutions he has in mind: 'Parliament, trial by jury, local government by local citizens, and even the beginnings of a free Press, may be discerned' by the turn of the fifteenth century.[24] Further, he ignores the significance of the fact that the constitution of the English language itself derives partly from the importation and assimilation of other languages (Norman French; German).[25] It is as if an already intrinsic and nascent or latent 'Englishness' is already present in England, where it can then smooth out these foreign imports and can circumvent their cultural norms, subsuming those norms under a more natural or original form that we know as the English language as it stands, here and now.

It would be easy to caricature all this as the residual bombast of an imperial power, consistent with the moment of its writing and the character of its author. Yet such a position regarding the absolute primacy of a given people through their language remains powerful even beyond that context, and it is repeated in the writings of a more recent – and fervently right-wing conservative – historian, Andrew Roberts. In 2006 Andrew Roberts published a kind of supplement to the four volumes of Churchill's history, with his *A History of the English-Speaking Peoples Since 1900*. There, we see some of the ideological substratum of Churchill's attitudes being more or less openly acknowledged and celebrated.

The language of 'duty' in Churchill is reiterated by Roberts in terms of 'mission': 'Ever since the mid-1830s, the English-speaking peoples

---

[23]Ibid.

[24]Ibid.

[25]To this, of course, should be added the significant number of terms introduced into English from Arabic. Consider the etymologies of the many words beginning 'al-' (albatross, alcohol, algebra, algorithm, alkali, to offer only the most common examples associated mostly with maths and sciences).

had considered it their civilising mission to apply – with varying degrees of force – their values and institutions to those areas of the world they believed would benefit from them.'[26] It is interesting here that – in this 2006 iteration of this motif of the primacy of political English – the barbarism that Walter Benjamin would have seen underpinning this civilizational drive is simply glossed over as a mere intercalation in the application and supposedly unquestionably beneficent dissemination of positive values. Roberts cannot actually ignore the well-established and empirically evident history of violence that sits uncomfortably at the core of imperialist and colonial enterprises. However, instead of adopting Churchill's ideological tactic that takes for granted that English simply is the language of truth and logic and reason, Roberts has to endorse the principle of the primacy of the English-speaking while at the same time acknowledging the divorce and discrepancy between the language and the politics.[27]

In this, there is a wedge driven between politics and English, but one that Roberts kicks aside by eliding or excusing-by-explanation the political violence while retaining the unquestioned value of the linguistic primacy of English. In short, this is a rhetoric that operates by suavely and silently eliding anything other than rhetoric itself. In terms of providing us with any genuine insight into the material and empirical conditions of actual history, it is utterly vacuous, therefore. However, what is important for our purposes is not the historical vacuity of Roberts's exercise here; rather, what is important is the fact that underlying his writing is an assertion of English as the foundation of a kind of 'political correctness' or truth.

Like Churchill, Roberts too goes for the broad brush as he introduces his book: 'Despite the harsh methods occasionally adopted to protect

---

[26] Andrew Roberts, *A History of the English-Speaking Peoples since 1900* (2006; repr. Phoenix, 2007), 6.

[27] The issues here have led to a scholarly controversy in more recent times. Nigel Biggar's 'Ethics and Empire' project, backed by the McDonald Centre in the University of Oxford, intends 'to measure apologias and critiques of empire against historical data from antiquity to modernity across the globe'; see http://www.mcdonaldcentre.org.uk/ethics-and-empire (accessed 9 January 2018). The validity and legitimacy of the entire project has been questioned by a very large number of international scholars, who see it as a project intrinsically focused on the validation, in ethical terms, of Britain's colonial past; see report at: https://www.theguardian.com/education/2017/dec/22/oxford-university-accused-of-backing-apologists-of-british-colonialism (accessed 9 January 2018), pointing out that the project aims to produce a 'Christian ethics of empire'.

their status and safety from Wilhelmine Prussian militarism, then the Nazi-led Axis, then global Marxism-Leninism and presently from Islamic fundamentalism, the English-speaking peoples would remain the last, best hope for Mankind [sic]'.[28] This extraordinarily succinct 'history' then becomes the primary means of establishing the tradition of Englishness that has its roots in Churchill's earlier work. Roberts notes that, in these and other great wars and struggles, 'the English-speaking peoples in the twentieth century … often suffered serious reverses in the first battle, or even the first campaign, before going on to ultimate victory'.[29] The picture here is one whereby the English-speaking peoples may be 'interrupted', as it were, but they will rapidly re-establish the volume of their own loud mouths and will drown out all linguistic or discursive competition.

The English character that underpins Roberts's description and analysis here is Optimistic, in the eighteenth-century philosophical sense that every setback is but a temporary stage in a great plan that will reassert an intrinsic and inevitable eventual realization of superiority. This English character is also typically 'plucky', like the underdog who can always face up to tyranny and overwhelm it. The Optimism is important: it says that, while other ways of describing the world may interrupt the smooth ongoing fluency of English speakers, nonetheless English will always ensure that this is but a temporary blip in history, the rude but insubstantial interruption of a foreign sound. The pluck is also an important characteristic: England may be a small geographical state in material terms and may indeed (by 2006) have become a medium-range state of limited significance, but, through the fact that its language ensures an intimacy with greatness, 'so British post-imperial greatness has been preserved and fostered through its incorporation into the American world-historical project'.[30]

English survives therefore – in American English. The third thing that Roberts asserts – alongside Optimism and pluck – is the myth of the strong man [sic]. He notes 'another aspect of the experience of the English-speaking peoples in the twentieth century' is 'the tendency for the right men to come to the fore in times of crises'.[31] Some ten years on from publishing this, Roberts might well have found what this means: the 'America First' bombast of the businessman-turned-president Donald

---

[28]Roberts, *A History*, 2.
[29]Ibid., 9.
[30]Ibid., 8.
[31]Ibid., 9.

Trump, admirer of the self-styled strong man bare-chested Vladimir Putin, and orator of a quite remarkably impoverished English vocabulary, full of solecism and semantic vacuity that nonetheless establishes what Howard Jacobson calls 'a symbiosis of inarticulacy'.[32]

It may well be the case that Roberts would be utterly content with this, for he adds the bizarre characterization that English is also the language of wealth. English fluency and world currency literally coincide here. In a quite extraordinary passage, he 'proves' the value of English by calibrating the GDP of a nation to the number of English speakers it has. 'Despite Britain having just 1.3% of the world's population – and taking up less than 0.2% of the world's land area – English is today both the language of wealth and, just as importantly, of aspiration to wealth,' he writes. The people who speak English as first or second languages 'have ... higher per capita incomes than those who speak the other great world languages'. Mandarin speakers are worth a measly £448 billion in total, Russians £801 billion, Germans £1,090 billion and Japanese £1,277 billion. Set against this 'English-speakers are worth a staggering £4,271 billion – more than all the rest put together'.[33] No contest, it seems.

On Friday, 24 February 2017, Nigel Farage, MEP and occasional leader of UKIP (the United Kingdom Independence Party) addressed the Conservative Political Action Conference (CPAC) of the American Conservative Union, following the inauguration of the newly installed President of the United States, Donald Trump. He spoke to his audience about Brexit, the 2016 vote that led to the UK government saying that Britain would leave the European Union. In doing so, he presented himself first as the plucky individual, fighting against the odds, pointing to what he called 'the twenty years of abuse' that he claimed to have suffered as a victim while campaigning to take the UK out of the European Union. He was fighting against all kinds of establishment interests, he claimed, including a 'bunch of unelected old men in Brussels', and he hailed what he claimed as 'his' victory in the Brexit referendum of 2016, along with Trump's election as President, as merely the beginning of 'a great global revolution' that would now roll out across 'the rest of the free world'.[34]

---

[32]Jacobson, 'Point of view', 13.
[33]Ibid., 574.
[34]The full address, including all passages quoted here, is available at: https://www.youtube.com/watch?v=Ww5Vzb1Y5TQ&index=26&list=PLmqnjF1D2hhYONeFVItHvLgmH_HPjRbv4 (accessed 15 August 2018).

All of these claims were subsumed under one great motif, however. The key to his politics, he said, was that he wanted to be able to 'make trade deals with our real friends in the world'. Then he clarified this: 'It's funny,' he said, 'our real friends in the world speak English, have common law, and stand by us in times of crisis.' Let us leave aside, for the moment, the precise identification of who might be included in this 'we' and 'us', except to note that it seems to embody only English speakers. Yet more significant is the identification of 'us' with 'the free world' and with the very idea of freedom itself. The logic is clear within this: if anyone wishes to have freedom, they must join the free world, and to join the free world is to speak English, like 'us'.

As with Roberts, however, this is a new and very specific English: American English. Farage ingratiates himself with his audience in a massive paradox or self-contradiction. He effectively sheds his English national identity, while claiming that his political position rests entirely upon the reassertion of what he called 'nation-state democracy'. At the beginning of his address, he refers to himself in faux-surprised tones as a 'foreigner' in the United States, but then adds that he has really now discovered his true inner self, which is American: 'since the election of Donald J. Trump, every time I come to America I'm feeling a little bit more American,' he says. When he does refer to ethnicity, he does so in terms that are meant to address the latent racism and less latent xenophobia that governs his talk.

'We', he says, are not opposed to Muslims or to any religions, 'we're not against anybody', in fact, and, just to be clear, 'we are for ourselves'. It is at this point that the 'we' should be considered more fully. This, it turns out, is the 'we' of Farage and Trump, themselves extraordinarily rich individuals, united really in one major characteristic: a mode of oratory that some might describe as demagogic, but which – less controversially – might be better characterized as a rhetoric that believes that it need not say anything of substance precisely because it is expressed in and through this new form of English. Like Churchill: they said that Brexit would happen; they said that Trump would win, and – against all the odds of rational debate and honest politics – lo, the word became the deed.

We might very reasonably draw two conclusions here: first, following Roberts, politics is now fully monetized, and all values (political, social, ethical, aesthetic, moral, personal) are calculated first in sterling and then in dollars. Second, and more fundamentally, money (and perhaps especially the dollar) has now replaced truth.[35] The value of English for Churchill, we recall, was its intimacy with fundamental truth. A half-century later, when Roberts is writing and when Farage is speaking, the value of English is its intimacy with money. From these two observations, it becomes clear that political English is now also financial English, and that the foundation of all meaning in this new rhetorical arrangement is money and its acquisition. This is why it makes sense in the English-speaking world to have a businessman as President and not quite the strong man of Roberts's fantasy. The merely strong – Russian – is only worth a pathetic £801 billion; at the time of writing, Trump's estimated personal wealth is calculated or estimated by Forbes at $3.5 billion.[36] On 20 December 2016, the net wealth of his (then only partially completed) Cabinet was calculated at $13 billion.[37] Betsy DeVos, Trump's highly controversial pick for Education Secretary, openly admitted in 1997 that 'I have decided … to stop taking offence at the suggestion that we are buying influence [through her extremely substantial contributions to the Republicans]. Now, I simply concede the point. … We expect a return on our investment.'[38] The return she appears to have been given is her governmental position under Trump.

At the same CPAC convention where Nigel Farage identified 'our' friends as those who 'speak English', Betsy DeVos also gave an address, her first at the convention in her new position as US Secretary for Education. Education – and the politics of education – is a significant issue in the United States as it is in the UK and elsewhere: everyone, it seems, would like it if the state could provide a good education for all children. However, DeVos, having rightly repeated the expected clichés around this – on equality of access to a quality education for all, regardless of income or zip code – then asked the audience if there were any college students there. There were; indeed, there was a good number. She then turned attention to them, telling them that 'our' struggle – by

---

[35]The backdrop for speeches at CPAC 2017 included a central image of the opening of the Constitution, where the words 'We the people' are very clear. The conference title that year was indeed 'We the people: Reclaiming America's promise'. It may be coincidence, but this is also the phrase that appears on the obverse of the $10 note ever since 2006.

[36]forbes.com, 'What's Donald Trump Really Worth', estimate dated February 2017.

[37]Matt Rocheleau, 'Trump's Cabinet picks', *The Boston Globe*, 20 December 2016.

[38]Betsy DeVos, 'op-ed', *Roll Call*, as cited on the website of The Center for Public Integrity, available at: www.publicintegrity.org (accessed 30 March 2017).

which she meant that of conservatives – was also theirs. 'The fight against the education establishment extends to you too.'

Faculty, DeVos claimed, tell students 'what to do, what to say, and more ominously what to think'. The evidence for this claim – if she had any – went unstated, except insofar as she suggested that Faculty apparently told students that a vote for Trump was a vote against the University community. It is somewhat hyperbolic, but let us remain with the claim that Faculty 'from Adjunct professors to Deans' essentially give a language and a script, as it were, to their students. Against this, she argued that 'the real threat is silencing the First Amendment rights of people with whom you disagree'. As was the case with Farage above, the tactic here is to present the victors in an election as the plucky underdogs, victims of an establishment that constrains their freedoms – here, the freedom to speak their own words and their own thoughts.

In principle, this may be a positive good, if it serves to extend academic and other freedoms within education. However, the argument is again somewhat self-contradictory. It is not the 'education establishment' that is monoglot; rather, it is precisely those who, along with Farage, identify truth and value with a politicized English that is now thoroughly financialized. 'Defenders of the status quo will stop at nothing to protect their special interests,' DeVos claimed; yet it is DeVos who has, in fact, deployed her own wealth to extend her own political influence. Her argument is based on the purest form of hypocrisy: it actually attacks DeVos herself.

The issues around this will take us, in the next chapter, into a further exploration of the working of English within the educational setting.

2 ENGLISH NATIVISM AND LINGUISTIC XENOPHOBIA

In the educational systems of most jurisdictions, the 'study of languages' is usually tacitly understood as the study of 'foreign languages'. This ostensibly totally innocent and entirely uncontroversial idea rests on the assumption that there exists a 'native' language that is somehow not a language that we learn in the same ways as we might learn those foreign tongues. Yet every native language is itself, of course, a language that we learn: we are not born speaking it but have to hear, understand, imitate the sounds, mimic the appropriate and necessary mouth shapes and so on if we are to become 'native' to a community or a place. This last element is often overlooked: the altering of a mouth shape involves a muscular dynamic that actually has a percussive effect through the body as a whole. Learning to speak a language is infinitely more than simply learning, in the abstract, a vocabulary and a grammar.

P.G. Wodehouse gives the comic version of this in his 1934–5 novel, *The Luck of the Bodkins*. The novel opens with a joke at the expense of the typical English attitude to foreign languages: 'Into the face of the young man who sat on the terrace of the Hotel Magnifique … there had crept a look of furtive shame, the shifty hangdog look which announces that an Englishman is about to talk French.' Almost immediately however, 'The strain was too great. Monty relapsed into his native tongue.'[1]

Howard Jacobson gives a political edge to the way in which language shapes the body in his satirical novel *Pussy*. The novel describes the rise of Prince Fracassus, obviously an analogue of Donald Trump. His father, the

---

[1] P.G. Wodehouse, *The Luck of the Bodkins* (1935; repr. Arrow Books, 2008), 7.

Grand Duke, shows Fracassus a 'winking crystal Sphinx' at the pyramid called 'the Nowhere Palace'. 'Classy or what?', says the Duke. The Trump character, Fracassus, responds and agrees, repeating the word: 'Classy ... He had never used the word before and liked the shape of it in his mouth. *Classy* – it seemed to open a whole new world of sensation to him. It made his mouth moist. It made his cheeks hot. *Classy*. It was as though he'd swallowed the softest of chocolates.'[2]

At its most fundamental, to learn a language is to learn how to occupy and how to become a body, and it is also to learn how to operate that body and its movements, sounds and rhythms in alignment with others. Monty's so-called 'native tongue' in Wodehouse is in fact a tongue that has learned a means of accommodation with others. It is a tongue that has led the rest of a single body to occupy a place in relation with other tongues and other bodies and to find comfort and safe refuge there. In this respect, it is not only intimately related to the shape of a polity as such; it is also informed by the necessity of attending to other voices and to other tongues within that polity. All such other tongues are, by definition, initially alien to it, and the task of communication in a native tongue is the task of forming a shared identity or a unity of shared political purpose. We sometimes call this latter a 'nation', and, as is well known, the articulation of a language in its various forms by individuals helps to organize and even to stratify that polity, giving it a shape and a specific configured identity.

This remains the case even and especially when that very unity, or nation, is itself shaped by conflict or debate. In this case, the mastery of a 'native tongue' becomes a marker of political or class difference. Conflict and debate is really nothing more or less than a different attitude or disposition – including a kinetic bodily disposition – towards a language and its mode of articulation. Different speech groups live their relation to the shared polity in different ways. Although we might have a 'united kingdom', for example, that unity is shaped by strains, conflicts and differences among its participating elements, and these differences are marked by different attitudes to language. The classic 'proud Yorkshireman' has a different relation to the semantic content of 'England' from that which is engaged by the 'nationalist Scot', say. While they might share a deep sense of the 'meaning' of the word 'England', they

---

[2]Howard Jacobson, *Pussy* (Jonathan Cape, 2017), 64.

nonetheless have a different disposition or ethos in relation to it. This constitutes a political difference based upon different modes of 'native tongue'.

Such a state of affairs has a profound effect upon education, especially with regard to language. The effect is, at the deepest level, political. Education, we might say, is a process in which at least three key things happen. First, there is the introduction of novelty: the essence of learning is an exposure to something foreign, to that which is previously undreamt of in our philosophies, to something 'other'. Secondly, this involves us in a process of a re-calibration of the relations between emotion and reason, such that reason becomes increasingly the basis for an understanding of our emotions, including an understanding of how we will relate to each other in a social formation or polity. Thirdly, education then becomes a process of acculturation. In conservative terms, this often means that the learner is taught how best to fit in with a society, to be sociable or to 'be socialized'. In a second possibility, it means that the learner is given the means through which to criticize the existing society and thus to propose historical progress by changing it. Education sits between compliance and critique, and the way in which we talk determines where we sit on that spectrum, or where others locate us on it.

* * *

A brief, anecdotal, but empirically true example will show what this means in matter of fact. I myself grew up, in the working-class east end of Glasgow, speaking in three different ways. I had the language that was used in the family home, to which I added the slightly more polite usages and a different register in my primary school, and, running alongside and behind all this, there was a third variant which consisted in the official language that I heard coming from British television, especially factual television. Learning these three different modes of speaking involved also three different modes of listening, or three different forms of attention. All three came along with three different attitudes or dispositions towards the voices I heard: intimate with family at home; slightly more self-aware and self-conscious at school, where a different kind of attentiveness was required; and more distanced when the then accepted modes of 'Received Pronunciation' put me firmly in my social, geo-cultural and class-located place with regard to 'proper' English.

Three different attitudes meant also three different communities and constitutions of identity. There were also three different kinds of 'body politic', or three different establishments of polities based on language, each of which involved either establishing an uneasy intimacy with, or taking my distance from 'home', from the homely, familiar, *Heimlich*. In the former case, when I was 'at home', I knew that the language I spoke – and the life that I lived – was regarded, by the 'official' language of Received Pronunciation, as lacking in legitimacy or authority. I 'knew my place', a place assigned to me, as it were, by the operations of the English language itself.

We no longer suffer in the same ways from the imposed and coercive norms of Received Pronunciation, of course, but the example shows quite clearly that speaking English not only 'locates' an individual but also places that individual in terms of a class structure and in terms of political legitimacy and authority. This persists, even in an age when we have accepted a multiplicity of accents and registers within 'official' political discourse. It is abundantly clear in those politicians who have become almost a Wodehousian self-parody and who attempt to claim the legitimacy and authority of their political stances simply through the adoption of what we now call 'posh' English.

The English Conservative Jacob Rees-Mogg is a prime example. He presents as an extremely polite and refined individual, eminently careful in his language. When he initially stood for election to Parliament in 1997, he found himself as the candidate for East Fife in Scotland. He rapidly gave up canvassing, saying that he could not understand people's accents. The journalist Suzanne Moore satirizes him as a man who is 'so posh that Latin is his first language'.[3] His language allows him to present not only as an interesting (and, for some, amiable) 'eccentric' but also as 'old-fashioned', and his reversion to older fashion is what permits him to present as the most authentic Conservative.

Often this is less a matter of actual speech and more a matter of decorous register and politeness. Rees-Mogg's antiquarian register and tone is illustrative of a profound political power, in fact. To argue with him is to argue against the weight of the authority of an entire cultural history. In this respect, 'calm' and polite reserve works to try to make the speaker unreachable and thus also ungovernable. We might

---

[3]Suzanne Moore, available at: https://www.theguardian.com/commentisfree/2017/sep/06/jacob-rees-mogg-isnt-old-fashioned-thoroughly-modern-bigot-suzanne-moore (accessed 16 March 2018).

properly characterize the underlying politics of this as a specific mode of Conservative Anarchy.[4]

In this way, through his politicized voice, Rees-Mogg is able to refer openly, for example, to the fact that he took his nanny with him when he went canvassing, and the implication is that it is completely normal for 'everyone' to have a nanny. To raise questions about the supposed norm here is to indicate one's own distance from a specific 'tradition' that enjoys cultural and historical legitimacy, and thereby to delegitimize oneself. Likewise, when he openly expresses more overtly political views – anti-abortion (even in cases of rape); anti-gay marriage; extreme harshness on welfare to assist the poor, the ill or the disadvantaged; anti-ethnic minority legislation; pro-repatriation of black people – the mode of expression presents these as acceptable and authentically Conservative views. This is what gives him a community and a legitimacy through the language norms and language-authority of that community.

The more celebrated example is that of Margaret Thatcher. Famously, Thatcher was a lower-middle-class woman who adopted a very posh accent and register as she went to Oxford. Her political adviser, Gordon Reece, realized in 1978 that this would not play well with potential voters, voters with whom she would need to be able to affirm community and empathy if she wanted political power. He arranged for voice-coaching lessons, through which she changed her voice tone with a view to sounding more authoritative while also sounding more 'like' her prospective constituency and community.[5] Once in office, she expected that colleagues would adopt her own regime of political discourse. The civil servant Ian Beesley, who worked closely with her between 1981 and 1986, stated that submissions presented to her had 'above all to use language which would resonate with her'.[6] She changed the voice of England thereby, and, in doing so, effected massive political change in the

---

[4]In this respect, Rees-Mogg shares much with the equally determinedly polite Conservative, Michael Gove. See David Laws, *Coalition* (Biteback, 2016), 389, where Laws quotes former Prime Minister David Cameron: 'The thing you've got to remember with Michael [Gove] is that he is basically a bit of a Maoist – he believes that the world makes progress through a process of creative destruction.' The fact that this is really a tenet of Schumpeterian economics and politics, and not Maoist, is beside the fundamental point here, which is that the strategy of a Gove or a Rees-Mogg is fundamentally anarchic.

[5]See David Cannadine, *Margaret Thatcher: A Life and Legacy* (Oxford University Press, 2017), 25.

[6]As quoted in Graham Goodlad, *Thatcher* (Routledge, 2016), 66.

way in which England constituted its political identity. She 'did more than anyone else to disrupt the political consensus that had existed from 1945 to 1979; she did shift the centre ground of public debate to the right'.[7]

The voice, indeed, became a focal point for political division. 'Powerful and persuasive, yet at the same time soft and cajoling, Margaret Thatcher's distinctive voice was one of her most potent political weapons,' argues Bill Gardner.[8] Simultaneously, one of her political opponents, Jonathan Miller, said that she had 'the diction of a perfumed fart'.[9] Her political advisers were aware, as soon as the extent of her political ambitions became clear, that she needed to change more than just her visual self-presentation if she were to be elected and to advance as a major political figure: 'Speech itself was subjected to radical change.'[10] This radical change was important because Thatcher had taken elocution lessons as a child (and had recourse to them many times later), and the resulting acquisition of a 'cut-glass voice', usually associated with social climbing, led to much criticism when she tried to make her way in 1970s British politics.[11] The artificiality of her elocution-trained voice had already irritated her peers in Oxford, where dinner tables in college were inhabited on class-lines. She was among the 'grammar school products' but was not fully accepted there: 'Her voice was part of the trouble. "When she talked, she was not natural,"' recalled one of her fellow students.[12]

Political voices – the actual and semiotic *mode* of speaking as opposed to the simple semantic content of the language – establish political identity and political difference. In establishing a certain kind of supposed 'authenticity', it is instrumental in generating communities or tribes: the 'authentic' native and the 'unnatural' foreign.

* * *

---

[7]Goodlad, *Thatcher*, 124.

[8]See Bill Gardner, available at: https://www.telegraph.co.uk/news/politics/11251919/From-shrill-housewife-to-Downing-Street-the-changing-voice-of-Margaret-Thatcher.html (accessed 16 March 2018).

[9]See https://www.independent.co.uk/arts-entertainment/books/reviews/margaret-thatcher-the-authorised-biography-volume-two-everything-she-wants-by-charles-moore-book-a6686351.html (accessed 16 March 2018).

[10]Hugo Young, *One of Us* (rev. edn; Pan Books, 1991), 428.

[11]Charles Moore, *Margaret Thatcher: Authorized Biography, Vol. 1: Not for Turning* (Allen Lane, 2013), 30–1.

[12]Moore, *Margaret Thatcher*, 42–3.

As the examples above all show, however, that which is 'native' is itself always shaped by alterity, by a certain degree of 'alienation', and certainly by a high degree of conscious and determined control. A so-called authentic voice is always an 'educated' voice: a voice that has been tutored, either determinedly or through cultural circumstance. Those who suggest that there is something intrinsically 'homely' or *heimlich* about a 'native tongue' that makes it constitutively different from an 'acquired' or 'foreign' language are fundamentally trying to circumvent this simple fact. They are nativist, isolationist, in very literal senses, and they are caught up in a logic that is essentially one based upon a politically fundamentalist claim regarding 'natural privilege' in questions of power. The jocularly presented English-language nativism of Wodehouse's Monty covers a more menacing political ideology. Those we might call 'English-language nativists' are shaped by a politics of race or eugenics. One such figure is Toby Young, the controversialist journalist, whose proposal for what he called 'progressive eugenics' partly contributed, firstly, to his being appointed to the Board of the UK's 'Office for Students' (OfS) and, then, secondly, to his removal from the same Board.[13]

In his paper 'The Fall of the Meritocracy', Young focused his attention specifically on education. He argued that the political left opposes the idea that scholarly attainment corresponds with what he referred to as 'children's natural abilities'. It might be more accurate to say that the political left might be suspicious instead of a case that rests on a subscription to the primacy of such abilities, especially when they are supposedly intellectual abilities. Interestingly, in this paper, Young takes it for granted that cognitive abilities can be measured and evaluated according to the financial wealth and social status of individuals. Such a position echoes more or less exactly the position outlined by Andrew Roberts, discussed in Chapter 1, regarding the natural primacy of English-speaking peoples. The 'evidence' of cognitive superiority, it seems, is wealth: in what is essentially a very claustrophobic and smug marriage, the clever are rich, and the rich are clever.[14] Further, this symbiosis is

---

[13]See reports at: https://www.theguardian.com/media/2018/jan/03/toby-young-quotes-on-breasts-eugenics-and-working-class-people; http://www.bbc.co.uk/news/uk-42617922 and https://www.theguardian.com/media/2018/jan/09/toby-young-resigns-office-for-students (all accessed 10 January 2018).

[14]See Toby Young, 'The Fall of the Meritocracy', *Quadrant Online*, 7 September 2015, available at: https://quadrant.org.au/magazine/2015/09/fall-meritocracy (accessed 10 January 2018).

allegedly naturally given. As we saw in my previous chapter, the political right appears to assume that wealth is a measure of value, and that its acquisition is thus a measure of both legitimacy and merit or desert. Worse, in Young, this is being tied to a spurious notion of 'children's natural abilities' in terms of education, and it stands in direct opposition to the observation that an education starts by introducing the learner to the possibility of being open to that which is foreign.

The subscription to 'progressive eugenics' presupposes an acceptance of genetic difference as itself a satisfactory basis for the resolution of conflicts. While Young may want to argue that political differences can be resolved by our acceding to whatever the wealthy deem to be true and valid (since they are 'naturally' greater than the poor in their cognitive talents), there is something even more sinister at work in such thought. Speaking is a physical activity, and communicative language has a material effect upon bodily and motor activity. Young's argument leads back to a further position, one that would hold that physical might is right, for the simple reason that physical might is, indeed, genetically given. Clearly, he would be reluctant to make such a statement, and he may not even consciously think it. However, it underpins the logical substructure of his argument. His 'escape route' from such crass politics is provided by his recourse to money. Essentially, he displaces physical might onto wealth and its acquisition: wealth becomes a displaced form of bullying, the medium through which force is exerted. A simple way of summing this up is as given to us by Bob Dylan, who reminds us that money doesn't just talk; rather, it swears. In the same song, Dylan advises us never to fear hearing sounds that are foreign to our own ears.[15]

English-language nativism completely eschews the more democratic idea that the proper or better way of resolving a conflict is not by the imposition of one's own physical presence, strength or force: throwing one's weight around. It nonetheless finds legitimation in those who throw their money around, in ostentatious displays of wealth, as if that were a sign of some intrinsic goodness, value or legitimate political authority. The means of gaining authority, in Young's logic, however, remains indeed physical and material, albeit in a very different way from the use of the body for violence. It requires speakers each to modify their tongues and thus their bodily attitudes, thereby finding ways in which

---

[15]Bob Dylan, 'It's Alright, Ma (I'm only bleeding)', in *Bringing It All Back Home* (Decca Records, 1965).

the modification of a language can help different parties to establish an agreed commitment to modes of living together or to accommodate each other's actual and material presence. Young is not in favour of the social dominance of physical force, but he is in favour of a mode of social domination in which the material powers of physical force have been displaced onto money. Put simply, given that he identifies value with wealth, this means that he submits to the language of market fundamentalism.

The history of our attitudes to education here is politically instructive. In 1918, the UK government passed 'the Fisher Act'. The Act, presented by Herbert Fisher, had two main achievements: it rendered child labour illegal, and it extended the school-leaving age to fourteen. Fisher had previously been the Vice-Chancellor of the fledgling University of Sheffield. During the war years, he had followed governmental directives in ensuring that the University served the war effort, in the case of Sheffield by attending to munitions manufacture and to medical technology. However, Fisher also ensured that the University extended its work in both politics and translation studies: the politics of language and of communication is at the core of Fisher's thinking, and it informs the logic of the Act.

This is significant for the question of political English. The Second Reading of Fisher's Bill took place on 13 March 1918, where the Liberal MP, Francis Acland, presented it to the House of Commons. The Bill's fundamental proposition was for an equality of access: 'there is ... a solid determination that there shall be for all classes an extension of publicly-provided education throughout the years of adolescence, as there has long been for the small class that has been able to afford to pay for that education,' he said. He commended to the House 'the central principle which is enshrined in the bill' which was that 'there should be a really bold application of day part-time continuation schooling for young persons of both sexes'. These, in fact, were comments attending to the possibility of extending education of the poor onwards into third-level work.

Basil Peto, Conservative MP for Devizes, led the opposition. His rhetoric is revealing. The bill, he says, 'constitutes a very large advance towards the Socialist theory that children belong to the State, and that the men and women, who are citizens of the State, are to be regarded as mere breeding machines'. With the reference to the 'Socialist theory' of the State, Peto is drawing attention to something that is decidedly non-English. He is reminding his audience that, just some six months or so previously, the Bolsheviks in Russia had effected a revolution, in which they had proposed free universal education for all children, educating both sexes together, from three to sixteen. The Bolsheviks – as everyone knew – realized that the best way to consolidate their revolution was by spreading it across the advanced capitalist countries of Europe. Peto, here, is not just opposing Fisher's Bill; he is opposing an entire political ideology that he claims is enshrined in its basic educational principles. Moreover, he gives legitimacy to his position by indicating that the Bill is operating essentially in line with the norms of a foreign power. Fisher's is a *foreign* idea and is to be resisted on those grounds. This kind of education is simply *un-English*, as it were.

The thing about foreign ideas is that they get expressed first of all in foreign languages. A suspicion of foreign ideas goes together with a suspicion not only of foreigners but also of foreign languages. Such languages offer new and unfamiliar ways of thinking and of speaking, certainly. They also thereby offer new ways of living in and through the physical body, and this offers a different way of bringing individual bodies into ethical relation with each other. Foreign languages offer politics as the site of debate and change, through the exploration of new meanings, new modes of communication, the expansion of all that is familiar in our existing intellectual world into an unknown – and thus, also, the exploration of different social modes, different polities.

* * *

The anecdotal issue of my own mode of childhood speaking, then, seems small only at first glance and without taking seriously the fact that one's native tongue is itself always shaped by the shadow of all that which is foreign, not yet 'homely'. My own linguistic experience, of course, is far from unique: on the contrary, it is utterly standard. Consequently, this becomes a much more serious and extremely significant issue when we start to consider the relation of language to truth and place, as we saw above. It is yet more significant when we consider our attitude not to foreign languages but to anything and everything that we designate as 'foreign' to ourselves, or as 'alien' to our identity: our attitude to 'learning', in fact. And it is significant when we think of political English, say, in terms of a supposedly global or world language. David Crystal knows the importance of this when he writes that 'Any discussion of an emerging global language has to be seen in the political context of global governance as a whole'.[16]

The greater significance of this is evident when we compare some contemporary political rhetoric today with the inflammatory racist and nativist rhetoric of Enoch Powell, for the most obvious example, in his 1968 speech in Birmingham, usually referred to as the 'rivers of blood' speech. Let's clarify that misnomer first. In the speech, Powell refers – without direct attribution – to a line from Virgil's *Aeneid*, Book VI, line 87. Looking towards a future that he predicts will be disastrous because of immigration into the UK of people of colour, he says that 'Like the Roman, I seem to see "the river Tiber foaming with much blood"'.[17] (The original Latin is *et Thybrim multo spumantem sanguine cerno*, and Powell was on record stating that he wished he had used the original Latin.) It is interesting that Powell, himself a distinguished linguistic Classicist, should turn to the foreign text – and an ancient language made determinedly contemporary – as a clinching moment or climax in a speech that explicitly indicates a rejection of all that is alien, and equally interesting that he renders it in English.

Powell's infamous speech hinges on his account of two conversations. The first is with one of Powell's constituents, 'a decent ordinary fellow-Englishman', who remonstrates with Powell, saying, 'In this country in 15 or 20 years the black man will have the whip hand over the white man.'[18] The claim that he founds his politics on the talk of 'a decent ordinary fellow-Englishman' would be echoed some half-century later by Nigel Farage, when this latter claimed that the Brexit vote was 'a victory for real people, a victory for ordinary people, a victory for decent people'.[19] Powell uses the voice of the 'decent and ordinary' as the cornerstone of an argument about numbers, because 'The significance and consequences of an alien element introduced into a country or population are profoundly different according to whether that element is one per cent or 10 per cent'. A half-century later, right-wing rhetoric continues in this same vein.

---

[16]David Crystal, *English as a Global Language* (2nd edn; Cambridge University Press, Cambridge, 2003), 25.

[17]Powell, *Freedom and Reality*, 219. The most recent verse translation of the lines from Virgil is by Seamus Heaney, in his posthumous *Aeneid Book VI* (Faber and Faber, 2016), 7–8: 'I see wars, / Atrocious wars, and the Tiber surging with blood'.

[18]Powell, *Freedom and Reality*, 213–4.

[19]See report at: http://www.bbc.co.uk/news/uk-politics-eu-referendum-36613238 (accessed 16 March 2018).

The Conservative Party, under both David Cameron and Theresa May, focuses attention on numbers in the contemporary argument as well, with their insistence on reducing net migration into the UK to 'the tens of thousands'.[20]

For Powell, immigration obviously suited immigrants but damaged 'the existing population', who 'found themselves made strangers in their own country'. This, clearly, begs the obvious question given by my observation that the anecdote regarding my own speech is utterly standard within the UK. When set against the official political English of my childhood, I, too, was made a stranger in my own country, and the point, again, is that this is utterly standard and not specific to my own individual case. Powell constructs the myth of English nativism here, and does so by a populist appeal that is given dignity by its classical allusion, an allusion that needs to be domesticated into the English language rather than left as foreign. 'Whose nation' is this, and what makes it 'their own country'?

Powell rehearses stories that still persist right up to the present day, about how this existing population find 'their wives unable to obtain hospital beds in childbirth, their children unable to obtain school places, their homes and neighbourhoods changed beyond recognition, their plans and prospects for the future defeated' and favouritism working against them in the workplace.[21] The locution is itself telling here: 'the population' has wives, which rather implies that Powell does not regard women as legitimate members of 'the population'. It is as if the 'Representation of the People Act' of 1918 that started to extend the franchise to women had not happened. Powell's rhetoric excludes women here from the 'native population': his address is to the Englishman. It is exclusive not just of those from foreign lands but also of those who are foreign in terms of gender.

However, women can be useful for his rhetoric, especially if they hold racist views. The second conversation recounted in the speech comes through a letter to Powell about a situation again in his own constituency. This letter comes from a woman, bereft of husband and sons after the

---

[20]Interestingly, unlike Theresa May, even the more obviously extreme Enoch Powell thought it improper to include numbers of students, especially medical students, in the official immigration figures: 'These are not, and never have been, immigrants.' The May position, though expressed not in terms of colour, turns out in fact to be more extreme than Powell's racism.

[21]Powell, *Freedom and Reality*, 217.

1939–45 war, who turned her seven-roomed house into a boarding house, in order to maintain herself financially. The appeal here to the case of a woman is one that exploits sentimentality, a classic trope of right-wing (and far-right) political rhetoric. Sentiment, after all, appeals to the primacy of emotion over reason and thus calls into question the value of an education which, as I argued above, should afford reason a proper place in political discourse as a mechanism for the proper calibration of our emotions.

The woman in this case is now the only white woman in her street, according to Powell's correspondent. 'The immigrants moved in. ... The quiet street became a place of noise and confusion.' Presumably the previously all-white population never uttered a sound and never spoke to each other.[22] Foreign tongues here are reduced to the status of 'noise' and 'confusion', in the same way that (as Powell was well aware) ancient Greek and Latin referred to foreigners as 'barbarians' because their speech sounded like 'bar-bar-bar'. 'Native English', by implication, is music, harmony and quiet order. The woman's white tenants moved out, and 'Immigrant families have tried to rent rooms in her house, but she always refused'.

Powell's point is that it is this woman – not the immigrants to whom she refuses accommodation on the grounds of their skin colour – who is the victim of discrimination, precisely because she is not being permitted by the State to practise her own racial discrimination any more. 'When she goes to the shops, she is followed by children, charming, wide-grinning piccaninnies. They cannot speak English, but one word they know. "Racialist", they chant.'[23]

The key element here is that Powell casts suspicion on the very legitimacy, the social standing of these children, because they do not speak English, and this simple and straightforward fact about their linguistic identity somehow induces fear, suspicion and a literal alienation. In calling them 'piccaninnies', Powell also uses an intrinsically abusive word, but one that derives again from a foreign source: Spanish *pequeño* or Portuguese *pequeno*, both meaning 'little', combined with

---

[22] Julian Barnes, *The Only Story* (Jonathan Cape, 2018), 61–2, writes of a very specific 'English silence': 'I got in, and as we drove my mood switched from pert indifference to furious humiliation. An English silence – one in which all the unspoken words are perfectly understood by both parties – prevailed.'

[23] Powell, *Freedom and Reality*, 218.

'ninny' implying stupidity or a simple-minded lack of civilization and culture. The word, quite literally, 'belittles' those whom it describes.

However disturbing we might find this, it remains the case that Powell's rhetoric is itself repeated, again some half-century later, by the Conservative MP Boris Johnson. Johnson was forced eventually to apologize for a speech in which he alleged that the reason the British Queen loved the Commonwealth was because 'it supplies her with regular cheering crowds of flag-waving piccaninnies' and ensured that she was surrounded by people with 'watermelon smiles'.[24] The political language of a specific kind of xenophobic Conservatism appears not to have changed. However, what has changed is something else: Powell was sacked from the opposition front bench by Conservative leader Ted Heath for his unacceptable and inflammatory rhetoric; Boris Johnson, by contrast, was appointed *to* the front bench, by Prime Minister Theresa May. As if that was not bad enough, he was appointed into the position of Secretary of State for Foreign Affairs.[25]

This suggests that the rhetoric of racism has now made its way right into the centre of government in the UK, and, worse, that it has become no longer shocking but entirely acceptable and even conventional. For Johnson, it is a matter for joking. For anyone with a sense of the importance of foreign tongues and the place of English in the world, Johnson's buffoonery and outrageous linguistic 'jokes' surely make his appointment to the Foreign Office as the UK's most senior diplomat extremely disturbing. My point is that it is precisely his English, his political rhetoric, that has made racism not just acceptable but an integral part of the contemporary British political disposition under Conservatism. That, however, is a fact that cannot be acknowledged openly, obviously, and hence it must be expressed in the language of the clown, the would-be adorable buffoon with his 'antic disposition', as it were. Such a rhetoric – in which the speaker presents himself as jocular buffoon, supposedly ironically undermining his own status – allows a pernicious idea to enter or be expressed in the public sphere without

---

[24]See report in Owen Bowcott and Sam Jones, 'Johnson's "piccaninnies" apology', *The Guardian*, 23 January 2008, available at: https://www.theguardian.com/politics/2008/jan/23/london.race

[25]Goodlad, *Thatcher*, 32, claims that, when Heath told his cabinet of his intention to sack Powell, 'Thatcher's was a lone voice urging the leader to stay his hand', though she also knew that it would be politic to distance herself from open support for his racist views.

the speaker assuming responsibility for the ill intention that it contains. It distances Johnson from his words, or, in the contemporary parlance, gives him 'deniability' while allowing those words to gain currency and even authority, given Johnson's official political standing.

Johnson, like Powell, studied Classics; like Powell, he makes occasional references to Classical literature, but does so in a way that undermines the learning involved in gaining the knowledge of such foreign tongues and domesticates the intrinsic foreignness of the language and the culture. In doing this, he trivializes the relation between the words and the world. Like Powell, he tacitly mocks the 'primitive belief that the word and the thing, the name and the object, are identical',[26] but he goes further than this and – like Donald Trump, his buffoonish US counterpart – brings a suave deniability into any and every statement. In short, his rhetoric depends upon no facts but only upon superficial prejudice, and it becomes all the more politically powerful and successful precisely because of that.

As Foreign Secretary, Boris Johnson takes the English language abroad with him, and it is this – English as a *political* (and not merely 'instrumental') world language – that will now be our focus.

* * *

In many ways, David Crystal's analysis of how English emerges as such a major world language has some surprising overlap with the narrative that Churchill told in his *History of the English-Speaking Peoples*. Crystal indicates that the English language spread with English travellers, as they moved across the world from the sixteenth and seventeenth centuries onwards. That historical and empirical factor, however, has to be placed alongside the major cultural factors that helped to consolidate the presence and persistence of English as its speakers took a vocabulary and a grammar into commercial trade across the world, exporting words and incorporating foreign vocabularies in a lexicon that contains numerous borrowings – including inheritances and modifications of words – from other languages.

Crystal also indicates a major factor that sits fairly comfortably, if again surprisingly, alongside Roberts's controversial thesis regarding the intimacy of English and wealth. As Crystal points out, English was the

---

[26]Powell, *Freedom and Reality*, 213.

language in which the first major Industrial Revolution was formed, and with it the technologies for forging new kinds of capitalist wealth-making and commerce. If other nations wanted similar kinds of economic development, then they essentially not only had to learn English-language technological terms but also had to keep in communicative contact with the nation that seemed to be leading the way ('pointing the finger' as Churchill would have had it), the nation that was 'the natural choice for progress' in the words of Crystal.[27]

The historical and the commercial combine with each other, to yield a very special political power: the power of a symbolic unity. As Crystal puts this, 'the language is a guarantor, as well as a symbol, of political unity' across the diverse countries of the British Empire.[28] Indeed, even when the Empire falls away after 1945, and in the absence of British English-speaking people, many of the people who were using English as the imported or imposed language of imperial power retained its use, because it helped them to retain communications internally and nationally among the many diverse languages that had previously been spoken even within their own nations. As Crystal explains, 'indigenous communities' were enabled 'to continue communicating with each other at a national level' through the ongoing use of English as the preferred medium.[29]

In short, then, as English became this world language, it also became a language that symbolized and even brought into actual being an idea of political unity. Further, we see the centre of gravity of the language moving to its specific American inflection in more recent times, given that the United States 'has come to be the dominant element' in many domains, and especially in the domain of technology and the web. Thus – and in many ways this is the logical summation of Crystal's observations regarding the intimate relations between the shape of a language and the shape of world governments – 'the future of English must be bound up to some extent with the future of that country [the USA]'.[30] At the time of writing, the United States has elected as its presiding voice the tweet-language of Donald Trump, and that is a

---

[27]Ibid., 83.
[28]Ibid., 79.
[29]Ibid., 79–80.
[30]Ibid., 127.

significant factor in the politics of nationalist isolationism that menaces democracy in our time.[31]

All of this surely helps us to understand that what we might think of as a 'native language' can, in fact, be an element in trade and thus a kind of commodity that can be 'owned' by anyone, at least in principle, without being tied to a specific geographical locale, nation or biographical location of birth. Further, it is not even necessarily tied to the body or tongue that speaks it, as the fundamental fact of mimicry shows. Aristotle was among the first to note that education, and perhaps especially linguistic education, depends primarily upon mimicry. We are thus all at a distance from our so-called 'native' language. Those who make a claim for the naturalness of that language, for the way in which it might yield a cognitive advantage on truth or reality or for its intrinsic value as given by any measure, including that of money, are simply making a tendentious political claim. It is a claim that lacks legitimacy, no matter in what tongue it is made.

The logic should now be clear. Every language becomes a foreign language. In both classic English literature and US popular culture, the status of English as an international – and even a universal – language becomes of interest. In Shakespeare's *The Tempest*, the young Ferdinand sees Miranda for the first time, and when she speaks – in English – he utters the amazed 'My English!' Ferdinand quickly overcomes this surprise, however, but his immediate response is one that raises issues of *how* the language is spoken and what it says about class and about political authority or legitimacy. 'I am the best of them that speak this speech / Were I but where 'tis spoken,' he says. The ostensibly foreign woman, Miranda (who, of course, is not 'foreign' at all) provokes the colonial incomer, Ferdinand, to assert his position, precisely through his *claim* upon an intimacy with the language. '*My* language!'

The same play dramatizes how it is that the colony might speak back to the 'native-English' speaker, when Caliban confronts Prospero. Prospero suggests that this foreigner was not only savage but also that he was unaware of meaning at all: 'when thou didst not, savage, / Know thine own meaning, but wouldst gabble like / A thing most brutish, I endow'd thy purposes / With words that made them known'. Caliban's

---

[31]For more explicit detail on Trump's threats to democracy, see Steven Levitsky and Daniel Ziblatt, *How Democracies Die* (Viking, 2018), 195–207.

celebrated response is 'You taught me language; and my profit on't / Is, I know how to curse'.

Such examples offer the early modern version, from within classic English literature, of the famously bizarre question that arises more recently in US popular culture: how come all these extraordinary forms of life from other galaxies that are discovered by the *Star Trek* picaresque travellers or cosmic colonialists all speak such good American English? This is not just Shakespeare's early modern English as an emerging world language; rather, it is contemporary American English staking its claims to be a fully cosmic or universal language.

'To imagine a language means to imagine a form of life,' said Wittgenstein.[32] The weirdness of the Shakespearean Ferdinand-meets-Miranda and of the *Star Trek*-meets-Klingon situation derives from the fact that, in both cases, the only real form of life imaginable – the only true and authentic form of life as such – is that centred on English (in Ferdinand's case) or American English (with Captains Kirk or Picard[33]). On board the Starship Enterprise, however, was the engineer, Scotty, played by James Doohan with a broad Scottish accent, and it was Doohan who made the first ventures into the invented language of 'Klingon'.

For many, this will sound banal or facetious: an invented language for a TV science-fiction series being taken seriously in a book about Political English. However, there are literally hundreds of such 'invented languages' – known as 'conlang' – around the world, Esperanto being only the most well known and highly regarded of them.[34] The point, however, is that *all* languages are, to some extent, invented languages. It is just that the invention is usually not mechanical and imposed, as with Klingon, but rather is organic, dynamic and carried through for the instrumental purposes of establishing a polity of some kind. As invented, therefore,

---

[32]Ludwig Wittgenstein, *Philosophical Investigations* (trans. G.E.M. Anscombe; Basil Blackwell, Oxford, 1958), §19.

[33]Those names are themselves politically significant. Kirk is Scottish for Church, and the character embodies a White Anglo-Saxon Protestant culture. Jean-Luc Picard retains echoes of Jean-Luc Godard and thus the sophistication of French avant-garde cinema, but it also alludes to Picard, the French frozen-food retailers, with their icy cool attention to taste and science combined. It also hints at the Hispano-American 'picaro', the rogue-like adventurer.

[34]For a view of Klingon, see https://www.youtube.com/watch?v=h9UEIQtafww. For a brief interview with its inventor, Marc Okrand, see https://www.youtube.com/watch?v=9YnYTSy0iYs; and, for a 'lesson', see https://www.youtube.com/watch?v=e5Did-eVQDc

all languages are also political, and, as inventions, they are subject to endless modifications and organic developments, developments that must be coterminous with developments and changes within the very polity that they constitute.

Political problems arise precisely when this simple fact is forgotten and when individuals assume an intimacy with their first-learnt language, letting them assume that it is 'natural'; that its existence and semantic content somehow originates with, and is coterminous with, the instance of their own birth; and that it is shaped entirely and autonomously by themselves in the free choice of mouth-movement, breath and sound. This is what yields the political conservatism – the claims by and for 'my language' – that we saw in my preceding chapter here. It is of especial importance in relation to English as a world or universal language. The proper response to this nativist English must surely be through a consideration of what it is to learn a language, even a first language, and also through a further consideration of what is at stake in according some intrinsic superior value to the understandings at which we arrive through the medium of that first language. How do we 'know' what we mean, and why do we act as if our spoken words somehow 'embody' that meaning?

Historically, the contemporary question has a very serious precursor. Christopher Hutton has explored the operations of what he has labelled as 'mother-tongue fascism' under the Nazi regime. Among the many turns to emotional sentiment that the Nazis exploited, there was also this identification of the German language with the mother. Nazism encouraged an attitude of reverence to both. This enabled a specific political attitude to 'foreigners' to take root. As Hutton puts it, 'One key aspect of the ideology of the mother-tongue was its importance – in the context of Nazism – as an anti-Semitic ideology. For Jews were held to lack a sense of loyalty to their mother-tongue and were therefore regarded as having an "unnatural" relationship to language. Jews lived in many countries and spoke many tongues; they were rootless nomads with loyalty only to their race.'[35]

The simple fact of having an expertise in more than one language is now a marker of the supposed 'elitism' of the 'cosmopolitan' Jew, and the fact of such expertise becomes instrumental in legitimizing the Nazi assault.

---

[35] Christopher M. Hutton, *Linguistics and the Third Reich: Mother-Tongue Fascism, Race and the Science of Language* (Routledge, 1999), 5.

This is a direct precursor of the political rhetoric of Theresa May, to give a most recent example from the UK, arguing in her Conservative Party conference speech of 4 October 2016 that 'if you believe you're a citizen of the world, you're a citizen of nowhere. You don't understand what the very word "citizenship" means.' In the same speech May stated that 'we' would now 'take control of our own destiny', and she made the repeated populist claim that she is sticking up for 'ordinary working-class people', and sometimes for 'the people' as such. She used these claims to identify a specific form of 'Britishness'. It is a form that allows her to 'state one thing loud and clear: we are not leaving the European Union only to give up control of immigration all over again'.[36]

Some months later, in July 2017, Vince Cable was poised to become the leader of the UK's Liberal Democrat party. He vigorously attacked May's speech on the grounds that 'It could have been taken out of *Mein Kampf*. I think that's where it came from, wasn't it? "Rootless cosmopolitans?"'[37] To say such a thing, of course, seems scandalous and excessively extremist. The point, however, is that the political English involved in May's speech has a subterranean link with all ideologies that are suspicious of the foreign as such, all ideologies that are nativist and that celebrate such nativism through an idealization of the 'mother-tongue'.

May's was a speech that encouraged suspicion not only of the cosmopolitan but also of the foreigner as such. However, crucially, it was a speech that was shaped almost entirely by the demands of a neologism, a made-up word that derives from foreign languages: the word 'Brexit', whose meanings haunt the entirety of the speech's content. It is a word worth exploring.

* * *

Poetry is where we often look for linguistic surprise, for a turn of phrase that can turn a mind. In 2001, Giulio Lepschy gave the Presidential Address to the UK's Modern Humanities Research Association. During his address, he turned to the vexing question of translation and, behind

---

[36]For the speech in full, see https://www.telegraph.co.uk/news/2016/10/05/theresa-mays-conference-speech-in-full/ (accessed 16 March 2018).

[37]See report at: http://www.independent.co.uk/news/uk/politics/theresa-may-mein-kampf-adolf-hitler-nazi-vince-cable-liberal-democrat-conservatives-a7825381.html (accessed 16 March 2018).

it, the question of the status of native languages. He told his audience that 'no one is a native speaker of the language of poetry', and he went on to remind his audience of 'a line of Marina Tsvetaeva, made famous by Paul Celan: "All poets are Jews". ... The language of poetry is a language of outsiders'.[38] Historically, English-language poets have revelled in using 'the language of outsiders', and this has sometimes involved the making up of neologisms.

On 11 July 2016, Theresa May became the UK's new Prime Minister, acceding to the role as the last candidate standing among Conservative contenders to assume the role of Conservative Party leader. That same day, she made her now famous pronouncement, that 'Brexit means Brexit; and we are going to make a success of it'. There is a poetic, almost incantatory rhyme there: 'Brexit, success-of-it'. Its structure is exactly the same as the infantile word for magic, 'abracadabra'. Yet even on its own, the first half of the phrase – 'Brexit means Brexit' – has assumed a massive political importance, shaping everything in British politics since that day. It operates as a newly minted and invented word that shapes and dominates UK politics. How does it work?

The phrase seems, on the face of it, to operate like any political slogan. It is pithy and easy to repeat, and its novelty as an invented word makes its speaker feel as if she or he is up to the minute in terms of political engagement. It's the newest and most attractive – because most fashionable – thing. Like many policies that are reduced to a slogan, however, it represents a danger to the fundamental principles of democratic government, in that it aims to do two things: first, it reduces the scope for dialogue and debate; secondly, it hands governance and government over to the control of one individual, who now stands over and in control of 'the people' whose voices the slogan silences. It deprives its very speakers of democratic political engagement precisely at the moment when, by speaking the phrase, they can believe themselves to be given voice. These are big claims for a small phrase, and they need to be laid out patiently.

First, 'Brexit' itself is a neologism whose roots lie in foreign words and usage. It is like a German composite noun, rolling together 'Britain' and 'exit'. The second of these words, of course, is Latin, but a Latin that has been fully domesticated into English, such that its speakers no longer

---

[38]Guilio Lepschy, 'Mother tongues and literary languages', *Modern Language Review*, 96:4 (2001), xlviii.

consider it anything other than pure English. The compound, running the two words together, is also itself a borrowing, for it echoes an earlier compound term, 'Grexit'. This latter was used to describe the potential forced expulsion of Greece from the Eurozone and, hypothetically, from the European Union itself, in 2015, a year before the British referendum. Given that the point of the 'pro-Leave' campaign was to 'take back control' of all decisions affecting the British people and their political situation, the term itself has to be fully 'domesticated': that is to say, control of its meaning has to be brought fully within the realms of political English, and the potentially inflammatory or even explosive power of any 'foreignness' in the term has to be defused.[39]

The simplest way to do that, of course, is to give it an English 'meaning'. Thus, Theresa May tells the British people exactly what it means. It means 'Brexit'; it 'means' itself. Saying this suggests that the meaning is, literally, self-evident, self-evidencing. It therefore needs no further explanation, for, given that it is self-evident, it operates like a truth universally acknowledged and requires no further gloss. This is part of the first stage: through the rhetoric of repetition in this context where foreignness must be domesticated, the slogan deprives its speaker of meaningful dialogue. There is no need for any debate as to what the meaning of the word might be. Full clarity has been provided; and, if you would like a further gloss, just repeat the rhyme: 'success-of-it'. Given this claim for self-evidencing, there is to be no further discussion or debate about what the political content of the word signifies.

Yet, questions can still, surely, be asked. Even though we may be 'charmed' by the abracadabra magic of all this, nonetheless we are left still seeking a substantive content for the term. As things stand, 'Brexit' is a term whose *semiotic* force is very powerful, but whose *semantic content* remains unclear. At this point, we turn to its originator to ask her directly what it means. As an exercise in semiotics – and in a kind of political signalling – it is full of force, but in what direction is that force taking us? Theresa May must know, for it is she who spoke the phrase first. In raising the question and putting it directly to her, however, we find the fulfilment of the second part of my claim. The meaning of this foreign neologism has been so utterly domesticated that it finds its 'home' not

---

[39]The slogan 'take back control' implied that something had been stolen improperly from the British people. I explore this, in detail, in 'Brexit: Thinking and resistance', in *Brexit and Literature*, ed. Robert Eaglestone (Routledge, 2018), 181–95.

just in England or in English but in the literally occult intention of its speaker. This is an example of how political rhetoric can slip from being authoritative into being authoritarian. The former would entail a speaker gaining recognition for her or his political English through a process of reasoned debate in which an authoritative position becomes clear. The latter is what happens when a speaker simply asserts authority, without earning it, and thus lacks legitimacy, claiming a speaking access to meaning that is denied to the rest of us.

'Brexit' is a semiotic term in search of semantic content. Theresa May implies that she knows that content, for she knows the meaning of the word. However, it is history that will determine what the word eventually means, as political realities start to fill it with sense. At the end of the process, Theresa May can claim that 'this is what it meant all along', that 'I told you'. Thus, she attempts to retain control of and governance over political reality, while in fact she is at its mercy. However, she manages to retain political power throughout the process. That is, authoritarianism. It is at its most evident in all political jurisdictions when genuine authority is most obviously lacking. At this point, too, legitimacy also slips into mere legality.

All of this happens because of the sleight of hand in which a political term assumes the importance of an abracadabra. The effect is extremely useful and powerful for a politician such as May. It is the very semantic vacuity of the phrase that converts it into a slogan for enchantment, with the loss of political consciousness in those who hear it and succumb to its repetitive and incantatory charm. Its political power lies here, in ensuring that there is nothing serious with which to engage in debate: no one can disagree with this, given that there is nothing sensible in it with which one can disagree (or even agree – all we can do is enter the field of repetition). At the same time, the very emptiness of the phrase is instrumental in permitting Theresa May to fill the meaning of 'Brexit' eventually – that is to say, following the events that will occur as Britain seeks to leave the European Union – in any way whatsoever that she chooses, and then saying that whatever she determines in political practice as the meaning of 'Brexit' is what it always meant and what it always was. As she said, as she dictated. It is a statement that is designed to justify and legitimize itself *in retrospect*, and its speaker is thereby proposing that she will have yet greater political power *after* the meaning becomes clear, not through the present making of the statement now. It is a political prophecy and thus entirely consistent with the very religious impulse that informs it: 'I am that I am.' That phrase is how the God of the biblical Old Testament identifies to Moses.

This religious prefiguration is apposite, given Theresa May's own background as the daughter of a vicar. As I will show in the next chapter, all contemporary authoritarian political English finds its source in theology. Here, however, it is worth recalling where in the Bible we get, in the 'I am that I am', the verbal prefiguration of 'Brexit means Brexit'. It comes, appropriately enough, in the book of Exodus, the book in the Old Testament that outlines how Moses will lead his people out of political oppression under the power of Egypt. The implicit parallel is with the supposed political oppression of the English by European foreigners. In Exodus, 3:7, we find 'the Lord said, I have surely seen the affliction of my people which are in Egypt, and have heard their cry by reason of their taskmasters; for I know their sorrows'. Moses has had his vision at the burning bush, certainly, but for Theresa May in the conference speech in which she uttered the 'Brexit means Brexit' phrase, 'a vision is nothing without the determination to see it through'. The speech describes a more general 'revolution', one that she is determined to lead as she leads 'the people' out of the European Union and into the fulfilment of their destiny, as she explicitly calls it. The rhetoric of the speech is one that is based on repetition throughout, and, paradoxically, the phrase that is repeated is itself the one that demands change: 'A change has got to come.' In the Bible, Moses is told to 'deliver [the people] out of the land of the Egyptians, and to bring them up out of that land unto a good land and a large, unto a land flowing with milk and honey' – and £350 million a week for the NHS, as it were.

The literary precursor is Humpty-Dumpty in Lewis Carroll's *Through the Looking-Glass*, for whom words can mean whatever he wants them to mean: 'The question is, which is to be master, that's all.' In this state of affairs, democratic parliamentary politics is reduced to the nonsense that Carroll satirized. It is not just coincidence or serendipity that saw Kenneth Clarke – pro-EU Conservative MP – allude directly to this precursor text when he explained why he could not support his party's whip over Brexit policy. On 5 February 2017, he described the policy as one where 'apparently, you follow the rabbit down the rabbit-hole and emerge in a wonderland' where a series of protectionist and authoritarian leaders – Trump and Erdoğan were the two he named – will suddenly be begging to trade with the UK, outside of the European Union. 'No doubt', he added, 'somewhere there's a hatter holding a tea party with a dormouse.' His point is that the policy is one that would suit a mad hatter: irrational, nonsense, nostalgic for Victorian fantasies of grandeur aligned with the time when Carroll wrote.

Clarke's intervention exemplifies what has happened to democratic debate, after the incantation of 'Brexit means Brexit; and we're going to make a success of it'. It is, for him, a phrase more suited to nonsense literature than to real democratic politics. Its magic – and its political power – is such that it precludes reasoned debate. It thus essentially contains the demand to by-pass parliament, and, indeed, this is exactly what Theresa May's government proposes to do, under so-called Henry VIII powers.[40] In repealing European Union laws, the UK Conservative administration proposed that it should enjoy the power to make and amend laws without having to go through parliament: essentially, to rule by decree or dictatorial fiat. In sum, we can now see that 'Brexit means Brexit' actually means something else, once we subject its political English to scrutiny.

Thus, the logical sequence now follows, given what I have said earlier about every language – even a 'native tongue' – being always already and intrinsically a foreign language. If we reject the foreign, then we reject dialogue; and if we reject dialogue, then we reject the very principles of democratic debate that genuine dialogue subtends; and if we reject democratic debate, we reject the fundamental order of the UK's House of Commons and due democratic political process. This has turned out to be exactly what Prime Minister Theresa May wishes to do, asserting for herself the full authority – as with a monarch – to assume the right to direct all political power within the nation and even going to the law courts to try to assert that political position.[41]

* * *

---

[40] The power in question is that enshrined in the 1539 'Statute of Proclamations'. The text is available at: http://statutes.org.uk/site/the-statutes/sixteenth-century/1539-31-henry-8-c-8-proclamation-by-the-crown/ (accessed 19 March 2018).

[41] The reference here is to the case brought by Gina Miller, requiring the government to ensure that parliament had the right to debate and to decide upon whether the Prime Minister had the right and authority to send a letter to the European Union saying that Britain would invoke Article 50 of the Lisbon Treaty, indicating the intention to leave the European Union. Miller won the case. In a further twist worthy of Lewis Carroll's upside-down world, MPs in Parliament then voted to deny themselves a vote on the matter.

As I indicated, the UK example is hardly exceptional. Every political action comes with its own slogans. Sometimes, the slogan can be reduced to single words, and this was the case in the Soviet Union as it transitioned to becoming the Russian Federation. At issue here is the language of two different leaders: Gorbachev and Putin. There is an interesting linkage that can be traced between the two different kinds of 'political Russian' deployed by these two politicians.

Masha Gessen describes the rise of what she calls 'The Autocrat's Language' in her 2017 Arthur Miller Freedom to Write Lecture, given in association with PEN International on 7 May 2017. She had already written extensively about the rise of Vladimir Putin in Russia in her 2012 study of *The Man without a Face: The Unlikely Rise of Vladimir Putin*. There, she noted the power of his language. Rather like the first impression that we might have of the language of Donald Trump, Putin's demotic consistently sought out cloacal vulgarity and deployed it fully. This presents us with a sense that political discourse is in a state of degradation; and the implication is that the conditions of both politics and of the people of Russia are also being systematically degraded, and that the language is instrumental in bringing this degradation about. Further, the deterioration of political language in Russia, she suggests, goes back to words that were in search of a meaning.

In around 1986, Mikhail Gorbachev 'floated the term *perestroika* – restructuring – though no one, not even Gorbachev himself, quite knew what he meant', Gessen wrote. This was an instantiation of our more recent 'Brexit' moment, in this respect. She notes that 'In January 1987, Gorbachev added another new term, *glasnost*, or openness'.[42] She reminds us that, in what was then the Soviet Union, while these terms did not mean the abolition of censorship, there nonetheless came about a loosening of State control, and libraries began to give readers access to previously unseen documents. The political consequence of this new language, as these words sought for a substantive meaning, was established – and in ways that Gorbachev himself had not openly intended.

Gorbachev did not intend to bring about the end of Communist rule, but the introduction of these new terms into the lexicon – and their legitimation through his own political deployment of them – led to a belief in the possibility of change in what had been experienced as a static

---

[42]Masha Gessen, *The Man Without a Face: the Unlikely Rise of Vladimir Putin* (Granta, 2012), 73.

and sclerotic regime. As Gessen puts it, 'Gorbachev had dangled the carrot of possible change – and so people began to talk about change as if it were possible.' In fact, although Gessen does not explain it in these terms, what is happening here is that a political language is looking for its historical realization: the words are in search of a reality that will be adequate to them and a reality that can be shared in a common understanding of the semantic scope and ambit of the terms themselves. Semiotics is becoming semantics; the 'noise' and 'confusion' (as Enoch Powell would call it) brought about in these new and unfamiliar terms seek proper understanding and communication. As they talk and engage these new words, 'Cautiously, people began to allow these conversations to spill out of their kitchens into other people's living rooms. Loose alliances began to take shape.'[43] In this way, a new polity was being formed, through the linguistic debate over the meanings of *perestroika* and *glasnost*. Within the late Soviet state, the language brought a hint of democracy.

By the time that Putin comes to power, however, the levels of political debate have been lowered, meanings increasingly constrained to the language of the sewer; and as they are lowered, so too is the threshold of social and political freedoms. A key aspect of this is the street language or scurrilous demotic used by Putin. Gessen points out that, when he intervened in Chechnya in September 1999, he described the Russian mission in scatological terms: '"We will hunt them down," he said of the terrorists. "Wherever we find them, we will destroy them. Even if we find them in the toilet. We will rub them out in the outhouse."'[44] It was this kind of language, with its scatological and 'authentic' gutter humour, that seemed to bring popular acclaim to Putin. No more talk of regular law enforcement, justice or virtue: instead, this former spy – a man whose language skills were really good (he excelled in German, for instance, and has a complete command also of English) – preferred the language of violence and a violence of language to gain and then to retain power.

After the disasters in Beslan and the Moscow theatre siege, a reporter from *Le Monde* quizzed Putin about State violence and about his use of heavy artillery in bringing these events to a bloody end. 'Putin, looking calm and even smiling slightly with the corners of his mouth, said, "If you are ready to become a radical adherent of Islam and you are ready to be

---

[43]Gessen, *Man Without a Face*, 74.
[44]Ibid., 26.

circumcised, I invite you to come to Moscow. We are a country of many faiths. We have specialists in this. I will recommend that the operation be performed in such a way that nothing will ever grow there again.'"[45]

This is an attempt to silence the reporter and anyone else who might dare to raise a voice in opposition to, or in criticism of, Putin. We should note, though, that the rhetoric here suggests that to silence a man is akin to circumcising him: your tongue is replaced by your penis, and either or both can be removed if you dare to speak.

Crazy as it may seem, this is one of the first political lessons in political language that Trump seemed to learn. Perhaps, of course, it is the case that he was already extremely fluent in it, and it was simply a matter of awaiting the moment when an American audience would be ready to legitimize it as the basis of their polity. Once that is done, it becomes unsurprising that he is elected. We became explicitly aware of the overlap with the kind of scatology familiar from Putin during the nomination debates within the Republican Party itself in the months leading up to November 2016. In those debates, when Trump was seeking the Republican nomination, his Republican rival Marco Rubio took issue with the fact that Trump always name-called him 'little Marco'. The name-calling was meant to demean and belittle, literally, but then literal meaning gets lost in the subsequent rhetorical to-and-fro.

Rubio concedes that Trump is about a foot taller than he is. 'About 6'2"', he says, but then adds 'that's why I don't understand that his hands are the size of someone who is 5'2". Have you seen the size of his hands? ... And you know what they say about men with small hands....' Having left the pause for the audience fully to get the intended double-entendre, his punch line, pretending that his comment is really about hands and not penis, is 'You can't trust them'. Trump, of course, picks up on it, and he spends the next series of debates and speeches boasting about the size of his 'hands'. Eventually, he crudely acknowledges the supposed double-entendre, and says that 'there is no problem' with the size of his penis. 'Look at those big hands,' he repeats time and again, calling them 'big', 'strong' and so on, essentially boasting about his virility as supposedly signalled by penis size.

In the late 1950s and early 1960s, it was a well-known fact among a number of people in the US President's inner circle and family that

---

[45] Ibid., 208.

John F. Kennedy had an insatiable sexual appetite, but this was never used as part of his rhetorical appeal to the public. Instead, it was kept largely secret. By contrast, Trump – in an age of transparency, perhaps – shows us a little too much and flaunts his sexual appetite, utterly shamelessly. This persists even when the public gets to hear of the secret recording in which he boasts that his fame as a TV celebrity allows him to do anything with women, up to and including assaulting them sexually as soon as he meets them. His penis becomes, for a while, his literal talking-point: he talks politics through it, to put things only slightly metaphorically here.

In her Arthur Miller Lecture, Gessen adverts to the Russian precedents for Trump Speak. She talks of Sergei Gandlevsky, a Russian poet, who 'loved the word secateurs', because, as Gessen puts it, 'Secateurs is a great word. It has a shape. It has weight. It has a function. It is not ambiguous. It is also not a hammer, a rake, or a plow.' Being able to use the word properly, being able to call 'secateurs' secateurs, is the mark of freedom; for in the political Russian world that she deplores, language can be used to mean anything: Humpty-Dumpty's question – who is to be master – is answered there by dictatorial authoritarianism. Trump's particular extension of this is that he has not only mastered the use of words to mean their opposites, as in Orwell's *Nineteen Eighty-Four*; he has also managed to 'take words and throw them into a pile that means nothing'. He is Humpty-Dumpty on steroids, as it were. He evacuates words of any semantic content, as when 'Everything is great and everything is tremendous', and he presides over a language where 'Any words can be given or taken away', as when NATO is both obsolete and no longer obsolete, for example.[46]

Politically, this is dangerous, for the simple and straightforward reason that – like May's 'Brexit' – it deprives political debate of any meaning. It reduces dialogue to drivel and consequently threatens 'the basic survival of the public sphere'.[47] This is the real danger not just of Trump but also of a politician such as Theresa May. The evisceration of language – the emptying out of semantic content and the preference for resolving difference merely at the level of semiotics – is not just a trivial side issue for politics. Trump Speak, or May's 'Brexit means Brexit', are anti-

---

[46]Masha Gessen, 'The Autocrat's Language', *NYR Daily: New York Review of Books*, 13 May 2017, also available at: https://worldvoices.pen.org/session/arthur-miller-lecture-masha-gesson-and-samantha-bee/

[47]Gessen, 'Autocrat'.

rhetorical devices masquerading as substantive comment, but they are themselves comments that drive the public sphere and the whole realm of politics into a void. The void will not remain empty, however, because whoever now controls the meanings of words not only controls language but also controls the speakers of that language and their material and physical human possibilities. This – the evacuation of semantic content from words – is one key method by which politicians seek to gain political power and to shape a polity in our time. It also presages the rise of political decision-making by the prevalence of emotion over reason, and, behind that, there lies eventually the iron law of the violent fist.

* * *

George Orwell was also interested in 'new words' and wrote an essay on that theme as war broke out, around 1940. He argued there that our existing language 'is practically useless for describing anything that goes on inside the brain'. As proof, he offers an experiment that recalls a famous suggestion made decades earlier by Virginia Woolf (though he does not see, or acknowledge, the borrowing nor the precedent that she offers). 'Examine your thought at any casual moment,' he writes, and you will find that 'The main movement in it will be a stream of nameless things – so nameless that one hardly knows whether to call them thoughts, images or feelings'.[48] In 1925, in her celebrated essay on 'Modern Fiction', Woolf had already advised novelists to 'Examine for a moment an ordinary mind on an ordinary day. The mind receives a myriad impressions – trivial, fantastic, evanescent, or engraved with the sharpness of steel', and, if we attend properly to that, we will reveal 'this unknown and uncircumscribed spirit' with 'whatever aberration or complexity it may display' and 'with as little mixture of the alien and external as possible'.[49]

For Woolf, as for Orwell, this attitude might yield something that encapsulates the reality of the human mind in action. However, it also captures exactly the incipient senselessness that we associate with Trump, or with the Brexit slogan. As Woolf indicates, the kind of stream of consciousness that follows yields a spirit that is certainly

---

[48]George Orwell, 'New Words', in *Collected Essays, Journalism and Letters, Vol. 2: My Country Right or Left, 1940–1943*, ed. Sonia Orwell and Ian Angus (Secker & Warburg, 1968), 3–4.
[49]Virginia Woolf, 'Modern Fiction', in *Selected Essays*, ed. David Bradshaw (Oxford University Press, 2008), 9.

'uncircumscribed', full of 'aberration' and utterly uncontaminated by the presence of anyone else, anyone 'alien and external' to the speaker. It might work as an exploration of an individual psyche, divorced entirely from the material realities of the world and thus appropriate to fictional explorations of 'character', but it is a recipe for political catastrophe.

Orwell offers a political corrective to Woolf's position. He argues that individuals cannot just invent new words, because the words only operate as words when they attend precisely to other people and their experiences. In this respect, something like Joyce's *Finnegans Wake* is only *seemingly* comprised of such 'new words'. In fact, they are not new, because they are portmanteau words that generously and hospitably invite the alien tongue into the heart of the text, such that the text becomes continuously foreign, calling forth experiences that are themselves new, and shareable. That is to say, for all its surface oddity, *Finnegans Wake* is actually a kind of 'commonplace book', a book where what we have in common, linguistically, is deliberately extended by the mixing of tongues.

As Orwell has it, it is precisely the making common of new experience that is the germinal seed of new meaning and thus of a new polity. 'Without common experience … no word can mean anything. … it is not desirable that any one man, short of a genius, should make a show of his inner life. What is wanted is to discover the now nameless feelings that men have *in common*.'[50] The problem with the political rhetoric of Trump, say, is that it is not just meaningless drivel; it is rather that it is, in the end, largely incomprehensible because it is utterly solipsistic, utterly self-regarding, with no interference from anything alien to himself. This is why his most important vocabulary is simply an endless repetition of his own name and why he has 'earned' the soubriquet of 'The Donald'.[51]

As a language that fails to attend to the foreign, Trump Speak is not actually a language at all. Every language, insofar as it is a language as such, must attend to the fact of dialogue, which means simply the

---

[50] Orwell, 'New Words', 9, 11.

[51] It was notable that, during his presidential campaign, he took to referring to himself in the third person, as 'Donald J. Trump', as when (for a typical example) he said, 'Donald J. Trump is calling for a total and complete shutdown of Muslims entering the United States', on 7 December 2015. See report by Jenna Johnson for the *Washington Post*, available at: https://www.washingtonpost.com/news/post-politics/wp/2015/12/07/donald-trump-calls-for-total-and-complete-shutdown-of-muslims-entering-the-united-states/?utm_term=.8000034149db. For the speech, see https://www.youtube.com/watch?v=LRxozK6Bpvk

'contamination' of some kind of would-be noble nativism with words that require that the speaker mix with those alien to herself or himself. Anything else is racism, posing sometimes as a form of 'nativism' or, in the worst of cases, nationalist patriotism or patriotic nationalism.

The German philosopher, Theodor Adorno, found a certain exoticism in foreign words and sought them out eagerly. In 1959, he gave a radio broadcast, entitled 'Words from Abroad' ('*Worter aus dem Fremde*'). He celebrated what he called 'the exogamy of language' against those who preferred the homely, the *heimlich*, the utter familiarity of a supposed native German. His argument there rested not just on his liking for the sensuality of foreign words on the tongue but also on the fact that a foreign word disturbs one's already-formed prejudices and ready-made fixed ideas. It is not the imported word itself that his detractors find irritating, he argues; rather, it is the fact that the foreign word introduces ideas with which they are unfamiliar. Those unfamiliar ideas, signalled in the foreign sounds, demand that the listener attend to experiences that are also new and that disturb our consciousness. In short, words from abroad propel us into thinking, and thus into being intellectually alert and alive to the words that we already know, our own lexicon. Words from abroad expand consciousness and make us live and inhabit our bodies and our social world differently.

He personalized this in his broadcast, in ways that are at once themselves troubling as well as illustrative of what is at stake in any serious political language. 'The early craving for foreign words is like the craving for foreign and if possible exotic girls,' he writes, and what this signals is a desire 'to escape from the sphere of what is always the same, the spell of what one is and knows anyway'. Through this detour, he returns to politics, concluding that 'National groups who want one-dish meals even in language find this ... hateful'.[52]

The fact that the metaphor of the erotic here may be disturbing in our time – though it would have been largely ideologically accepted as untroubling and even 'normal' in 1959 – is itself precisely the point. In our own moment, we may well be accustomed to avoiding the incipient heteronormative masculinism that sits silently within Adorno's phrasing and metaphor; and it is this that makes his language 'foreign', even in its English translation. The foreign can be that which comes from a different

---

[52] Theodor Adorno, *Notes to Literature*, vol. 1, ed. Rolf Tiedemann (trans. Shierry Weber Nicholsen; Columbia University Press, New York, 1991), 187.

historical moment, every bit as much as that which comes from a different geographical space. The past is indeed 'a foreign country', as L.P. Hartley signalled as the opening gambit of his 1953 novel, *The Go-Between*, a novel appropriately enough about passing between different voices.

Hannah Arendt also, somewhat inadvertently and perhaps intending to contest the argument that I am advancing here, has something of significance to say about native and foreign tongues. In an interview given to Gunther Gaus on 28 October 1964, she said that 'there is a tremendous difference between your mother tongue and another language. For myself I can put it extremely simply. In German I know a rather large part of German poetry by heart; the poems are always somehow in the back of my mind. I can never do that again.'[53] In this, she is indicating the special value that she gives to the intimacy that she feels between her sense of her self and the first language she spoke, German.

Yet this is, in fact, a problem, for she is indicating that 'the poems are always … in the back of my mind', suggesting that there is a constant backdrop that is unchanging and only ever available for repetition and rehearsal. The key, though, comes in the sentence with which she prefaced this comment, for there she said that 'I write in English, but I have never lost a feeling of distance from it'.[54] That feeling of distance is, in fact, precisely what makes her able to think anew: it is precisely this distance between self and speech – this alienation that she calls 'distance' – that brings the foreign into the heart of what she says.

Two decades after Adorno gave his broadcast, Hans-Georg Gadamer was awarded the 'Sigmund Freud Prize' by the German Academy for Language and Poetry. In his acceptance speech, given in Darmstadt that year, he took as his topic 'Good German'. What he finds in the speech is that 'good German' depends upon a kind of poetic or artistic attitude. Languages are governed by rules and conventions, certainly, he concedes. However, even if this is so, it does not follow that the best way to learn a language is by learning those rules. Rather, as he says at the opening of his speech, 'One can only learn from examples'.

Further, as with language, so also with living. Gadamer asks, 'Is our behavior really governed just by the application of rules?' He answers his own question, indicating that rules really just 'constitute a dead

---

[53] Hannah Arendt, *Essays in Understanding, 1930–1954: Formation, Exile, and Totalitarianism*, ed. Jerome Kohn (Schocken Books, New York, 1994), 13.
[54] Arendt, *Essays in Understanding*, 13.

framework of rectitude'; and if we want to do as, say, Virginia Woolf or George Orwell or Theodor Adorno wanted to do – that is, to grasp something of the reality of a life as it is lived – then we will find that such a life 'is revealed to us in the exceptions, the deviations, and the ventures beyond what is correct and regular'.[55] Once more, we find here a praise of a language that 'ventures beyond' that which is already known. 'Good German' involves us in a process whereby we realize that to obey the rules is to keep our thinking stultified – and thereby to refuse to think at all. Rules may seem to govern precision, but, as Gadamer argues, an obedience to such rule-governed behaviour will predict its own results and will produce only what we already know: the familiar, the self, the self that identifies only with itself. This is what will yield the most extreme and damaging form of prejudicial nativism, a belief that 'this is so' only and entirely because 'I say "this is so"'.

Such a self talks only to itself, and thus knows and can know nothing of the world or of the polity in which it speaks. It has no place in politics and, as in the extreme example of Trump, fails to engage with real material conditions of life, even as it claims to be simple, straightforward, unambiguous and directly referential.

Politics starts – we might say as a logical consequence of this argument – from foreign policy, and domestic policies can only genuinely offer themselves as political if and only if they are themselves shaped by the conditions of the world beyond our own 'native' tongue. The subscription to the belief that there is indeed such a thing as 'native English', say, is precisely what produces not only nationalist consciousness but also the denial of the very existence of the public sphere, the existence of a real democratic polity. 'Native English' and its political counterpart in 'the Anglosphere' is a construction – a fabrication – designed to deny English-speaking people the very possibility of engaging properly in politics. Instead, it gives such speakers only the already familiar, without the political openness of having that disturbed by any possibility of change. It is not only conservative politically; it is the very denial of politics. It is the mark not of a self-assuredness but of a profound fear of anything foreign: xenophobia in its purest form.

---

[55]Hans-Georg Gadamer, *Praise of Theory* (1983; trans. Chris Dawson; Yale University Press, 1998), 135.

3 FUNDAMENTALIST ENGLISH: THE STIFF UPPER LIP

On 28 March 2017, Leslie Fielding was interviewed on the BBC's flagship morning news programme, *Today*. He had been invited for interview because, on the eve of Theresa May initiating the process of Britain leaving the European Union, via Article 50 of the Lisbon Treaty, the editors of *Today* thought it a useful idea to look back to the day when Britain initially entered what was then the European Economic Community. At that time, in 1973, Fielding was the first British diplomat to go to Brussels and begin the process of integration into the Community.

He spoke of his first day and said that it was rather disorganized and chaotic. 'But that was understandable,' he said, because 'after all, I was a newcomer, a dreaded Englishman, thought to be unable to speak any other language than English'. However, he may well have surprised colleagues in Brussels, because he was indeed fluent in French. He said that 'I was told by Ted Heath [the UK Prime Minister at the time] to speak French all the time: he didn't want any linguistic chauvinism'. Fielding went on, 'I spoke French all the time and it was OK. The problem was that it was twenty-four hours a day. The French language demands facial exertions different from those required when one mutters away in English with a clipped manner. My throat, cheeks and lips began to rebel after 8-10 hours of that.' However self-deprecating Fielding may have intended to be, the words here show that, culturally and as part of the English unconscious, P.G. Wodehouse's Monty was alive and well in 1973.

It is interesting here that Heath – whose own French was very poor – was aware of the issues around 'linguistic chauvinism'. Heath could see that there may have been some suspicion among the other European nations at the arrival of a British complement who, according to type, might simply expect the whole of Europe to speak English, as had been the expected norm among the English in the days of Empire. Fielding, in fact, held something of that legacy, for he told the radio listeners that, although Brussels functioned extremely well, 'I thought that on the whole our methods were better than theirs. As a Brit, I had better man-management skills than most of them.'[1]

Why might the simple fact of being British be a determining characteristic of good 'man-management skills', unless the governing assumption is that British people are or were used to finding themselves in the position of managers: that is to say, in a position where others – foreigners, non-British people – worked under their leadership and direction? Further, why might such a thing be associated in Fielding's mind with the fact of being an English speaker, unless, again, a question of linguistic chauvinism did indeed ghost the relations between the UK and what would eventually become the European Union?

Official and political superiority is tied here to an assumed superiority of language, and especially of the English language. Fielding may well have mastered the tongue of the foreigners – French (there was no mention of Flemish or Walloon) – but he finds that his very body rebels against it almost immediately, almost by natural reflex: 'my throat, cheeks and lips began to rebel after 8-10 hours of that.' Obviously he resists 'going native', as it were, but in doing so, he remains conscious of an assumed 'naturalness' of speaking English, as against a presumed unnatural and rebellious contrivance by foreigners to determinedly speak French and to pervert and distort the otherwise natural body in doing so. The political superiority that is identified with the speaking of English relates also to an *innate* superiority of the person, of the Englishman's body itself. The Englishman and especially the English imperialist may be a manager of others, but he is also, prior to that, a manager of himself: managing not just his language but also his bodily bearing and demeanour, above all. The fabled 'stiff upper lip' – that rebellion of his throat, cheeks and lips – denotes both language and behaviour.

There is a history to such linguistic imperialism, in fact. It is akin to the nativism that we have just explored in my preceding chapter here, a nativism that is actually a cover for an implicit legacy of racism. It relates not just to Empire but also to social class and to the fundamentals of

---

[1] Listen to the interview in full here: https://www.bbc.co.uk/programmes/p04y8w5q (accessed 16 August 2018).

linguistic education: the place of English in our educational curricula. It was on 2 May 1919, in the wake of the Great War and the massive turmoil of the Russian Revolution that had shaken the stability and self-assurance of European governments, that the UK government asked Henry Newbolt to chair a 'Departmental Committee Appointed by the President of the Board of Education to Inquire into the Position of English in the Educational System of England'; and in 1922, George Sampson, who had himself been a member of that Committee, also produced his own separate book, *English for the English*.

In his 'Programme' for the education of the English in the language of English, Sampson already indicates – here as early as 1922, a half-century before Fielding went to Brussels – the global standing of English as a *spoken* world language, and asks, 'Where should the standard of spoken English be found if not in England?' Such a standard, he suggests, is crucial for proper communication among those speakers of the language across the world. He laments that, in England in 1922, 'there is no standard'. Counties and towns across the country essentially have their own autonomous versions of English, with no common standard form, and this, he says, 'is not independence, it is merely provincialism; and it is not the duty of the schools to encourage provincialism, but to set the standard of speech for the Empire'. This is part of his argument for establishing standards of spoken English, which he claims as a kind of social right: 'The English boy [sic] has an indefeasible right to the King's English.'[2]

We will look in more detail here at the history of English and its relation to imperialist politics further. However, for the moment, we can take our cue from this reference to 'the King's English' to examine a more recent interest in political speech, as seen in the popular and successful 2010 film by Tom Hooper, called *The King's Speech*. This film shows a man struggling to speak through a stutter, and it is not just any man, but it is that man who is supposed to embody the very being of Empire, the King. Like Fielding in Brussels, this man's very body is also in a state of turmoil and even rebellion, but the point is that in coming to make 'the King's speech' – fluent English – that resistance is completely (and, in the true popular cinematic manner, 'heroically') overcome.

---

[2]George Sampson, *English for the English*, with an introduction by Denys Thompson (Cambridge University Press, 1970), 67–8.

The truth of English political superiority, symbolically embodied in the speaking of the English language, becomes associated with an almost complete 'state of nature'. As we will see in this chapter, English-speaking is political through and through because it is associated with the very fundamental possibility of having access to a quasi-God-given truth. Indeed, the 'King's English' is also rooted in the cultural and linguistic importance of the King James Version of the Bible, and it is imbued with a fundamentalist sense of its own innate authority: it operates as if it is the very origin of any authentic speech at all. As a consequence of this, as we will see here, it is as if the world and all of its natural and proper being, politically, is the articulation of an English voice. How does this happen? How can such a totalizing condition come about?

* * *

Tom Hooper's 2010 film, *The King's Speech*, tells the historically true story of how King George VI overcame an extreme and incapacitating stutter, thanks to the speech therapy that he had with Lionel Logue. George was a reluctant king who did not want to accede to the throne but was required to assume the role of monarch as a consequence of the abdication crisis provoked by Edward VIII's decision to marry the divorced Wallis Simpson. The film places speech – 'the King's English' indeed, and thus a very specific version of speech – at the heart of that fundamentally political situation. The scenario is one that, historically, is not too distant from the moment in which George Sampson and Henry Newbolt were advocating, a mere two decades before in the early 1920s, that a 'King's English' should be a more or less essential condition of civic and political existence, and thus a fundamental cornerstone of an English school education.

Although based on the true story, the film is not entirely accurate historically. It gives a positive role to Churchill, one that historically he did not entirely deserve. Churchill himself, of course, had his own speech impediment, briefly alluded to in the film. Indeed, at one moment he had a real breakdown in the House of Commons and became unable to speak. It was on 22 April 1904, when he was distancing himself from the Tories, and while he was speaking about improving the rights of the trade unions. Knowing of his discontent with Conservative protectionist trade policies, the Liberals had advanced repeated invitations to Churchill, asking him to stand as a Liberal candidate in various constituencies.

On 18 April, just four days prior to this speech, he had finally edged closer to them. The Liberals in Manchester told him that they would support him if he stood as a 'Free Trade' candidate; and he accepted their support.

By some accounts, when he stood in the Chamber on 22 April, Churchill simply forgot a speech that he had committed to memory. The committing of political speeches to memory has been a fundamental aspect of rhetoric at least since Cicero, and Churchill was simply following a standard, if classical, procedure. Indeed, the classical model gave him an authority over others who had not mastered the necessary techniques of memorization.[3] In full flow, some forty-five minutes in to his speech, Churchill simply fell suddenly into a silence, before sitting back down, the speech incomplete, and Churchill humiliated. He sat down and 'covered his face with his hands', reduced to muttering.[4] Whether it was simply a lapse of memory, or due to the stresses that he felt in his increasingly awkward political position, the speech was completely impeded. It was as if his stutter had completely taken him over, and he collapsed under the sheer pressures of its weight.[5] It is important, however, to note that the fundamental circumstance here is that he found himself in a politically sensitive position, and that the stress of his political condition – distancing himself from those with whom he had long shared allegiances – is not merely incidental to his inability to speak.

The political situation of the film's historical narrative, likewise, is important for the argument here. George V, who is reigning as the film opens, was the first of the inherited German line to adopt the name 'Windsor' (in 1917). Names too are political in this context. His parents were from the unambiguously German House of Saxe-Coburg and Gotha, and the day-to-day language of the family had been German until

---

[3]Much more recently, Ed Miliband famously tried to do the same thing when he was leader of the Labour Party. The contemporary political world may not remember Cicero, but speaking thus, without notes, gives the appearance of authenticity. In Miliband's case, it also led – in his Labour Party conference speech on 23 September 2014 – to him omitting a section dealing with the UK's deficit, opening him thereby to mockery and humiliation, and fundamentally damaging his prime ministerial credentials.

[4]A full account is given in Gilbert, *Churchill*, 163–4, and (in less detail), Jenkins, *Churchill*, 87. Both biographers refer to the breakdown of Randolph Churchill as a possible predetermining inherited problem.

[5]There has, of course, been a long historical dispute as to the nature of Churchill's speech impediment. Some describe it as a lisp, with the inability to pronounce the letter 's' properly; but others indicate that the real problem, in fact, was the stutter, and the mispronunciation was itself a means of trying to overcome the impediment of the stammer.

the mid-nineteenth century. George V was thus the first modern King to be named in an English style, after an English place and land, and he was among the first of the generations to speak English routinely. The reason for the name change was itself associated with political demands: a Royal Family with a German name sat very uneasily with the great and rising anti-German sentiment of the English both during the Great War of 1914–18 and then also in its political and cultural aftermath.

However, it is the later historical period, the lead-up to the war of 1939–45, that forms the central political focus of the film, for its narrative covers the period from around 1925 – just after the Duke of York (at that time called Albert or 'Bertie', subsequently to become George VI) makes his first public speech, stammering embarrassingly and disastrously through it – up to the rise of Hitler in Germany the 1930s, and on to the eve of war. George VI, the central figure in the film, made that first public speech as Duke of York in 1925, at the closing ceremony of the British Empire Exhibition in Wembley, and it was an embarrassing disaster.

The disaster had two sources, in fact: the first was his stammer, which marred the speech to the extent that parts of it were incomprehensible; the second was the fact that it was among the first major public addresses by a member of the Royal Family to avail of the new technology of radio. The stammer was broadcast not just to the immediate audience in Wembley but also to the nation as a whole and, indeed, around the world and through the British Empire. The mythic and ideological stiff upper lip was obviously somewhat tremulous here, and, as a result the very idea of England and of the innate superiority of English and of the English was at stake.

George V had opened the Exhibition, on 23 April 1924: St George's Day. It was to be a celebration of British imperial power, and its opening ceremony was marked by technological efficiency in communications. As George V opened the ceremony, he broadcast his speech across the Empire through radio – the first time such a technology had been used. He also sent a telegram to demonstrate the speed of new modes of electronic communication, as it returned to him from going round the world not in a Jules Verne style eighty days but in just over one minute. However, a year later, the Exhibition was formally closed not by George V but by the future George VI, his son the Duke of York. Having opened with fireworks, the British Empire Exhibition literally stuttered to a close one year later, going out not with a bang but a stammering whimper.

The technology is itself politically important. The broadcasting of a language across the world is tied firmly to the very idea of modernity as inscribed in the technology and is associated with the commercial opportunities that a world-broadcast language makes possible; and the film rightly attends to it. The opening series of shots is of a microphone, followed by a BBC announcer going through an extended ritual prior to introducing the speech that is about to be made by the Duke. The announcer's preparations include not just standard formal dress (for a medium that was aural only) but also a series of ritualized mouth-washings, throat-sprayings, loosening of the lips to ensure no plosive sounds during the broadcast, and a careful measuring of the distance between mouth and microphone. All of this is followed by an announcement in standard Received Pronunciation English, rich in its own special sounds: 'Empiah' for 'Empire' for instance.

As Gary Love has pointed out, one thing that the film catches well 'is the response of educated elites in the 1930s to the importance of radio as a national unifying medium, which could be used for the projection of Christian values and democratic constitutionalism against revolutionary ideas of both left and right'.[6] The technology itself is not neutral, in fact; rather, it is identified with a specific imperial power, a power that aspires to mediation or to taking the median way between what are seen as the political extremes of both left and right. It is centralizing, and focuses attention on the voice – and language – of the King as it transmits an idea of hierarchical unification over the radio. This is a fully politicized English, made all the more political by the simple fact of the international broadcasting of the speech. 'English' travels over and round the world, encircling, comprising and 'containing' the world through the English speech itself.

Sampson and Newbolt had written in the aftermath of the Russian Revolution, and in both the Newbolt Report and in Sampson's *English for the English* there is a deep anxiety about class and an abiding sense that class struggle and conflict have to be resolved if Britain is to avoid a political revolution. There is therefore great emphasis here on a benevolent patrician conservatism, in which the poor and under-

---

[6]Gary Love, 'A Churchillian view of the 1930s? Cinematic representations of politics and monarchy in "The King's Speech"', 30 August 2013, available at: http://www.cardiffsciscreen.co.uk/article/churchillian-view-1930s-cinematic-representations-politics-and-monarchy-kings-speechrom

privileged or under-educated will be given access to the beauties of the English language. George VI, at the later historical moment during the Second War, was trying essentially to do something similar. The task was to 'nationalize' the King's English and the King's nation, using the medium of radio, faced as Britain was in the 1930s, not with socialist revolution but rather with the rise of the radical right in Germany. George V, in fact, adverts directly to the predicament that he says the country is in during the mid-1930s, with 'Herr Hitler intimidating half of Europe, and Marshall Stalin the other half', putting Britain 'between the jackboots and the proletarian abyss', as he puts it.

The film's opening sequence, after the lengthy shots of the microphone, is set up as a funereal execution scene. Bertie, the Duke of York, is filmed ascending a narrow staircase, as if ascending an executioner's scaffold, with the microphone at Wembley set up to evoke visually the hangman's noose that awaits Bertie as he mounts the steps. He has been 'prepared' for the moment by the Archbishop of Canterbury, who stands with him – as if shriving him – at the base of the stairs in a solemnity associated with the ceremony of the religious Last Rites; and the general solemnity and silence in the scene mark this out as a tragic moment. It is a moment that, within the film's narrative arc, signals the symbolic execution of 'Bertie' and the start of what will become his resurrection as 'George VI'. It is the start of the process of 'George' making his name the name he will adopt as King, and it is thus appropriate that the word that gives him the greatest trouble in this opening speech is the word 'King' itself.

The film's narrative then follows the mythic narrative logic of a descent into the underworld, as Elizabeth, the Duke of York's wife, comes out of a car, its modernity in 1925 almost submerged under the Styx-like London fog. She emerges at a house in Harley Street, where she takes a lift downstairs to the basement rooms in which Lionel Logue, the Australian speech therapist from a literal 'down-under', awaits her. She has come as 'Mrs Johnson', to make initial inquiries about help for her husband. This is the moment that sets up a distance between English propriety and Australian vernacular and relaxed behaviour.

Logue is in the toilet when she arrives, and he enters to the sound of water flushing behind him: he enters, literally, from the scatological and taboo realm of the cloaca with which his language will later identify him. However, the cultural distance between the two is immediately mitigated and complicated by the fact that, as they greet each other, Logue quotes Shakespeare in lines from *Othello* (spoken by Iago) that the very 'proper'

English Elizabeth fails to recognize: 'poor and content is rich, and rich enough'. Bertie, at this point, is not there, and Logue tells 'Mrs Johnson' to bring her hubby and pop over on Tuesday when he will take some personal details for his assessment.

Language here again asserts itself, and with the language comes status and class. 'Mrs Johnson' says 'I don't have a "hubby"; we don't "pop"; nor do we talk about our private lives'. Logue starts to turn her away, but then she says, 'What if my husband is the Duke of York?' The 'proper' English vocabulary, combined with a very precise pronunciation, the quality of personal reserve, class and the regal status of a name all come together at this point to set up what the film is actually going to be about.

The substantive narrative of the film is one in which we see someone – Bertie – coming into language, as if learning his language for the first time. The language that he will enter, however, is very precisely the English of 'the King's speech'. Throughout, the link between language, empire and war is made clear. There is the cultural and even political suspicion of the establishment when faced with Logue – a great admirer of Shakespeare and a man who knows the plays by heart – purely because he *sounds* Australian. When he auditions with an amateur group for the part of Richard III, he stutters (paradoxically, of course) over one word, at which point the audition is cut short because the theatre director 'didn't know that Richard III was king of the colonies'. In similar vein, Bertie makes disparaging remarks about what an Australian might do for money. Towards the end, when preparing for the coronation, the Archbishop of Canterbury suggests that it would be only right and proper to provide an *English* specialist, instead of an Australian.

Logue insists on his own language throughout. He speaks in the Australian vernacular, encourages Bertie to swear – but with more vim and vigour than a 'public school prig', getting him to abandon the mild 'bloody' and 'bugger' and to shout 'fuck, shit, arse' essentially as an aid to overcome his impediment. This is indeed a kind of linguistic underworld, the language of the cloaca, through which Bertie must pass if he is to acquire 'the King's English' and become George VI.[7] Logue also insists on the familiar names throughout, and, for him, the name – the proper and

---

[7]Structurally, the film repeats what Northrop Frye once called 'the argument of comedy' in Shakespeare. In those comedies, the characters face an initial crisis, and then must all enter the 'green world' (a forest, Arden, fairy-land and so on), in which they experiment and come to find some proper sense of self and identity, before returning, refreshed, anew and purged,

familial name, 'Bertie' – is central to his therapy. At one point, Bertie tells Logue to 'Stop calling me that', to which Logue replies, 'I'm not calling you anything else', and Bertie's final reply to this is 'then we shan't speak'.

To speak fluently, for Logue, is to come to inhabit a name, with all that that entails. As he reminds Bertie, late on in the film and when claiming his one-shilling bet, pretty soon it will be Bertie's name on the coins. The name is associated with both fluency and currency, and both are associated with wealth, and even with the legitimation of wealth and capital itself. When Churchill asks Bertie what name he will adopt as King, he advises against Albert, on the grounds that it is 'too Germanic', and he suggests 'George' instead, thereby establishing a continuity with George V and establishing legitimacy itself with English and with the continuity of a kind of currency of authentic value.

Bertie's brother, David, as Edward VIII, taunts Bertie about his stutter, especially when Bertie complains about David's relation with Wallis Simpson, portrayed as she is in the film as a wealthy but somewhat vulgar American. When she and David talk, their language is that of phone-sex, in which they flirt and speak about 'making drowsies': their private euphemism for sex or drugs. This childish code works to establish their own private realm from which others are excluded. David, historically, is isolated because of his abdication, but, in the film, he is essentially isolated with Wallis because of this secret language that they and they alone share. The bedroom is their polity: David's speech is not a 'King's speech' at all and is thus delegitimized in the film's narrative arc. When Bertie confronts David about the political situation in Europe, David simply replies that Hitler will sort everything out, before rushing back to talk and drink again with Wallis. Their private language and private realm is aligned, in the film, with David's failure to treat the rise of Nazism seriously.[8]

Bertie, terrified of the new technology of radio, actually starts to come into speech through the recording that Logue makes of him speaking. Logue makes Bertie listen to Mozart through headphones while recording him simultaneously speaking some lines that he reads from Shakespeare. Interestingly, given that we witness the metaphorical execution of Bertie at the start of the film, in this scene we see him pondering life and death;

---

to the 'real' world. It is also obviously, a classical 'visit to the underworld' structure. See Northrop Frye, *The Anatomy of Criticism* (Princeton University Press, 1957), esp. 163–86.

[8] One historical flaw in the film is that it rather underplays David's Nazi sympathies.

for the speech he reads is Hamlet's 'To be or not to be'. He reads the speech flawlessly, of course (though not yet realizing himself that he has done so because of the noise of the music), and the irony here is that this speech is Hamlet's own great speech of hesitations, his stammering between life and death. For Bertie, it will be the start of his coming 'to be', but what he comes to be is not Bertie but King George VI, whose radio broadcasts – his political English – during the 1939–45 war were to become key to maintaining a sense of national identity and strength among the population at war.

Eventually, when Bertie is crowned as George VI, the ceremony is filmed. The family watches the film of the coronation at home, accompanied by the Archbishop of Canterbury, and it looks like a great success. However, at the end, when the Archbishop goes to switch the film off, a newsreel is just beginning, and it is a film of Hitler speaking at a Nuremberg rally. The young princess Margaret asks 'Papa, what is he saying?' George VI replies, 'I don't know; but he seems to be saying it rather well.' This is a crucial scene in the film. It is essentially setting the King's good English up against the ranting rhetoric of Hitler's German. This is certainly not the 'good German' that Gadamer praised. It is, however, a language of war, and it is this language that George VI sees, suddenly, that he must counter.

The King's speech – the King's English – is itself an act of war, and English is itself revealed as a language that is political in all its essentials, for it is legitimized and authorized as the language of the King. It has an absolute political authority – provided that it is spoken 'properly' and by a body that is comfortable with the shapes into which the language manoeuvres it. That is the language that Fielding spoke when he arrived in Brussels in 1973 and before he had to warp his tongue to speak French, and his position is that this language is itself one that neutralizes politics as such, by implying that to speak English is part of the natural order of things, all other languages contorting the human face and body into unnatural shapes.

Some political orators of the right have made much of the twisting of the face or body into odd shapes, a form of body-speak that is supposed to transcend national or local languages. Mussolini and Trump share a liking for the upturned mouth with its inverted smile, and the jutting stomach. Farage punctuates his speaking voice with an aggressive butting forward of the head, accompanied by abrupt bounces on his heels; and he disqualifies – and attempts to preclude – any criticism of him, prejudicially trivializing it with the disfiguring enormity of his gaping mouth in its rictus of the forced and false laugh. These gestures can be regimented, as they were in the Nazi salute (which has a disturbing tendency to reappear among far-right political groups), but Hitler made this his own 'signature' in its lazy casualness, at odds with the rigour and rigidity of the raised arm of his supporters. Not everyone shares in the body disfigurement in the same ways. The point of all this, however, is to find a way to make one's own language into a more universal language: to make one's meanings available to all who might not share your place and your point of view. It is the technology of the body primed to overcome linguistic difference.

The King's Speech shares this interest in the desire for communication beyond the immediacy of one's place. It is not just about someone coming into a 'native' language. It is about how that 'native' language is situated in and even shaped by war and other modes of violent conflict. The film explores how such a language relates to the difference not just between nations but to the difference between linguistic authority (George) and linguistic authoritarianism (Hitler). It is about establishing a link between English, the kingdom of the nation state, and fundamental ethical, social, and political values. It is the great paradox, of course, that the lesson in how to do this comes from a supposedly uncultured Australian (uncultured *because* Australian is the ideological view – the 'improper' underworld of English – that the film subverts), a man who has in fact no formal qualifications.

The roots of this authentic, legitimate, political English derive from the colonies, those colonies that were ideologically associated with a political underclass and – in the Australian example – associated with criminals, with those carrying the most fundamental of all *illegitimacies*. Logue, we learn at the end, is not a 'doctor' at all; he gained his knowledge of speech therapy by treating Australian shell-shocked soldiers from the Great War, using his actor's ability to speak the lines of Shakespeare.

* * *

The King's English as spoken by George VI derives from precisely the period in which Sampson and Newbolt were writing: the Great War of 1914–18. The language and rhetoric associated with this period persists not just through the war of 1939–45 but also right up to the political rhetoric of our own historical moment. The two world wars of the twentieth century figure centrally in a great deal of the political rhetoric of England. Indeed, it often seems that 'Political English' is pretty constantly at war, in one way or another. Perhaps the most obvious examples of this today are to be found in the lexicon of Boris Johnson.

Johnson is well known for his flip and suavely glib comments, often in the middle of extremely serious political situations. The effect of the introduction of somewhat chummy and often localized patois is quite different, in his case, from that of the character of Lionel Logue. For Johnson, the rhetorical language is intended to reduce the significance and especially the political import of the situation in which he finds himself. World politics can be reduced to an Eton classroom, with an eccentric teacher (always remaining in charge but) always somehow diverting the listener from serious engagement with thought and replacing that with the assuredness of intrinsic privilege. The rhetoric works to focus attention on the cleverness of the speaker, rather than on the substance of the argument to which the speaker is supposed to be making a contribution. Yet, for all its supposed cleverness, Johnson's rhetoric is also often gaffe-ridden, and perhaps no more so than when he calls upon the language, vocabulary and imagery associated with the Great Wars of the twentieth century.

In January 2017, for example, Boris Johnson warned the then French President, François Hollande, not to try to 'administer punishment beatings' to Brexit Britain 'in the manner of some world war two movie'. In May 2016, as part of the campaign leading to the Brexit referendum, he compared the European Union to Napoleon and Hitler, stating that the European Union had the same ultimate goal as the Nazis, albeit by different methods: the unification of Europe. 'The whole thing began with the Roman Empire,' he said, adding that 'various people and institutions' have tried 'to rediscover the lost childhood of Europe, by trying to unify it. Napoleon, Hitler, various people tried this out'. The British, he added, could essentially repeat their historical success in the Second World War, becoming 'the heroes of Europe' once again.[9]

This – and perhaps especially the populist reference to films – played handily into the rhetoric of the UK's far-right newspapers. Perhaps paradoxically, one of the most determinedly influential newspapers that campaigned for the Brexit vote was the *Daily Mail*, whose own

---

[9]See report at: http://www.telegraph.co.uk/news/2016/05/14/boris-johnson-interview-we-can-be-the-heroes-of-europe-by-voting/

history includes a period of open support for Hitler and for Fascism. Its journalism retains the martial vocabulary that was the staple of Nazism and 1930s Fascism, while the newspaper's editorial line proclaims it piously to be a supporter of Johnson's supposedly anti-Hitler position.

The vocabulary of the populist press is, of course, often direct and lacking in nuance or subtlety. Johnson's rhetorical demeaning and diminishing of the reality of politics behind the gaffe-filled and would-be jocular language plays directly into this. In the newspapers, the actual violence that underpins Johnson is clearly revealed. People do not have disagreements: they 'clash'. They never speak with emotion: they 'rant', 'lash out'. They cannot hold to a view consistently: they are 'defiant'. They never say anything new: they 'drop bombshells' to 'scupper' the opposition; they 'savage' their enemies, often giving them 'a kick in the teeth'. News doesn't emerge: it 'explodes'. An argument is a 'spat' in which someone 'roasts' or 'slams' or 'blasts' their opponent.

One such standard term in populist journalism contains a perfect example of how a serious issue can be dramatically shrunk when a foreign idea is thoroughly domesticated into political English. Boris Johnson knows well the tragedies of Aeschylus in the *Oresteia* or Euripides in *Orestes*, plays whose chorus members are identified firstly as 'the Furies'. The plays dramatize very specific ideas related to justice, and this includes a sense that the root of earthly injustice is often found in the sexual predations of men. The Furies are, in at least one sense, an invitation to consider the politics of the ancient world as failing because of a masculinist ideology of force and violence.

In contemporary populist journalism, however, all of this is lost in translation. People can never simply be unhappy with a political position opposed to their own: they are instead always 'furious'. In this – a populist jargon fully exploited by many politicians, including those who know the classical roots – the possibility of reasoned argument becomes, instead, simply the expression of brute emotion; and the emotion in question is one that invites precisely the kind of masculinist violence that the root idea opposed. Now, instead of understanding contemporary politics in terms that would invite analysis of the male-gendered basis of power, the deployment of 'fury' simply seeks to validate and even extend that power, into conflict, violence and war if required. This, in turn, is then indulged by those politicians who, even though aware of the language here and its classical references, encourage such masculinist ideologies by their situating of all conflicts in the terms of war. In England, that reference is almost always to the two twentieth-century world wars; and those wars become symbolically construed as a defence of England and of all that is quintessentially English, and, yet more specifically, a heroic defence of male pluck as seen in the essential 'Englishman'.

At the same time, this populist vocabulary is intermixed with another vocabulary, of the kind that is reminiscent of the sauciness that Orwell liked in the seaside postcard cartoons of Donald McGill. The populist press are extremely fond of printing images of women who seem simply unable to control or restrain their sexuality, revealing their 'sideboobs' or 'underboobs', having 'X-rated wardrobe malfunctions', being caught in 'romps' that are sometimes 'shameless' and sometimes – if those involved are in favour at the newspaper – 'naughty' or 'flirty' or just 'hot'.

Boris Johnson's faux-common-people approach, falling into the vernacular or slang and accompanied by occasional forays into the sexually risqué, is designed to keep readers of these newspapers on board for his political preferences. It is a straightforward exercise in manipulation, and one that is all the more troubling precisely because it is a mixture of patronizing and fooling those who have had a less expensive classical education than he. Perhaps even worse is the underlying motivation for this: violence.

I suggested above that the populist press lays bare the incipient violence in Johnson's rhetoric. In fact, he often uses exactly the same crude lexicon, immune from any nuance. Yet the violence is more dangerous than this might suggest. Politics and political language, we might say, is there for one key reason: it allows us to resolve disputes or contrasting views without falling into the crude methods of war or of violence. In Churchill's famous terms, it represents 'jaw-jaw' over 'war-war'. Johnson – who knows a few things about Churchill – also might know this; and he perverts its sense in that he evacuates the political rhetoric of any meaning and sense, diminishing its value and leaving instead only the tendency to straightforward fighting.[10] We have precisely the kind of

---

[10] As Richard Evans points out in his review of Boris Johnson's *The Churchill Factor*, in *The New Statesman*, 13 November 2014, Johnson actually gets a very substantial number of his claims about Churchill – and indeed about most of twentieth-century European history – simply wrong. See '"One man who made history" by another who seems just to make it up: Boris on Churchill', available at: https://www.newstatesman.com/books/2014/11/one-man-who-made-history-another-who-seems-just-make-it-boris-churchill (accessed 16 August 2018). Evans draws attention to Johnson's casual populist slang and sees it for what

priggish public school-boy jargon that Logue derided: the language of the wizard wheeze, the jolly jape, the whoopsee and so on.

Perhaps the greatest scandal of all this, however, is that the rhetoric that Johnson deployed in the Brexit campaign is all based on what Johnson himself knows to be falsehoods. As Brendan Simms pointed out in 'The Great Huckster: Boris Johnson's distortions of history' in *The New Statesman* of 22 May 2016, Hitler was completely opposed to the idea of a European political project, preferring instead – and openly arguing for – a continent of national and nationalist independent states. In fact, it was the opponents of Nazism who helped to build the European project precisely out of their resistance to the Nazis. Likewise, Churchill – whose biography Johnson had just written when he made his remarks – had a much more nuanced view of Europe and a European union than Johnson allowed in his Brexit campaign political rhetoric.

The issue of political lying is matter for a subsequent chapter. The immediate point here, regarding the fundamentalist turn in political English, is that Johnson finds the 'foundation' of his rhetoric in an English identity that derives from the Second World War. In turn, that language has its roots in the politicization of English as a discipline identified with the England of the post-1918 settlement. Johnson, of course, is not unique in this; and what makes it an interesting observation is that he is but a paradigmatic example of an entire conservative ideology of political English, an ideology whose roots lie in imperial England. It is embodied in the very idea of 'the King's English' as a spoken mode.

In one of its key particulars in recent times, the Brexit campaign – as simply the most explicit recent political campaign fought in the UK – based a good deal of its rhetoric on reminiscence regarding the wars of the twentieth century. It is not for nothing that Decca released a reworked version of Vera Lynn songs right on the eve of Prime Minister Theresa May signing her Article 50 letter. Vera Lynn – popular darling of the wartime forces – became herself part of the rhetoric of the campaign for a plucky Britain fighting to secure its borders against the invading foreigners. Countless 'vox pop' interviews referred to how 'we' had 'fought two wars', seeing Brexit essentially as a continuation of that same struggle.

---

it is: a means of avoiding argument amidst 'huge condescension'. He also compares Johnson, pertinently enough for my arguments here, to the fictional Bertie Wooster.

The great sorrow here is that the fact of the matter is completely opposite to the rhetorical images. Those who advocated UK independence – especially among the UKIP party – base their politics on the far-right political philosophy against which Britain fought in those wars. The people who vaunt themselves as patriots in this, especially when they use the language, images and insignia of the war, are, in fact, proponents of a far-right nationalism from whose vicissitudes those soldiers fought to try to sustain the very idea of politics – and of a democracy of voices in debate – in the face of a crude violence that relies on the might and force of the body itself. The rhetorical mastery here, in which one side manages to harness the power and symbolism of its opponents, resides in two things: the domestication and disabling of all that is foreign (or all that provokes new thinking) and the subscription to a very specific set of fundamentalisms. Those fundamentalisms lie in the monarchy and the established church, king and the Bible – as I will show.

* * *

First, however, we should note that there exists a prehistory of such political language, and one that should disturb those who find Boris Johnson's influential buffoonery attractive or even simply mildly amusing. We have seen it in another country, at another time. Viktor Klemperer made an extended analysis of the political language of Nazism, in his *The Language of the Third Reich: LTI – Lingua Tertii Imperii*, and we will find there some troubling similarities between the political German language of the 1930s and the political English of the Brexit campaign. Hitler, too, had his popular and populist speaker: Hermann Göring, who, as Klemperer notes, was 'the people's comedian'.[11] Göring, like Johnson, had serious leadership ambitions for his party. Famously, in fact, Göring went so far as to arrogate to himself the leadership of the Nazi Party, on hearing of Hitler's likely demise in the bunker. His was a leadership that lasted for a mere few hours for, as soon as Hitler heard of it, he placed Goebbels in charge and demanded Göring's execution.

Like Johnson, Göring was often the butt of jokes, yet he was also – again like Johnson – a man of some intelligence who knew how to deploy the mockery of himself in a manner that would allow him to accrue real

---

[11] Viktor Klemperer, *The Language of the Third Reich: LTI – Lingua Tertii Imperii* (1957; trans. Martin Brady; Athlone Press, 2000), 128.

power to himself. Richard Overy's description of Göring could easily be a perfect description of the posturing of Johnson: 'For all the popular image of Goering as the butt of popular jokes and rumour, too idle to do a job properly and too fond of the good life to abandon his position without a struggle, there was much more to his personality.'[12] Overy describes him as a man who appears to be politically opportunistic, but was really politically committed to his party's fundamental cause. He was 'a deceptive personality, charming and larger-than-life in the right environment, but a callous bully in others'.[13]

In an extraordinary rhetorical piece, Matthew Parris – Johnson's former friend and ally as a Tory MP – made a sustained attack on Johnson's character. In rhetorical terms, the piece depends upon the cumulatively powerful effect of repetition, whose purpose is to expose the reality behind the humour. It is not acceptable politically, he says, to 'laugh everything off', and he goes on to write that 'Incompetence is not funny. Policy vacuum is not funny. Administrative sloth is not funny. Advising old mates planning to beat somebody up is not funny. Abortions and gagging orders are not funny. Creeping ambition in a jester's cap is not funny. Vacuity posing as merriment, cynicism posing as savviness, a wink and smile covering for betrayal … these things are not funny.'[14]

What makes this powerful is the relentlessness of the attack, combined with the simple clarity of the language. It undercuts the typical Johnsonian bluster, a bluster that is informed fully by populist slang that works to half-obscure Johnson's real intentions at all times, to allow Johnson to get ideas into the public mind without him having ever to acknowledge responsibility for those ideas himself. There is a world of difference between Parris – rhetorical amplification by repetition – and Johnson's own mode of hyperbolic exaggeration. Exaggeration is, indeed, another of those rhetorical gestures in political English that we have seen historically, and, again, it has its historical precedent in the language of the Third Reich.

In contemporary political English, the exaggeration is numerical: the classic contemporary example would be that of Johnson and Michael

---

[12] Richard Overy, *Goering: Hitler's Iron Knight* (1984; new edn, I.B. Tauris, 2012), x.
[13] Overy, *Goering*, xii.
[14] Matthew Parris, 'Tories have got to end their affair with Boris', *The Times*, 26 March 2016, available at: https://www.thetimes.co.uk/article/tories-have-got-to-end-their-affair-with-boris-35lc9p06w

Gove, leading the Vote Leave campaign in the Brexit referendum, suggesting that some 76 million Turks – many of them allegedly criminals and rapists – were poised and ready to enter the UK unless we left the European Union and closed our borders against them.[15] In Craig Oliver's insider account of the Brexit political campaigns, Michael Gove, chief ally of Johnson during the campaign, wrote a piece for the *Daily Mail* in which Gove 'warns of the threat from the East, with a potential 77 million Turks and Albanians coming here with their criminal gangs'.[16] Gove and Johnson used these exaggerated numbers to help them present the case for leaving the European Union as British people 'taking back control' over what, numerically, is an overwhelming and dangerous situation. I showed in Chapter 2 how precisely the same tactic had been used by Enoch Powell in his so-called 'rivers of blood' speech in Birmingham in 1968, where he conjured up exaggerated numbers of immigrants, projecting exponential rises as 'their' women took up places in the hospitals to give birth to many more, displacing 'our' women thereby. The yet more revealing precursor, however, is, once again, the language of war, of the rhetoric of the 1939–45 period, and of the Third Reich.

As Klemperer points out, 'The bulletins of the Third Reich' use the tactic of rhetorical exaggeration (as opposed to Parris's trope of amplification) at every available opportunity. They typically 'start off in a superlative mode from the very outset and then, the worse the situation, the more they overdo it, *until everything becomes literally measureless*' (italics mine). At this point, any attempt to make the language appropriate to the reality of empirical fact dissolves, and 'the fundamental quality of military language, its disciplined exactitude' is twisted 'into its very opposite, into fantasy and fairy-tale'.[17] As I explained above in relation to far-right politicians such as Farage and Johnson and May, the task is to evacuate politics of meaning. Wild over-exaggeration is key to this.

For Klemperer there was a method and a political attitude that underlies this. 'The extraordinary thing', he writes, 'was the shameless

---

[15]See, for example, press report at: http://www.independent.co.uk/news/uk/politics/eu-referendum-boris-johnson-michael-gove-turkey-migration-deliberately-lying-to-voters-yvette-cooper-a7072661.html and http://www.dailymail.co.uk/news/article-3556924/Gove-warns-migration-free-Britain-votes-stay-EU-expansion-hand-millions-five-nations-including-Turkey-right-freely-UK.html

[16]Craig Oliver, *Unleashing Demons* (Hodder, 2017), 211–12.

[17]Klemperer, *The Language of the Third Reich*, 217.

transparency of the lies revealed by the figures'. In our contemporary context, the shameless lie would be the figure printed in huge letters on the side of a bus: '£350 million' that 'we' supposedly send to the European Union every week (we do not) and that could go to the NHS instead (a move against which Johnson and Gove expressly voted in Parliament, having touted the lie). The logic during the Nazi regime was clear: 'one of the fundamentals of Nazi doctrine is the conviction that the masses are unthinking and that their minds can be completely dulled.'[18] Or, as Michael Gove might have it, 'the people of this country have had enough of experts'.

* * *

In the period immediately following the Great War of 1914–18, advocates of a reformed education in English were clear in their own minds and writings that politics was always present in any formulation of what constitutes English speech. Newbolt saw that English and especially its literature could and should replace the Classics as the primary ground on which we might build a society in which, citing Arnold, 'Culture unites classes'.[19] Interestingly, in 1921, Newbolt's Committee saw that every language is a foreign language. What makes English and its literature so very special, they argue, is that it is always a bastard language: 'There are mingled in it, as only in the greatest rivers there could be mingled, the fertilizing influences flowing down from many countries and from many ages of history.' However, the foreign has been integrated, and even domesticated, because 'all these have been subdued to form a stream native to our own soil'. The consequence is that our own native life is itself always already informed by this ability to hold, within ourselves – and our own place and time – the now domesticated riches of elsewhere: 'The flood of diverse human experience which it brings down to our own life and time is in no sense or degree foreign to us, but has become the native experience of men of our own race and culture.'[20]

---

[18] Ibid., 217.

[19] Henry Newbolt et al., *The Teaching of English in England: Being the Report of the Departmental Committee Appointed by the President of the Board of Education to Inquire into the Position of English in the Educational System of England* (HMSO, 1921), 6.

[20] Newbolt et al., *Teaching of English*, 13–14.

This, of course, is not all a simple positive. Indeed, it forms part of the imperialist mindset – and economics – that sees the foreign world as a resource to be plundered and domesticated.[21] It is the Elgin Marbles in the form of our 'native' spoken English, as it were: the translation of the Greek Parthenon Marbles into the English Elgin Marbles.[22] Yet a conservative benevolent paternalism is also apparent here. Newbolt was aware that the country was driven by social and class divisions, and the argument is that every English person had a right to share in the spoils of the English language and its literature, which had hitherto 'been the privilege of a limited section' of society. It is important for the Committee that 'the common right' to a liberal education with English at its centre, 'the common discipline and enjoyment of it, the common possession of the tastes and associations connected with it, would form a new element of national unity'.[23] Central to this is an education in the language, in order to unify the classes that are currently divided by the 'marked difference in their modes of speech'; and the task would be to ensure the disappearance of 'the difference between educated and uneducated speech, which at present causes so much prejudice and difficulty of intercourse'.[24]

Shortly before Newbolt published his Report, George Bernard Shaw had premiered *Pygmalion*. The play tests the hypothesis that class is a matter of language, and that the physical manipulation of the tongue can effect social change. At the close of Act 2, Higgins tells Liza to say her alphabet. She pronounces the letters in her own regular way, and Higgins winces physically. When she pronounces 'a cup of tea' with an emphasis on all the possible glottal stops, Higgins instructs her to 'put your tongue forward until it squeezes against the top of your lower teeth. Now say cup.'[25] This is, as it were, the stiffening of her upper English lip. Higgins explains to his mother that the question of making Liza speak like a duchess is tied to money: his bet with Pickering that he is determined

---

[21] A similar attitude prevails in the right-wing account of 'managed migration', in which 'we' will 'bring migrants in when we need them'. The world's population becomes a human resource for English business.

[22] One might be tempted to say – rhetorically and cheaply – that we have here the appropriation of the marbles that Demosthenes allegedly put into his mouth to help overcome his speech defects.

[23] Newbolt et al., *Teaching of English*, 15.

[24] Ibid., 22.

[25] George Bernard Shaw, *Pygmalion* (1913; Penguin, 2000), 51–2.

to win. He tells Mrs Higgins that Liza 'has a quick ear, and she's been easier to teach than my middle-class pupils because she's had to learn a complete new language. She talks English almost as you talk French'.[26] His only problem now is to change the content of her speech, but the fundamental hypothesis of the play – the bet that Shaw makes with his audiences, like that which Higgins makes with Pickering – is that the mode of speech determines political status, and therefore that to change the mode of speech is to change political and social class-structures.

The Newbolt Report acknowledges – in a kind of parallel with this and as a quasi-validation of Higgins' bet – that literature has consequences, moral and political. It is thus important to decide what is to be read, and the first text to which it turns is the Bible, and specifically the King James Authorized Version of the Bible. That book, 'though a translation from an eastern original, is a true part of English literature', and 'it is historically true that for five centuries and more no other English book has been … so closely connected with our national life'.[27]

Two things emerge here. The first is that the Bible is tied firmly to an idea of the nation, and the second is that the Bible, as somehow intrinsic to English and to literature, becomes a text that binds English language and the English nation into a theological ground in some absolute and fundamentalist truth, the kind of truth that is theologically associated with the Bible and the theocratic word of a God. Politically, therefore, English becomes an absolute language, a fundamentalist language. English is not just one special and national example of a 'political' language: it *is* politics, and what it says is identified with the Scripture. In short, English claims its special prominence because it is the word of God, according to this.

It follows, logically, that all other languages are not only foreign, but they are also foreign to the truth as inscribed in a fundamentalist religious text. They are deviant with respect to God, so to speak. This goes some way towards explaining the extraordinary claim that I exposed at the start of this chapter. Leslie Fielding, remember, found it axiomatic that, as a Brit, he was in a better position to manage the world than anyone who was not a Brit. The rationale is now clear: he was speaking the truth while everyone else, because of their national language, was deviant. In

---

[26]Shaw, *Pygmalion*, 55–6.
[27]Newbolt et al., *Teaching of English*, 341.

time, those who are 'deviant' in this way become characterized instead, in a neat linguistic slippage, as 'devious': a classic populist depiction of the foreigner.

For Newbolt, while literacy has in general increased by 1922, it remains a troubling fact that the generality of people are less and less inclined to read the Bible. He puts this down to the fact that parents of children have essentially delegated full responsibility for education to the State and to the national institutional system of education. The hinterland of this suggestion is also itself instructive. Prior to the Newbolt Report – and as I noted earlier – Parliament had passed the Education Act of 1918, conventionally known as the Fisher Act, after its proponent, the Liberal MP and former academic historian and Vice-Chancellor of the emergent University of Sheffield, Herbert Fisher. The Conservative opposition to Fisher's Act – which extended the school-leaving age to fourteen and rendered child labour illegal – was based in a fear that the State would be intervening too much in individual private lives. Basil Peto, the leading Conservative opponent of the Act, explicitly referred to this as a semi-Socialist condition. He claimed that the Fisher Act was completely consistent with the 'Socialist theory that children belong to the State' and not to their parents and families.[28]

Newbolt is clearly aware of the same wider political condition of the time, in the aftermath of the Russian Bolshevik Revolution. The consequence of this alleged delegation of parental responsibility to the State, he argues, is that family reading and instruction in the Bible is less common. So, although 'we are on the way to becoming a reading nation', nonetheless we are increasingly ignorant of this one text that, 'for centuries gave something of a common form, a common dignity, to the thought and speech of the people'.[29] Indeed, for Arthur Quiller-Couch, a member of the Newbolt Committee, the Authorized Version 'is in us, in our blood' as English-speaking people.[30]

This thinking goes some way towards explaining the special status of 'the English-Speaking Peoples' that were so central to Churchill's idea of history, and, indeed, to all right-wing political accounts of the

---

[28] See report in Hansard, available at: http://hansard.millbanksystems.com/commons/1918/mar/13/education-bill. I describe the political conditions of this more fully in my closing chapter.
[29] Newbolt et al., *Teaching of English*, 342.
[30] Ibid., 344.

'exceptional' status of 'the English'. English is exceptional, according to this, because it is the language of God. Insofar as it is thus 'fundamental' to any and all social and political life, it also becomes *fundamentalist*. 'The English-speaking people' are not 'the exception to the rule', because, in fact, they *are* 'the rule'. At this point, Newbolt's Report closes: no more need be said.

The idea that the politics of a specific nation is tied to the alleged primacy of its language and speakers permeates the ideological undercurrents that flow everywhere through the Authorized Version. Gordon Campbell has traced the history of the translation, and he reveals the principles that governed it. The first attempt to render the Bible or part of it into English, he points out, was carried out by the Venerable Bede, who started the task with the translation of John's Gospel sometime in the early eighth century. 'It is a happy coincidence', writes Campbell, 'that the man who first tried to translate the Bible into English was the same person who tried to create the idea of the English people', through his work, *The Ecclesiastical History of the English People*, written originally in Latin but designed to unify the nation of English speakers.[31] The translation of the Bible, into the English of Bede's own historical moment, was designed to bring a people together around a book that could be shared by those who spoke the language.

By the time of the Reformation, the alignment of the language of God with the language of English was being fully established: 'John Milton's attitude was typical. When God speaks, Milton explained, he speaks first to his Englishmen.'[32] The Authorized Version was political English laid bare: it claims an absolute authority not by legitimizing the content of what is being said, but rather because of the absolute authority of the medium itself. English cannot lie, because it is the language of God, and it is henceforth from English that the meaning of the entire world derives. Copernicus may have destabilized the world when he set the earth off on its dizzying revolutionary circling of the sun and instead placed the sun at the centre of the universe; Lenin may much later have destabilized the world's politics by establishing a political revolution in the world; but truth and stability are restored by an appeal to the Authorized Version

---

[31] Gordon Campbell, *The Story of the King James Version, 1611–2011* (Oxford University Press, 2010), 7–8.
[32] Campbell, *The Story of the King James Version*, 10.

placing English – and the English-speaking people – at the core of all truth and historical realities.

King James saw the Authorized Version as being instrumental in helping to advance his own ideals regarding a union of peoples, the myth of a 'united kingdom'. Its effects went further, given the historical importance of England as an advanced economy in the early 1600s. Diarmaid MacCulloch describes the scope and ambit of the translation in stark terms: 'Within seven years, a remarkably efficient and scandalously under-financed set of committees had cooperated to create the text that was to prove one of the most lasting commemorations of the first person to rule the entire Atlantic archipelago.' In his account of the significance of the English text, MacCulloch draws attention to the genealogical tables of characters in the Bible purporting to show the ancestry of Christ and of Paul. These, he claims, are there 'to convince the good folk of Jacobean England that the Twelve Tribes of Israel and the notables of the Old Testament were gentry families rather like those who ruled the shires of England in 1611 – or better still, that the whole people of England were like the Twelve Tribes of Israel'. Once again, the translation into English serves the function of stressing English exceptionalism. It turns out to be not so very odd that – as I argued in Chapter 2 – Theresa May might find the appeal of an alignment between herself (as leader of Brexit) to Moses (as leader in Exodus) to be not just an attractive but also a profoundly proper proposition.

The Bible now becomes the text that serves to demonstrate an innate superiority of the English people, thanks to the primacy of their language. It had 'the potential to become a uniting symbol for English-speaking Protestantism', as MacCulloch argues. He then follows the logic of this politicized English quite clearly: 'So it was that when England and Scotland jointly stumbled on a "British" world empire, the unifying Anglophone book which they took to new lands was the KJB [King James Bible].'[33] The colonies were formed, in their relation with the British Empire, as 'legitimate' to the extent to which they adopted political English, as a form of religious fundamentalism, as the cornerstone of their existence.

This may go some way towards explaining why it would be unusual or awkward for the United States to have a President who allies herself or himself with anything other than religiously Christian fundamentalism.

---

[33]Diarmaid MacCulloch, 'How Good is It?' *London Review of Books*, 33:3 (3 February 2011), 20–22.

Many – perhaps most – make this alignment quietly, but, not only do they swear their allegiance to the Constitution on a Bible at the moment of their inauguration, they have also tended, historically, to acknowledge – even if only tacitly – the primacy of faith as a condition of their politics.

This is the meaning of English as a fundamentalism. It ties language to religion, and religion to imperial politics, and that combination operates in such a way as to make English a fundamental condition of government and of all truth-telling, all language that works in accordance with a fundamental religious claim upon absolute knowledge. In the early twentieth century in England, this was advocated as the very fundamental element necessary for the English to be fully English. Being fully English also meant eschewing not only the politics of socialism (as in the impetus behind the Russian Revolution of 1917) but also, later, the politics of Nazism. The result is that English (as both language and people) presents itself as a 'natural' condition of human existence, natural because it claims as its fundamental condition an avoidance of all extremes in politics. At the same time, however, this avoidance of extremes generates a specific kind of political English that might be characterized as the politics of 'the extreme centre'.[34] This is a centre that is entirely shaped by its own politics, while pretending to be – like God – above the political as such. Yet it is political through and through. This is the essence of any form of fundamentalism, be it religious or economic or politically totalitarian: it presumes its own absolute truth, its basic position as a 'degree zero' or 'ground zero' from which all else will derive.

* * *

We ought to draw together some common themes that have now emerged in the argument. The first thing to note, once again, is the relation between English and other languages, English and alterity. As R.S. Sugirtharajah asks, 'how did this text [of the King James Bible] that emerged in hot, dusty West Asia come to be seen as the book of "England's green and pleasant land"?'.[35] This was an act not just of translation in any 'innocent' or basic

---

[34]See Tariq Ali, *The Extreme Centre* (Verso, 2015). The same logic applies to the thinking of Slavoj Žižek, *Violence* (Profile Books, 2009), when he indicates that the everyday is marked by its own tacit forms of violence, that violence is in fact the actual condition of everyday social, political and cultural living.

[35]R.S. Sugirtharajah, 'Postcolonial Notes on the King James Bible', in *The King James Bible after 400 Years*, ed. Hannibal Hamlin and Norman W. Jones (Cambridge University Press,

linguistic sense; rather, it was an act of domestication and appropriation. At the centre of this is money and capital. We usually describe the six sub-groups of translators who established the Authorized Version as six 'committees', but in fact they were 'companies'; and 'company' in Jacobean England was a term used not only to describe a troupe of actors but also to describe 'trading and investment organizations'. Sugirtharajah shows what is at issue here, for 'These companies emerged at a time when Europe was "discovering" a new world – a world which offered potential commercial opportunities'.[36]

Once we know and acknowledge the importance of this, other parts of the fundamentalist jigsaw start to fall into their proper place to give a clear image of what is going on. The Bible becomes instrumental in expanding the empire and is related firmly not only to commercial activities but also to political power, and both of these relate to the primacy of the English language. 'While the commercial companies of their time were importing cotton, silk, indigo, and spices, these six companies of translators were transferring the textual ideas of the Jews and ancient Christians and turning them into an English product.' The further product of the colonial and eventually imperial exercise, of course, was the production of the cultural other as a 'failed English person', a derivative of the original, dependent upon the original for any and all legitimacy in cultural and political terms, but forever condemned to a secondary place because of how they spoke. Their English was 'acquired' whereas that of the Englishman and Englishwoman was, supposedly literally, God-given: natural.

The foreigner is erased in this. From now on, 'to be' is 'to be English'; the speaker of every other language stands at one remove from the originary language, the language that is at the origin and centre of the world: the word from which the world springs. For Milton, for example, the Reformation owed more to an Englishman than it did to Luther. Christopher Hill explains how, for Milton, Wyclif – with his initial attempts at translating the Bible – anticipated Luther and Calvin 'whose names might never have been known if the English reformer had not been silenced'.[37] This is what leads Milton to believe that the logical expression of Reformation is English, and also that Reformation finds its

---

2010), 148.
[36]Sugirtharajah, 'Postcolonial Notes on the King James Bible', 148.
[37]Hill, *Milton and the English Revolution*, 85–6.

proper articulation in the English Revolution. Indeed, the Reformation for Milton had never played a unique part in human advance. Wyclif, perhaps because he was an Englishman, was equally important. In his *Defence of the People of England* in 1651, Milton essentially speaks up for the primacy of English nationalism, where the Revolution becomes emblematic of the heroic instance of a 'victory for civil freedom'. For Milton, the famous freedom of the press and of speech that he advocates in *Areopagitica* lies expressly within the English language itself. Those who speak true English demonstrate, thereby, their innate inclination to freedom as such. It is no wonder, given this, that Bishop Aylmer was eventually able to declare that 'God is English'.[38]

If this is indeed the case, then we might ask how it is possible that political rhetoric in English is so thoroughly marred by lying?

---

[38]Ibid., 279–80. See also ibid., 280–1 for Milton's belief in English exceptionalism, an exceptionalism grounded in English speech and language that brings forth 'the first tidings and trumpet of reformation to all Europe'.

4 ON TRUTH AND LYING IN A POLITICAL SENSE

In his essay 'On liars', Montaigne made a useful distinction that has served political discourse well, directly and indirectly and, in many cases, without the politician really acknowledging the nuances involved. 'I know quite well', he writes, 'that grammarians make a distinction between telling an untruth and lying'. Few politicians would be willing to state that they were telling an untruth, and fewer still might admit to lying, or giving what Shakespeare's Touchstone called 'the Lie Direct'.[1]

Montaigne's grammarians 'say that to tell an untruth is to say something that is false, but that we suppose to be true'. Such a position offers the obvious get-out clause of acknowledging a mistake, while maintaining ethical dignity and moral uprightness. It suggests that the politician who 'tells an untruth' has herself or himself been the victim indeed of someone else's lying, and as long as this does not veer into a characterization as 'gullible' or 'naïve', the politician will find their reputation potentially enhanced.

By contrast, lying, for Montaigne, 'is to go against one's conscience', and it follows that liars as such are 'those who say the opposite of what they know'.[2] Had he been aware of this distinction, Tony Blair could have called upon it in his self-defence over his decisions regarding participation

---

[1] Shakespeare, *As You Like It*, 5:4. I shall explore the relevant passage from the play, on the relation of diplomacy to lying, further below.
[2] Michel de Montaigne, 'On liars', in *Essays*, ed. and trans. J.M. Cohen (Penguin, 1958; repr. 1973), 30. For the original French, see 'Des menteurs' *Essais: Livre 1* (Garnier-Flammarion, Paris, 1969), 72–3: 'Je sçay bien que les grammairiens font différence entre dire mensonge et mentir; et disent que dire mensonge, c'est dire chose fauce, mais qu'on a pris pour vraye, et que la définition du mot mentir ... porte autant comme aller contre sa conscience, et que par conséquent cela ne touche que ceux qui disent contre ce qu'ils sçavent.'

in the Iraq War. His case has consistently been that he acted in good faith, believing firmly that the evidence available to him showed that Saddam Hussein had a substantial arsenal of weapons of mass destruction, and that he would be able and willing to deploy those weapons at a mere forty-five minutes notice. In Montaigne's terms, he 'told an untruth', but he did not lie. This case shows both how fine and yet how determining the nuance is, while also revealing something that is even more fundamental with regard to the question of truth and lies in political discourse.

Blair, it seems clear, acted in line with his predisposition or, in his own words, his beliefs. Famously, he said, 'I only know what I believe', and his belief became the basis for what he thought of as his knowledge.[3] The knowledge – however much of an 'unknown unknown' it proved to be – was thus shaped by the pre-existing belief or predisposition. Yet this – a mode of basic ideological conditioning – is something that is really pretty fundamental to all human activity, and indeed to all dialogue or debate. Each participant goes into a debate – or entertains a political question, puzzle or issue – with an already pre-formed set of beliefs or predispositions. Indeed, those predispositions – many of them determined by language in all its complexity as we have seen thus far – are exactly what constitute an individual's identity.

Thus, if we asked someone to describe her or his predispositions or ethos, we would find that they are predispositions that are shaped by the language. To describe oneself in these terms is to tell a story about oneself, to insert the self into a narrative. The narrative need not be true, of course (in fact, it probably rarely is). It simply needs to be credible, subject to a belief rather than a proof. This is all the more evident if we ask someone to describe their political ethos. That is given by the way in which they inhabit their language and their narratives of political life. Political English, in these terms, is the very cornerstone of political identity.

The beliefs that constitute a political ethos may be as far-reaching as a fully settled ideological position, or they may simply be based upon prejudices – pre-judgements and habits – of various kinds. No matter

---

[3] See Tony Blair's speech to the Labour Party conference, 28 September 2004, and the report of the speech, available at: https://www.theguardian.com/uk/2004/sep/28/labourconference.labour1. See also Laura Kuenssberg's interview with John Chilcot, one year after the publication of the Chilcot Report, available at: http://www.bbc.co.uk/news/uk-politics-40510539

how, they are there, and they are largely unavoidable. Habit is absolutely necessary to us if we are to live our lives in a reasonable fashion; and it operates by precluding thought. Although this sounds like a bad thing, we should consider how utterly paralysing and crippling it would be if we were to think about absolutely everything that we do, from blinking our eyelids to keep water stimulated in our eyes through to sighing as we remember to breathe, or every single motor activity that is required simply to get out of bed in the morning. Habit helps us to live, through a kind of creative forgetting of the everyday, but it depends upon our having some settled beliefs about how the world works. To have moments that we will characterize as 'thoughtful' at all, we need a solid ground of habit against which thought itself will stand out and become foregrounded by being spoken. 'Thinking' thus becomes something that has a real and material historical substance, for it irrupts into and disturbs the quotidian calm of the routinized everyday. In doing so, thinking marks itself out as something that enables the possibility of radical fundamental and political change – in the literal sense of both 'radical' and 'fundamental'.

Another way of describing Blair's Iraq situation would be to say that Blair is typical of most human agents in having some kind of overarching theory or general set of narratives that govern how he will see any particular event, and to which he habitually turns for analysis. This, we would say, is the very language, the linguistic frame, in which he thinks and knows his politics. Such a mentality is, indeed, pretty fundamental to anyone forming any understanding of any event at all: it is how we make sense of the world. The problem arises when such a habitual position determinedly asserts the validity of the habit and precludes the possibility of the disruptive thought. That is to say, it is a problem when our linguistic frame is so settled and closed off from the world that we cannot hear other foreign voices and thus cannot seriously engage with anything other than 'what we already believe'. This – a mode of internal 'confirmation bias' – is Blair's predicament, given (perhaps unconsciously) in his statement that he only knows what he believes. Blair found himself in the position of the addict, helpless in the face of his habit and unable to think a way out of succumbing to it.

The point of democratic engagement, however, is to find a mode of talk that gets behind the ideological conditioning that shapes what is essentially a prejudice, a pre-judgement based on ideological predispositions to believe what we would prefer the truth or facts of a case to be. Democracy works by breaking with habit, upsetting how it is that an individual subject characteristically sees and analyses the world. It works if it changes my disposition: that is, if it makes me change my mind or if it modifies in some way my relation to my existing political commitment. This is the only politically legitimate way in which an individual might be required to change her or his mind, and that – changing one's mind – is basic to anything that we can call 'democracy'. This is also a matter of language, for the change of disposition or ethos is – as my logic above argues – a change of language, an opening to the voice of others. It is not often enough noted that democracy involves listening as well as talking: it calls for a particular form of attention or mode of attentiveness to other voices.

Frank Kermode famously described what is at stake in this, in his *The Sense of an Ending*, the 'Mary Flexner Lectures' given in Bryn Mawr in 1965 and published in 1966. He was not addressing political language directly, but his observations, as I will show, are central and pertinent to my case here. One thing we can learn from those lectures is that we tend to organize our lives according to the functional operations of narrative and of fiction. In reading a novel, for example, part of our engagement involves us inescapably in hypothesizing possible endings or resolutions of the intrigue or plot, and, as in fiction, so also in daily living. The key point that Kermode makes and that is relevant for our purposes here, however, is that these hypothesized endings are never fixed: given their merely hypothetical standing, they have to be modified always in the light of new evidence. In this way, fiction threatens the stability of habit and opens us to the possibility of futures ('endings') that differ from those that our habits made us envisage as necessary.

That is to say – as Keynes was once reputed to have said – 'when the facts change, I change my mind'. As a matter of fact, as John Kay has told us, it was Paul Samuelson who was the origin of the pithy aperçu here, not Keynes, and the statement was actually this: 'When my information changes, I alter my conclusions.'[4] As I will show later in this chapter, that distinction is as important as the distinction made by Montaigne. It is a distinction that is not merely epistemological but also political: it is a use of language that brings truth and falsehood into the political domain.

A politician who does not alter their conclusions when they have new information can become a dogmatist (or, as in the terms of my previous

---

[4]John Kay, 'Keynes was half right about the facts', *Financial Times*, 4 August, 2015, available at: https://www.ft.com/content/96a620a8-3a8d-11e5-bbd1-b37bc06f590c?mhq5j=e1

chapter here, a fundamentalist), and, as that position becomes standard, she or he veers into lying directly. They know that the facts of the world no longer fit into their proposed narrative of history; yet they persist in their 'belief' (oddly, a belief that they no longer actually hold, and thus now a fantasy) that that narrative will unfold and proceed precisely as their theoretical or ideological position determines that it must. This is, in fact, what puts lying – in Montaigne's sense – at the cornerstone of all totalitarian, authoritarian or fundamentalist political regimes. Political dogmatism like this is a form of fundamentalism, like an absolutist religious faith, and fundamentalism is the antithesis of democracy and of history. Fundamentalism brooks no opposition and admits no possible histories other than its own predetermined – predetermining and thus prejudicial – version, its 'authorized version'.

If authoritarian and totalitarian rule both depend upon lies, in the strict sense of that term, does it follow that democratic polities are based upon truth-telling? Remember that, following the grammarian's nuanced distinction, the politician can escape being tarnished as a liar, while yet 'truthfully' repeating 'the thing that is not', as Jonathan Swift's Houyhnhnms described it in *Gulliver's Travels* in 1726.[5] In the case of Blair and Iraq, the view that emerges in the determination to save Blair's reputation is that, when he gave evidence to the Iraq Inquiry, 'it was, from his perspective and standpoint, emotionally truthful'. John Chilcot's Inquiry suggests that Blair found a form of words – in the famous dossier that was used to justify military intervention – that essentially misinformed its readers while nonetheless being stated in good faith. Chilcot remarks that Blair said, '"I believe the assessed intelligence shows beyond doubt." Pinning it on "my belief". Not on the fact, what the assessed intelligence said. You can make an argument around that, both ethical and – well, there is an ethical argument I think.'[6]

Above, I put this in terms of Blair acting in accordance with his 'predisposition'. I choose that word carefully, because it is linked, fundamentally, to matters of ethics and of character. The ancient Greek *ethos*, from which we derive our own word 'ethics', indicates something close to what we would call a personal disposition or 'character', for it

---

[5] Jonathan Swift, *Gulliver's Travels* (1726), Part 4, chapter IV. See Jonathan Swift, *Gulliver's Travels and Other Writings*, ed. Louis A. Landa (Oxford University Press, 1976), 193–7.
[6] See Laura Kuenssberg interview with John Chilcot, available at: http://www.bbc.co.uk/news/uk-politics-40510539

signals the inclinations, attitudes and moods – the habitual predispositions – of an individual. When Blair, as in this paradigmatic example, says that he only knows what he believes, what he is signalling is that he acted 'ethically', meaning by this that he acted in a way that was fashioned and predetermined by his attitudes and inclinations or according to his own character/*ethos*.

It is, of course, straightforward from a rational point of view to refuse to accept that there can be such an ethical escape route for Blair: his critics will want to rest their case on the argument that holds that, in democratic politics, reason should trump ethics. So-called 'deliberative democracy' holds to the ideal, most clearly formulated by Habermas, that through non-coercive rational discussion, we can arrive always at 'the better argument', and that the political legitimacy of any position depends upon such an operation of reason itself.[7] At the same time, it is also true that we know that politics is never fully determined by reason, nor is political argument or rhetoric. Indeed, if politics were to be determined purely by reason, we might well find ourselves in Plato's *Republic* and have philosophers in positions of political rule, or in Huxley's *Brave New World*, with scientists determining the conditions of human existence at its most basic biological levels. Neither of these positions would really be an enhancement of the democratic credentials of a polity: democracy clearly needs to retain at least some aspects of reasoned argument and logic, combined with an acknowledgement of the non-intellectual components of our commitments (love being only the most obvious such example – an ethical example – of a politically pertinent commitment). We can remain sceptical about the intrusion of emotion into a politician's claims on truth, but it would be irrational indeed to deny that emotion plays a part in political rhetoric and persuasion.

One of the key factors to be accounted for is that there is no straightforward and incorruptible link between what we know to be true and what we want to be true, between what we know and what we would believe. Blair's bad or flawed political judgement on Iraq comes about because he conflates the two, and gives priority to his belief, proceeding therefrom as if what he wants to be true is indeed factually and referentially true. In the end, Blair gets what he wishes for: he asks not that we judge his call regarding the war but rather that we judge him

---

[7]See Jürgen Habermas, *Legitimation Crisis* (trans. Thomas McCarthy; Heinemann, 1986), 107–8 for the detailed description of how this works.

and his character. Accordingly, this self-described 'straightforward kind of guy' is then judged in the court of public opinion (and in the court of the Chilcot Inquiry) to be not quite so straightforward after all and is characterized for many, quite simply and without hesitation, as a liar. We come eventually to judge the person rather than the judgement that the person made. There is an uneasy and discomfiting relationship, at best, between ethics and politics in this respect.

It is clear that the attitude shown to be operative in Blair's Iraq judgement leads into a kind of obstinacy: a determination never to recant, and never to review. That is at odds with the position of Keynes and Samuelson. Blair's stance claims the virtue of 'consistency', while merely becoming stubborn; and it has an account of the truth that eventually says that truth is independent of facts, for truth is essentially a matter of belief, essentially a personal and even private matter. Montaigne had also considered obstinacy such as this, and, interestingly, he places it in direct alignment with lying. 'Lying', he writes, 'is indeed an accursed vice …. Lying – and in a lesser degree obstinacy – are, in my opinion, the only faults whose birth and progress we should consistently oppose'.[8] Obstinacy such as that which we see in those politicians who claim never to have to change their mind, so certain are they of the truth of their convictions – an obstinacy that is the same as lying, but only different in its degree – is tantamount to making a belief into a myth.

Here is where Kermode is at his most instructive for a consideration of political English. Having argued in *The Sense of an Ending* that fictions are narratives that we live by, and that they are primarily characterized by the fact that their endings are always provisional and subject to modification – the opposite of obstinacy – he turns attention to a specific type of debased fiction, the fiction that is inscribed in myth. 'Fictions', he argues, 'can degenerate into myths whenever they are not consciously held to be fictive'.

This is what constitutes the difference, argues Kermode, deliberately taking a political example – between Nazi anti-Semitism and a fiction such as *King Lear*. Myth subscribes to the presupposition that we can have 'total and adequate' explanations of material realities, and myth is

---

[8]Montaigne, *Essays*, 31. For the original French, see Montaigne, *Essais: Livre 1*, 73–4: 'En vérité le mentir est un maudit vice … La menterie seule et, un peu au-dessous, l'opiniastreté me semblent ester celles desquelles on devroit à toute instance combattre la naissance et le progrez.'

therefore 'a sequence of radically unchangeable gestures', argues Kermode. By contrast, 'Fictions are for finding things out, and they change as the needs of sense-making change.' He goes on to make the fundamental distinction in these terms: 'Myths are the agents of stability, fictions the agents of change. Myths call for absolute, fictions for conditional assent.'[9] In this way, myth is akin to a belief that has forgotten that it is merely a belief and that then parades as immutable truth. Myth, in this sense, is a fiction that becomes unchangeable because of the obstinate ethos of the individual who subscribes to it and who becomes addicted to it.

If Kermode can properly indicate that myth such as this is best exemplified by the anti-Semitism that was basic to Nazi politics, it becomes clear just how high the stakes of truth-telling and lying in political rhetoric are. We are here in the presence of truth and lies in much more than any kind of moral sense. This is also a matter of life and death, visible in the radical extremes of the Nazi Holocaust and slaughter of individuals who are killed because they are Jewish, homosexual, Romany or physically disabled in some way. The high stakes are also visible in the case of Bush and Blair engaging in the Iraq War, itself a war for which motivation was found or adduced after an Islamist terrorist attack – involving no Iraqis – in New York in 2001.[10] Yet we need not rest our case upon extremes such as these, for the same issue regarding truth and lies in political rhetoric shapes many more everyday political and social matters as well.

* * *

For Nietzsche, dissimulation – a form of lying – is as natural to humans as the weather: we need it to survive at all, at least insofar as we exist in societies where individuals congregate, and our only political issue is, as with weather, how to accommodate ourselves most comfortably with it or how we negotiate a political life that we know must embrace the fact of dissimulation. The inevitability of lying is a motif that is carried on in more recent times by Leszek Kołakowski when he argues that 'The deliberate transmission of false information is ... part of the natural order

---

[9]Frank Kermode, *The Sense of an Ending* (Oxford University Press, 1966), 39.

[10]None of the nineteen terrorist attackers involved in 9/11 were actually from Iraq. This fact alone should indicate that the decision to attack Iraq derived from some pre-existing beliefs or habitual coding of the political situation.

of things. The butterfly says to the bird, "But I'm not really a butterfly at all, I'm just a dead leaf"; the wasp says to the bee guarding its hive, "But I'm not really a wasp at all, I'm a bee."[11] These ostensibly simple examples reveal the full bio-political condition in which we have to negotiate the fact of political lying.

It is worth noting that, in his explanation of this, Kołakowski has recourse to the presentation of a linguistic dramatic scene, and a narrative format. For Nietzsche, it was because we survive not just as individuals but also within social situations and in relation with others to whom we present as individuals with our stories, that dissimulations must be permitted silently to pass among us without disagreement or discord. For the sake of maintaining peaceful relations, we are complicit with each other in ignoring the fact of our shared lies: all parties know that their relations are based in lies, and all agree to pass over the truth of that fact in silence. We need to commit communally to agreed dissimulations, especially in our linguistic intercourse with each other, without probing those dissimulations too much lest we bring about social breakdown and, with it, the violence that will jeopardize our continued existence and peaceful survival in a shared polity.

In relation to truth, then, what happens, for Nietzsche, is that 'a uniformly valid and binding designation is invented for things, and this legislation of language … establishes the first laws of truth'. In this way, the social formation itself – the very condition that governs the possibility of establishing common and social life, a life lived together – is founded entirely upon an unacknowledged dissimulation, in which truths of fact can be ignored precisely because they are superseded by peacefully agreed and peace-keeping linguistic truths that we will all agree to hold precisely in the interests of keeping the peace and of self-preservation.[12] We have seen, up until this present moment in the argument, that this is often characterized as the triumph of emotion over reason, of *pathos* over *logos*. We can now advance this further. A liar, according to this latest stage in the development of the argument, is a kind of linguistic dissident, not a moral failure. The political liar acts like a comedian, capitalizing on

---

[11]Leszek Kołakowski, 'On lying', in *Freedom, Fame, Lying and Betrayal: Essays on Everyday Life* (trans. Agnieszka Kołakowska; Penguin, 1999), 25.
[12]See Friedrich Nietzsche, 'On truth and lies in a non-moral sense' (1873), in *The Nietzsche Reader*, ed. Keith Ansell Pearson and Duncan Large (Blackwell, Oxford, 2006), 114–23.

linguistic discrepancy.[13] The logic here is that politics itself becomes a kind of linguistic game, with its inbuilt rules and regulations, regulations that the politician-as-comedian can disturb, providing persuasive comic pleasure as he or she refuses to 'play the game' or 'play by the rules'.

Just as in the issue of Montaigne's account of obstinacy, there are set parameters here for what can be said within political discourse. My contention is that this 'obstinacy' is really just another word for 'ideology' or any general 'theory', when it starts to operate in the manner of myth or in the manner of a fundamentalist belief in having 'total and adequate' explanations and understandings of real states of affairs in the present, past and future. Montaigne's 'obstinacy' is what I call here an 'addiction to habit', but which some left-wing politics would describe – positively and with endorsement – as a 'totalizing' theory.

A subscription to any political ideology as something that offers total and adequate explanation of all realities generates an 'ethical belief' that becomes confused with truth. It thus determines the condition of what passes as legitimate comment in any political dialogue. If we want to advance political debate in terms of logic, rather than appealing simply to the comforting lies of pathos, then we face an awkward predicament when we are faced with the appealing political comedian or more general comic. In rational terms, if we are to be audible or to 'make sense' within such obstinate and now also obdurate discourse, and if we are to engage in political debate, then we must obey the rules that govern the obstinacy, the theory, the ideology *as if these are unquestionable and unchanging*, and this entails a requirement for conformity, or an acceptance that what is legitimately 'sayable' is itself circumscribed by the beliefs that are obstinately and 'ethically' held. We need, as it were, to engage (and engage with) the addict.

* * *

Yet it is not the case, in this, that rational politics is founded upon truth-telling. On the contrary, it seems to be founded upon our willingness pragmatically to act as if we are simply concerned to 'keep a conversation going', and thereby to defer any fall into physical confrontation and the resolution of differences by violence. While it may be admirable to avoid

---

[13] We recognize the lie because it is 'funny' – and much political lying is indeed designed to provoke laughter. It does not follow that the consequences of the lie always avoid tragedy.

violence, it is nonetheless troubling that politics here has been reduced to a language-game, without a purchase upon material reality and without having recourse to real material human conditions (as Marx would have it) from which we derive the validity and authority of our propositions.

The philosophical hinterland to the predicaments that I am addressing here is to be found in the generalized political crises of the 1980s, for which the category of 'the postmodern' can stand as key emblem. On one hand, this period sees the emerging power of market-fundamentalist economics, advocated by Milton Friedman, his Chicago School adherents, and indebted to F.A. Hayek and the 'free-market' libertarianism of the Mont Pelerin Society. The economic policies deriving from this kind of work were carried through in both Reaganomics and Thatcherism, and the associated ideology was in the ascendant. The business of persuading citizens everywhere to subscribe to that ideology depended fundamentally upon an act of linguistic re-description, in which all of human interaction was to be re-described in quasi-financial and quasi-business terms. Human relations became matters of personal investments and bargains (culminating in the logic eventually of the 'pre-nup' in some marriage ceremonies). All public sphere activities and associated institutions (universities, hospitals, schools, local governmental agencies and the like) were to consider themselves as businesses, driven by profit motives.

The political left of this same period had also turned to language as a key determinant of social change. Through the rise of a generalized 'Theory', especially in the field of literary and cultural study, thinkers began to consider political facts in terms of symbolic practices, and the period sees the massive rise in semiotics as a powerful tool of social, cultural and political analysis. This led, however, to a turn away from the materialism of Marxism, notwithstanding the determined attempts to describe the linguistic signifier in materialist terms. The actual economic analysis – the 'real individuals, their activity and the material conditions under which they live, both those which they find already existing and those produced by their activity' – that had derived initially from Marx now became a matter of the 'signs' of economics. Marxism had taken the linguistic turn thereby.

One obvious consequence of this – no matter how illuminating, exciting and intellectually charged and productive the eventual semiotic analyses actually were in fact – is that while the political left worried intensely about language, the world of material economics and politics marched relentlessly on, caring little about language and concentrating on the far-right revolution in the sequestration of wealth and capital.

It was in the midst of this – a genuine crisis for the political left deriving from its intense attention to vocabularies – that a specific kind of 'centrist' pragmatism comes to the fore, as a kind of poor substitute for Marxism itself. Its serious philosopher was probably Richard Rorty, who worked out his positions partly in contradistinction to Derrida, Lyotard and Habermas. Its popular form, as adopted by UK and other politicians, was the fabled 'Third Way' as advocated by the sociologist Anthony Giddens. This 'Third Way' more or less explicitly gave up on the primacy of economics as a determining force for the establishment of social justice and increased equality, replacing that with a concentration on ethical 'values'. In this way, value itself moves out of economics for the political left and becomes the site instead of dialogue and debate.

The position of Third Way politics is, in fact, presciently satirized – even before it is officially described and proclaimed by Giddens – in Monty Python's 1979 film *The Life of Brian*, where the fictional 'PFJ' or 'People's Front of Judea', headed up by 'Reg' (played by John Cleese) engage in endless debate while the Roman occupation continues to exert its violent control of the land and polity. Their response to the news that Brian has been arrested and is about to be crucified is to 'propose a resolution' for debate, instead of attending to the material bio-political facts that make such debate pointless.

The political equivalent of the pragmatism that emanates from the 1980s crisis of the political left and its linguistic turn is to be found towards the end of the New Labour era of Tony Blair. Steve Richards has pointed out that, in the case of New Labour, what began as a means of gaining and exercising power in a real and meaningful way degenerated towards the end, becoming 'fatally shallow'. Blairite pragmatism was what permitted New Labour to re-enter the political mainstream, as it were, in the three or four years leading to the landslide electoral victory in the UK's 1997 general election. In those years, 1994–97, what made the Labour Party into New Labour was the fact that it adopted the prevailing conservative language of the political moment, embracing a tendency towards de-regulation, the ideology of competition as determined by free marketeering, the extension of the market-fundamentalist ideology into new areas that had previously been the domain of the State, and the general idea that an individual's development was best served by minimizing her or his direct engagement with the general State. This position 'kept the peace' with the prevailing orthodoxies of neoliberal capital, bringing Labour into a position of economic orthodoxy so that the party no longer seemed to be dissident with respect to the 'truth' that there was no viable alternative to such an economic ideology.

This – the embrace of a language, to the point where Labour politicians started to command its tongue and lexicon more convincingly than the Conservatives (whose over-enthusiastic embrace of this same discourse had led them into 'sleaze' and generalized corruption) – brought Labour to power again. The problem that emerges as part of the political legacy of the New Labour years, however, is that the language did not manage to re-connect with material realities in some crucial ways. Having gained power by language – the near-obsessive and certainly obstinate control of all political messaging – they began to lose credibility through it as well, when the electorate lost confidence in their ability to make the conversation of Labour's politicians tie in accurately with the world as the electorate experienced it. Conformity to the language of an essentially conservative world view among the politicians eventually distanced them from having a mode of speech that conformed to the material realities of the world in which their voters lived. They were literally 'speaking to themselves' while the world went on its merry way, steadily moving further and further away from Labour's descriptions of it.

Thus, as Richards argues, the Blair pragmatic mantra – 'what matters is what works' – becomes visibly 'a phrase that reduces politics to a managerial vocation'. This is what he means by the shallowness of the Blairite philosophy: it manages the conversations about reality while leaving the material conditions of that reality untouched. When Blair finally did return to those material conditions, he did so through material engagement in the Iraq War, a violence that eschewed pragmatism in almost every sense. Richards argues, against the pragmatic mantra, that 'the essence of democratic politics is an ideological battle about what works but also why'.[14] That is to say, Labour had committed to specific political languages in the manner of subscription to a myth, rather than changing the language as one might do in a fiction that remembers that the goal is to change 'the sense of one's endings' or social and political outcomes as the material and historical, secular needs of the polity also change.

---

[14] Steve Richards, 'All shook up', *Prospect*, 23 July 2017.

What comes out of this is the realization that, in politics, there is a necessary mediating term that operates between truth and lies, and that term is 'fiction', or what we might call 'the political hypothesis'. The politician who advances her or his case by claiming an intrinsic privileged access to the truth of fact, as it were, is the politician who prefers to operate according to the logic of myth. Against this, democratic political discourse is underpinned, necessarily, by the logic of the hypothesis or the fiction. The statements made under the rubric of democratic discourse are neither truths nor lies. When Nietzsche wrote of truth and lies in a non-moral sense, he may not have known it, but he was opening a door to the language of politics itself. His text is important because it undermines the entire validity of the *Ubermensch* with which he is more usually associated.

Shakespeare had prefigured all of this, as I noted at the start of this chapter, in the figure of Touchstone in *As You Like It*. Touchstone outlines the structure of diplomacy in politics, which he describes as seven causes of a quarrel or seven degrees of lying. Asked to explain this, he gives the example of a dispute between himself and a courtier over the look of the courtier's beard. Touchstone told the courtier that he didn't like the man's beard, but there are seven stages of diplomatic lying before such a dispute can get to violence:

> If I said his beard was not cut well, he was in mind it was. This is call'd the Retort Courteous. If I sent him word again it was not well cut, he would send me word he cut it to please himself. This is call'd the Quip Modest. If again it was not well cut, he disabled my judgment. This is call'd the Reply Churlish. If again it was not well cut, he would answer I spake not true. This is call'd the Reproof Valiant. If again it was not well cut, he would say I lie. This is called the Countercheck Quarrelsome. And so to the Lie Circumstantial and the Lie Direct.

The key, however, to avoiding this seemingly inevitable fall towards violence as the means by which to resolve a dispute, is to establish the case that argument – all and any argument that might be determined to keep the peace and to retain the possibility of democratically keeping a political conversation going – is based entirely upon hypothesis. 'I knew when seven justices could not take up a quarrel; but when the parties were met themselves, one of them thought but of an If, as: "If you said so, then I said so." And they shook hands, and swore brothers. Your If is the only peace-maker; much virtue in If.'[15]

* * *

We can formulate this in terms of an opposition taken from within analytic philosophy. Essentially, the distinction I draw here is the distinction between coherence theories of truth and correspondence theories of truth. Within analytic philosophy, this is an extremely technical distinction, best explored in the work of Donald Davidson. For present purposes, it will suffice to say that the 'correspondence' theory is based on the assumption that a linguistic proposition will find its truth-validation in the material and non-linguistic conditions of a referent in the world. Davidson himself defends a correspondence theory, writing that 'I think truth can be explained by appeal to a relation between language and the world'.[16] Thus, 'it is raining' is true if and only if precipitation is actually happening, as shown empirically by a stream of drops of water falling from the sky towards the earth. The 'coherence' theory is based on the assumption that it makes sense in our language community to utter the phrase 'it is raining' in specific conditions as prescribed by the community. Thus, 'it is raining' is true here if and only if our linguistic community agrees that 'it is raining' is a meaningful sentence to utter within specific conditions and conventions, and its validity depends upon its iterability and in our consistency in uttering the phrase.

Beckett toys with this in *Molloy*. He opens part two of this novel with this: 'It is midnight. The rain is beating on the windows.' He will close the novel by referring back to his own writing of it: 'I went back into the house and wrote, "It is midnight. The rain is beating on the windows." It was not midnight. It was not raining.'[17] Referential validation of the rain is undermined; at the same time, the text's internal linguistic consistency is validated. This is so even if, in this instance, it calls into question the reliability of the narrator: indeed, the validation of a coherence theory

---

[15]Shakespeare, *As You Like It*.
[16]Donald Davidson, *Inquiries into Truth and Interpretation* (Oxford University Press, 1984), 37. The full argument is worked out in chapters 2 and 3 in this volume, with the defence of correspondence most fully elaborated in chapter 3, 'True to the Facts'.
[17]Samuel Beckett, *Molloy, Malone Dies: The Unnamable* (John Calder, 1959; repr. 1976), 92, 176.

is precisely being called into question by a 'correspondence-theory' that pre-empts it. That is the point.[18]

For the correspondence theory, truth is measured by the relation between language and fact; and, for the coherence theory, truth is measured by ideological agreement as to how we will communicate with each other and establish thereby a meaningful community, without having to call upon any pre-existing and non-linguistic reality in the world. The aims of both accounts differ in some fundamentals, therefore. The former requires a connection between proposition and material or empirical reality for its authentication, and it will base an argument upon an appeal to those material conditions and to the accurate representation of them in sentences. The latter is more inclined to seek agreement between or among participants, regardless of the actual material conditions of the world, and it will rest its arguments on how fully such concord is reached, and how pragmatically effective the communication is in establishing or maintaining that community of participants. The former demands that a politician's statements will be true if and only if they relate accurately to agreed material conditions in the world. The latter requires simply that the politician will engage her or his propositions in ways that we find linguistically agreeable, or persuasive, on grounds that are themselves essentially community-based and not reality-based. Coherence permits of agreeable fictions; correspondence is more absolutist and exacting.

In terms of the politics of the Iraq War, for example, correspondence says, WMD actually exist, and here is the empirical evidence, and there can be no further argument. By contrast, coherence says, let us all act as in agreement with the statement 'WMD exist', whether they do or not, for that will allow us to exist and cohabit peacefully together. Simultaneously, however, coherence also says that argument must continue, because all that coherence shows is the viability of the tribal allegiance of those who *wish to believe* that WMD exist. Other allegiances are possible and, consequently, other modes of engagement with the material reality of the case (whatever it may be) are also possible. Blair's tragedy is that he confused these two positions. Bush was clearer, when he stated that

---

[18]The philosophy behind this is worked out in detail in Hegel, *Phenomenology of Spirit* (trans. A.V. Miller; Oxford University Press, 1977), 59ff, where Hegel meditates on the meaning and semantic content of 'Now', where he begins the elaboration of his fundamental principle of negation. See also my commentary on this in my *Criticism and Modernity* (Oxford University Press, 1999), 188–96.

'Every nation, in every region, now has a decision to make. Either you are with us, or you are with the terrorists' – 'you are either with us or against us' – to which Blair replied, 'We stand side by side with you now, without hesitation. This is a struggle that concerns us all, the whole of the democratic and civilized and free world.' Famously, in secret, he said simply, 'I will be with you, whatever.'[19]

In regular political discourse, however, the correspondence and coherence theories are never fully distinct from each other. In fact, much of politics depends upon slipping and sliding unobtrusively between the two. It would be an error to describe the coherence theory as one that is based upon a democratic desire to establish community at any and all costs, and it would equally be an error to suggest that the correspondence theory demands assent to a specific politics because 'that's just the way things are', with its attendant refusal to debate and its tendency towards an authoritarianism that parades itself cynically under the terms of 'realism'.

The relevant example from UK politics might be the assertion that the UK government sends £350 million per week to the European Union, and that this is money that ought to be used for the NHS. In terms of correspondence, this is simply untrue. In terms of coherence, it established a community of people who found solace in it, who 'agreed' with its speaker, and who then voted accordingly. Two things now become possible, given that correspondence demonstrates that the claim is false. First, the voter might change their mind, recalibrating the relative weights of correspondence (i.e. rational fact) against coherence (i.e. being part of a specific community of 'believers'). Alternatively, however, the voter might see the demonstration of falsehood, yet still retain the 'belief'. In this latter case, the actual and empirical facts of the matter count for nothing. Instead, what is at stake is the question of a political 'identity'. The question that the voter asks herself or himself is: 'With whom shall I identify as a voter?' Identity trumps empirical political reality; tribes are classed and sorted. In this specific example, further, the referent is the NHS – an explicitly national entity identified with my health and well-being. The voter who retains this belief and prioritizes coherence over

---

[19]See report at 'Voice of America', available at: https://www.voanews.com/a/a-13-a-2001-09-21-14-bush-66411197/549664.html (accessed 6 February 2018), and Tony Blair's now declassified Memo to George W. Bush, dated 7/28/2002, reproduced at: https://www.theguardian.com/uk-news/2016/jul/06/with-you-whatever-tony-blair-letters-george-w-bush-chilcot (accessed 6 February 2018).

correspondence identifies with the national language in which the claim is made. In retaining the position, regardless of empirical fact, this voter is saying, in the simplest and purest terms, 'I am English'. If we need a further gloss, she or he is saying 'I am politically English', and I am of the tribe of those who speak these words.

* * *

This may all seem a little abstruse, but we can clarify it further by considering a specific representative example, from a classroom in literature. In 1854, Charles Dickens wrote *Hard Times*, featuring Thomas Gradgrind, the educationist who praises the learning and rehearsal of facts, and who can become our representative of truth-as-fact, the correspondence theory. In this example, truth-as-fact is shown to be essentially mindless and lacking in thought or emotion. Asked by Gradgrind to define a horse, Sissy Jupe, who lives surrounded by horses, is 'thrown into the greatest alarm', unable to speak. Gradgrind turns to another pupil, the much less attractively presented Bitzer, who gives the definition in cold, precise and factual terms: 'Quadruped. Graminivorous. Forty teeth, namely twenty-four grinders, four eye-teeth, and twelve incisive. Sheds coat in the spring; in marshy countries, sheds hoofs, too. Hoofs hard, but requiring to be shod with iron. Age known by marks in mouth.'[20]

The very formulation of the phrases here dramatizes Bitzer's distance from the horse as such: the *primary* qualification of his statement is that it assumes there is no subjective point of view, and all is presented robotically, as if from some entirely neutral (and neutered) place. Oddly, then, this reality-as-fact is a reality from which Bitzer himself is utterly distanced. However, his speech is entirely in tune with the speech of Gradgrind and the School Commissioner, and it is the combination of 'objective' truth-as-fact with the agreed discourse of the community of those in educational authority that gives legitimacy to his statement, that makes it 'true' and – more importantly – that gives Bitzer authority.

Immediately after this, we have an entirely different attitude to truth, and one that, being based *primarily* on a group's coherence and conventions, illustrates the opposing attitude to truth. The Commissioner for education intervenes in the classroom scene. Now that the class 'know'

---

[20]Charles Dickens, *Hard Times* (1854; Penguin, 1977), 50.

what a horse is, courtesy of Bitzer's description, he asks, 'Would you paper a room with representations of horses?' There is a pause, before half of the class chorus out, gaily, 'Yes, sir!' This may be *factually* true: perhaps they would. However, the other half of the class 'seeing in the gentleman's face that Yes was wrong, cried out in chorus, "No, sir!"'[21] With this, we see that what passes for truth need have no bearing upon the material reality of actual wallpaper in actual rooms; rather, it is merely a question of conforming to what the authorities or authoritative voices within the community have agreed. That authority is embodied in the figure of the Commissioner.

In this situation, truth thus becomes a purely linguistic matter, a matter of saying the right thing regardless of its veracity or contact with real facts. In UK parliamentary politics, the broad equivalent would be obeying the official Party Whip. In general political discourse, the equivalent is the endorsement of conformist thinking, obedience towards 'the will of the people' – to put it in the relevant pertinent contemporary terms – as if reality was something that was determined simply by majoritarian voting. Further, the 'majority' in this case is simply given by the volume with which one version of the world is rehearsed, and the further corollary is that this can operate as a means of diverting attention from real material concerns.

In *Hard Times*, having got this 'right' answer (the answer that is acceptable under the legitimate rules of this game and that is determined by those rules and by those in command of the rules), the Commissioner asks, further, 'why' would they not paper the walls with representations of horses. Once again, a 'corpulent boy' replies, truthful-factual, that it is because 'he wouldn't paper a room at all, but would paint it'. This is not playing the game, and the Commissioner immediately calls him back into the rules, into what passes for legitimate modes of speech or contribution to the discussion, and rules his statement out-of-order: '"You must paper it," said the gentleman, rather warmly.'[22] The language-game here is circumscribed by the rules that say that all rooms are papered; if he wants to continue as a member of this community, the corpulent boy must abide by those rules and must say whether he would or would not paper the walls with representations of horses. Indeed, the man in

---

[21]Dickens, *Hard Times*, 51.
[22]Ibid.

command of the rules here essentially menaces the boy, to ensure his conformist participation in the game, speaking to him 'rather warmly' as Dickens puts it.

Once more, in this example, we can see the seemingly intimate relation between a tendency to authoritarianism that is combined with a particular attitude to truth. The authoritarian politician is she or he who claims to have some fundamental direct claim upon truth-as-fact and who will use this as the grounds on which to rest the validity of her or his argument. However, in this case, what is also extremely clear is that such an authoritarian attitude can actually disregard facts (as in Sissy Jupe's 'emotional truth' about horses, say) while at the same time turning to truth-as-coherence or linguistic convention to coerce others into compliance with a specific view of the world. Dickens seems to have been implicitly aware of how the control of language can become the control of material realities, in a deeply political sense. Crucially, the example demonstrates power at work, and it does so in a way that reveals how education can itself be perverted for those explicit political ends, in which authoritarian figures will dictate what it is that constitutes reality.

Moreover, such an attitude towards political language also indirectly and secondarily establishes a community of 'insiders' and a separate community of 'outsiders'. Bitzer is an insider; Sissy an outsider. The distinction between insiders and outsiders is one that is made in another of Frank Kermode's books, his study of biblical narrative in his engagement with *The Genesis of Secrecy*. He considers there how Christ's parables work, and discovers that the parable already presupposes the existence of those who know the truth of what it signifies, and those who stand outside of that truth. The paradox of the parable is that 'Only the insiders can have access to the true sense of these stories', while those outside 'will pay a supreme penalty' for not being able to access their meaning. 'To divine the true, the latent sense, you need to be of the elect, of the institution.'[23] Kermode is discussing theological 'election' here. In the political sphere, the 'elect' are, in our time, more conventionally referred to as 'the elite' (the two words – elite and elect – are cognate). The Dickens example shows that Bitzer will get ahead

---

[23] Frank Kermode, *The Genesis of Secrecy* (Harvard University Press, Cambridge, MA, 1979), 2–3.

socially; Sissy will not. Bitzer will be 'co-opted' into the position of political authority; Sissy will become the object of Bitzer's eventual political authority. He will manage her.

* * *

This also indicates, however, another fundamental aspect of this way of understanding political discourse. Individuals will now be in a position to determine their political allegiances and alliances as a matter of language-games. The language of the political right differs not just in vocabulary but also in semantics from the language of the political left. Perhaps most obviously, the word 'freedom' has entirely different semantic content depending on its political context: the right would see it as legitimizing market-capitalism, the left as legitimizing the struggle against being controlled and subsumed by the very same market-capitalism. Furthermore, as with 'freedom', so also with many classic political concepts, such as liberalism, justice, equality, democracy, authority, socialism, communism and so on. In recent times, however, this kind of divergence (and confusion) has become more and more insistent, and the result has been a multiplication of language-games, with an attendant multiplication of political interests – and the result is a fragmentation of the social as a whole. Now, it is almost a commonplace to suggest that there are as many truths as there are interests.[24]

Alain Badiou argues satirically that, with this multiplication of identitarian language-games (or 'communities of interpretation', as we once called them), there is a corresponding bonus for capital, an 'inexhaustible future for mercantile investment' in all the 'redeemed communities' of 'women, homosexuals, the disabled, Arabs', breaking down further into yet more commercial opportunities for sub-sub-groups, such as 'Black homosexuals, disabled Serbs, Catholic paedophiles, moderate Islamists, married priests' and so on and on. 'Every time, a new social image authorises new products.'[25]

---

[24]The logic of this is explored in terms of psychology in Drew Westen, *Self and Society: Narcissism, Collectivism and the Development of Morals* (Cambridge University Press, 2009). See especially chapter 6 of the book, pp. 216–40, on 'Societal structure and dynamics'.

[25]Alain Badiou, *Saint Paul: La fondation de l'universalisme* (Presses Universitaires de France, Paris, 1997), 11 (translation mine).

Badiou's barely suppressed contempt here is based in the realization that – despite, and even contrary to, the supposed emancipation of such identity-groups – there is clearly money to be made in the multiplication of truths, and an almost proportionate calibration of growth in the capitalist economy with the growth in specific political identities. Multiply the 'communities of interpreters', this suggests, and you simply multiply the ways in which capital will continue to exploit. This is so, most insistently, precisely when you subscribe to the belief that your very identity is the thing that will help to undermine the control and power of capital itself. Identity itself here becomes a key resource for capital, the very means by which it will continue to exploit those who claim the identity in the first place. Badiou has a point, and his point demonstrates that the power of capital – money – can undermine any and every attempt to rest a political case for emancipation on the play of a linguistic game.

Writing about the UK's attitudes towards immigrants, Lyndsey Stonebridge indicates the more specific point that I am making in very exacting and precise terms. She reminds us that George Orwell, Simone Weil and Hannah Arendt understood fully that, in the wake of Nazism, a 'psychic uprootedness … was shaping the lives of supposedly secure national populations as much as those of the displaced and homeless'. Further, this sense was generated from a general political predicament rooted in issue of 'power, money and acquisition'. From this, the question of political fantasy, 'or, as Orwell and Arendt both understood it, political lying', enters directly into our consideration, especially our consideration of the position of refugees and of migrants, those who are psychically and materially uprooted.

Stonebridge then argues, correctly, that 'The dangerous thing about living in a political culture that openly trades in lies and fancies is not that we are duped'. It is not the case that people 'believe' that Donald Trump, say, is ever likely to be revealing a profound and previously unknown set of empirical truths about the world. The real danger is 'that we lose our sense of shared truth', with the consequence that the sense of community vanishes, and one is left with 'organised loneliness'. What follows is that 'you make up a version of community instead, which will, perforce, be a lie'. The specific lie that is of interest in relation to the question of immigration in the UK is, of course, the lie that governs nationalism, 'the political doctrine of the delusional fantasist'. As Stonebridge sums the position up, 'It is not so much that the nationalist doesn't know that two plus two cannot equal five, but the desire to live in a coherent fiction, to banish vulnerability, means that he doesn't care whether it does or not.'[26]

This 'coherent fiction' is the coherence account of truth elevated to the status of myth. That is to say, one gets one's truth from one's adherence to a specific linguistic community. The community that governs English nationalism, for example, as described in Stonebridge here, heavily influenced by Orwell and his critique, is that of English speakers, 'the Anglosphere', the 'English-speaking peoples' who are always in the truth because English is itself the language that has privileged access to truth. More generally, the same applies to all particular interest groups as they enter into political debate: each develops its own lexicon, its own code, and adherence to the code becomes the primary goal of political action. The term that has often been used for this – and which I will describe and engage with more fully below – is 'political correctness'. In this form, it is trite, but there is a serious political issue here, relating to whether one can change the empirical conditions of material history by changing the linguistic norms that describe it. What this means, in serious terms, is whether those who accord with a specific language-game can displace those in authority: can Sissy Jupe overcome Bitzer? Moreover, can she do it by persuading Bitzer to abandon the language of Gradgrind and to embrace hers instead?

* * *

As Hannah Arendt pointed out on many occasions, politics has an uneasy relationship to truth-telling. 'No one has ever doubted that truth and politics are on rather bad terms with each other, and no one ... has ever counted truthfulness among the political virtues.' She went even further, for the avoidance of doubt, writing that 'Lies have always been regarded as necessary and justifiable tools not only of the politician's or the demagogue's but also of the statesman's trade'.[27]

This is quite probably generally understood, and so it is not a crude cynicism that determines our suspicion of the truth-content of the words of politicians. Knowing, as we do, that politicians are involved in an act

---

[26]Lyndsey Stonebridge, 'Fantasy Island', *Prospect*, 13 July 2017. See also the extended argument in her *Placeless People: Writing, Rights and Refugees* (Oxford University Press, 2018).

[27]Hannah Arendt, 'Truth and Politics', in *Between Past and Future* (Penguin, 2006), 223. See also her 'Lying in Politics', in *Crises of the Republic* (Harcourt, New York, 1972).

of rhetorical persuasion that is designed to secure our tribal allegiance, we take it as read that they will be skewing information and presenting an explicitly biased case in the manipulation of information. This much, then, is clear, and it is an error to proceed in political activities as if politicians are wedded to a philosophical demand for an empirically verifiable truth as such.

To explain this simply, we might say that the important thing is not that Donald Trump or Boris Johnson are constitutional and inveterate liars; rather, the important and most troubling thing is that they disable the very demand for truth itself, by undermining the idea that political rhetoric can be validated by any claims upon either material reality or the establishment of peace. Their language is characterized – through the mechanism of inveterate lying – by a determination to undermine an electorate's belief that we can ever get to the truth about anything at all. The attack on all forms of institutions that are dedicated to getting at the truth – the 'mainstream media', intellectuals, journalists, scientists, researchers, experts and so on – is part of an attack on the very idea that anyone might even *want* to test hypotheses against empirical reality or to test the legitimacy of the position of one's tribe with its own internal coherent speech and fictions.

In the light of this kind of assault, it is, perhaps above all, the key characteristic of a proper and democratic spirit of critique that it requires us to seek to find the actual *motivations* behind the propositions in any politician's claims. 'From what reasoned perspective might such propositions as these be made?' is the correct kind of question to ask. 'What are the consequential implications for all political arrangements in general if we adopt this perspective in this particular instance?' These questions are designed to test the coherence against the correspondence theories of truth. It is not that we will reach some transcendent truth through this: it is simply that we can find the most appropriate calibration of the relative weight of one's tribal identity against the equally important weight of a public shared polity.

Questions such as these – questions that are basic to all democracy – indicate that all participants know that a particular kind of language-game is in play in political discourse. We do not judge these statements and propositions in terms of their fidelity to some absolute notion of truth; rather, we make our judgements based in terms of the larger and more general ideological predisposition that the statements imply. Such ideologies, we say, determine the content of the statements in what we acknowledge to be their 'interested' formulation. Biased information can thus be excused, given that it is information that does not exist in a pure form but rather a kind of information that is itself 'informed' by a preferred set of beliefs and political desires or preferences.

We do not expect some absolute fidelity to truth in the statements made by any and all politicians, but we do rightly demand that there should be some kind of serious analysis that lies behind and underpins those statements. It is that analysis that constitutes their predispositions and habits; and the task is to realize that such habits have the status merely of fictions and hypotheses, and thereby to disable the claim that the habit has the absolutizing and totalizing status of a mythic truth. That is to say, democracy requires not only that we acknowledge that every political position is determined by a pre-existing ideology but also that we discover and disarm most urgently those political positions that claim to be beyond ideology. The position that most needs such uncovering is the political position that claims to base itself not upon reality but upon realism. The mantra of democracy might be very clumsily stated: 'analyze the conditions that inform the politician's analysis.'

Two rival modes of conversation go on in all political English, therefore. On the one hand, we have the monologue of 'realism': 'the world really is like this, and nothing you can say or do will change these facts.' On the other hand, we have the dialogue of political hypotheses: 'if you were just to join me and share my world view, then we might make that view a reality.' For many, the securing of a tribal alliance or allegiance is absolutely primary. The belief is that if we can get a majority of people to side with us, then reality will become as we describe it. More succinctly put, we will be in command of the discourses that describe the world, and thus we will be the legislators of what constitutes truth. This is a specific but bastard form of democracy: majoritarian rule. It depends on ensuring that participants in a polity become 'one of us', an 'insider'.[28] In the particular context of a national politics, what this amounts to is a determination to give credence to those who share a specific national identity. 'How English is it? How English are you?'

* * *

---

[28]This is what lies behind the famous question reportedly always posed by Margaret Thatcher, when she was introduced to anyone new: 'Is he one of us?' The phrase yielded the title of Hugo Young's biography of her, *One of Us* (1989; rev. edn, Pan Books, 2013).

Enoch Powell gave an address in Trinity College Dublin on 13 November 1964. There, he spoke of a nation as what Benedict Anderson would one day call an 'imagined community', but Powell meant something different from Anderson. He used a different term as well, speaking of the nation as a 'corporate imagination'; and he argued that this imagination could, in some deep way, affect the material condition of the nation as a polity. Nations live according to the logic of myth, he argued, and he further identified all of history precisely as mythic, 'a pattern which men weave out of the materials of the past'. With this assertion, he was able to make a claim that my present argument shows to be extremely contentious. He said that 'the moment a fact enters into history, it becomes mythical, because it has been taken and fitted into its place in a set of ordered relationships which is the creation of the human mind and not otherwise present in nature'.[29]

Powell's argument is that myth is inescapable, and that the function of the politician is 'to offer his people good myths and to save them from harmful myths'.[30] As my argument has made clear, this is tantamount to saying that the task of the politician is to replace one totalitarian rule with another, to overwhelm one position to the point of eradicating it, while persuading people to subscribe to another, equally totalitarian position. If there remains anything 'democratic' in this at all, then it can only be the bogus democracy of an absolutist version of majoritarian rule. Such rule necessarily discounts – eradicates – the language of those who are not 'one of us'.

In his speech, Powell states, explicitly, that the people of Britain at that moment in 1964 accept two myths: (1) Britain was an imperial power that has lost its standing; (2) Britain was once the workshop of the world, but no longer stands tall in this way. These myths, he says, are false, and, 'being false, they entail upon Britain grave psychological damage and errors of judgment'. Consequently, 'they ought to be destroyed'.[31] Such thinking – such violence – is the antithesis of the democracy that Powell claims to be defending. Certainly, this is a speech in which he finds it difficult to entertain the possibility that the corporate imagination that is 'Britain' might constitute anything other than the myth of an enlarged

---

[29] Powell, *Freedom and Reality*, 246.
[30] Ibid., 246.
[31] Ibid., 247.

'England', the corporate imagination of 'Englandness' or of the being – and speaking – of 'English'.[32]

The Trinity College Dublin speech followed one that Powell had given earlier that year, to the Royal Society of St George on 22 April 1964. He rehearsed, in the St George speech, a position that he had laid out on several other occasions. He spoke of patriotism and imagined what might be the essence of Englishness. Inviting his audience to travel back across centuries with him, he asks 'the old English' to tell us 'what it is that binds us together' and goes on to ask old England to 'show us the clue that leads through a thousand years; whisper to us the secret of this charmed life of England, that we in our time may know how to hold it fast'. What, he asks, would the people of old England say when faced with the question of what constitutes the essential English?

In response, first of all, he attends to the medium in which they would say it. They would speak the truth, he says, because they speak English: 'They would speak to us in our own English tongue, the tongue made for telling the truth in.' This being established by mere assertion (though I have revealed its ideological substratum in these pages), he can go on to the substance of their message. We hear that the substance of this Englishness would be a combination of pastoral, centred on rural life, with a cultural existence, a place for meeting and communing together and a place 'to which men resorted out of all England to speak on behalf of their fellows, a thing called "Parliament"' from where justice is dispensed, as through the law'.[33]

Powell is essentially making a fundamentalist claim here, in which England is itself defined as some kind of original Edenic state of nature, from which all other states have undergone a quasi-Biblical Fall. Everywhere else is a deviation, delinquent and less 'natural'. Those other nations and states, exiled thus from the locus of truth, have 'learned' how to live properly through the adoption of institutions that are utterly 'natural' to England. In terms appropriate to this chapter, he is establishing *as if it were a truth of fact* (England as an original condition of all proper and

---

[32] An anecdotal but important aside is apposite here. When I taught in Trinity College Dublin, one of my colleagues – an eminent Professor of Anglo-Irish Literature – pointed out that, for many, Trinity represented the 'last bastion of British imperialism'. I think that 'English imperialism' might be the more appropriate formulation – as my argument here will show.

[33] Powell, *Freedom and Reality*, 256.

natural human being) what is *merely a rhetorical assertion* (his poetical and metaphorical account of pastoral idyll). This confusion of fact with rhetoric takes him inexorably into the far-right terrain, in which a certain authentic being is tied to blood, breeding and soil.

First, however, to do this he has to get rid of the extraneous matter and subordinate people around the English centre of all things. At the centre of this idyllic paradise and unity that is England, 'Englishness', and the English language, we will find kingship – but especially and specifically 'English kingship'. In his metaphors, further, he indicates his own right-wing affirmation of blood lineages. His specifically 'English kingship' is a kingship that springs 'as from the soil of England'. This kingship is determinedly English (not British), and we can safely disregard 'all the leeks and thistles and shamrocks'. Through this simple rhetorical trope of metonymy, Powell rids 'England' of entire peoples who are clearly not in the same truth-telling category as the English, even if they often largely speak the same language: Welsh, Scots, Irish. We can also ignore the little historical awkwardness that this English kingship might have a derivation that comes from 'Stuarts and Hanoverians' (with a couple of sweeping name-callings, any incipient Catholics or Germans can follow the Scots, Irish and Welsh out of the realm of paradisiacal truth). Powell can then turn to one of his favourite modes of thought and speech, using a vocabulary that is intimately related to ideas of breeding and eugenics: 'The stock that received all these grafts [Welsh, Scottish, Irish, German, half-Catholic] is English, the sap that rises through it to its extremities rises from roots in English earth, the earth of England's history.'[34]

Powell's speech was given on the eve of St George's Day: 22 April 1964. Exactly twenty-nine years later, 22 April 1993, John Major, at that time the UK's Conservative Prime Minister, also made a significant speech, in which he considered the place of Britain in the interconnected realms of Europe. Unlike Powell, Major did not want to stress a kind of English hierarchical exceptionalism, an England that was the *fons et origo* of truth. The occasion of Major's speech, after all, was different from where we left Powell. Major was addressing the Conservative Group for Europe, and he wanted, through the speech, to indicate that membership of an international polity was not something that would intrinsically damage or weaken the specific identity of the British. Being 'one of them'

---

[34] Ibid., 257.

(European) was consistent, for Major, with being 'one of us' (British). Yet it is interesting to note the rhetorical overlaps between the speeches of Powell and of Major in this present context.

Speaking of the persistence of a British identity within Europe, Major – like Powell – invoked a similar kind of pastoral image. 'Fifty years from now', he said, Britain 'will still be the country of long shadows on county grounds, warm beer, invincible green suburbs, dog lovers and pools fillers'. We will still see 'old maids bicycling to Holy Communion through the morning mist', and, 'if we get our way – Shakespeare still read even in school'.[35] The reference to Shakespeare in schools harks back to the urgencies and political drive in the educational policies of Newbolt and Sampson, and it is the single direct reference in the speech to a tradition that prioritizes modes of speech. However, Major's 'old maids' are in a certain sense not actually or empirically real individuals, for they are lifted from another text. They have no factual existence, so to speak, and their being is entirely literary: Major is quoting (actually slightly misquoting) from a literary source, George Orwell's 'England your England' in his 1941 essay *The Lion and the Unicorn*. Since Major's old maids are not underpinned by the truth of their factual existence, we can see that they constitute nothing more or less than a rhetorical device. It is not a truth of correspondence that Major effects here but rather an affiliation or coherence between himself and the culture of Englishness represented by Orwell.

Major, then, very clearly differs from Powell. Where Powell wanted to underline his idea of Englishness by stressing the constitutional identity of fact with English language, and both with an essential truth that is available only to the English speaker, Major by contrast establishes a formal distance between the truth of fact (that warm beer, those cricket grounds) and language (the argument that operates by a textual recalling of the voice of Orwell and the speeches of Shakespeare). This is not a mere difference of tone: it is an entirely different politics. Powell is far right, tending towards an English nationalist totalitarianism, and he is incipiently racist. The point about race, for the racist, is that race supposedly presents us with an ineluctable truth of fact; and arguments based on race are therefore not at all amenable to debate, their constituent

---

[35] See John Major, 'Speech to the Conservative Group for Europe', delivered 22 April 1993, available at: http://www.johnmajor.co.uk/page1086.html.

statements not available for discussion. As Kermode showed, this is the political power of myth in Nazism.

For Powell, the word is the deed. He refers his audience to 'a saying, not heard today so often as formerly': 'What do they know of England who only England know?' The phrase comes from Kipling's poem, 'The English Flag', a poem that laments how the English fail to attend sufficiently well to the expanded Empire. The clear implication is that to know England is to know the world that England controlled. Pondering this, Powell states that 'In that incredible phrase, which came upon the English unawares, as all true greatness comes unawares upon a nation, the power and influence of England expanded with the force and speed of an explosion'.[36] The discovery of English identity is entirely of a piece and entirely contemporaneous with the imperial expansion of that identity. The rhetorical word of the question *is* its own political answer, and the deed is utterly instantaneous and coterminous with the uttering of the uncontested word. Powell might equally well have cited Kipling's 'England's Answer', where he would find the advice 'Now must ye speak to your kinsmen and they must speak to you / After the use of the English, in straight-flung words and few', so that you can be 'certain of sword and pen'.[37] This is the classic English style: plain, honest, straightforward – and in fact allied to the sword.

Powell is ostensibly arguing against introspection, which he regards as 'an unhealthy attitude unless it be sparingly practised'. In that context, it is worth pointing out, even in passing, that Kipling prefaced his poem with a brief sentence indicating the source of the poem's sentiment, an image that spurred Kipling to write. The sentence describes an image taken from 'daily papers': 'Above the portico a flag-staff, bearing the Union Jack, remained fluttering in the flames for some time, but ultimately when it fell the crowds rent the air with shouts, and seemed to see significance in the incident.'[38] In fact, the event described occurred in Cork, where the Union Jack was set alight (and with it an entire courtroom) during the trial of five Irish men who were charged with riot. The flag in question, then, is not 'the English Flag' at all, but, given Powell's casual dismissal of Scots, Welsh and Irish, one can see why he might have been caught by the poem and its poignant phrase. Yet one must obviously ask Powell

---

[36] Powell, *Freedom and Reality*, 254–5.
[37] Rudyard Kipling, 'England's Answer', in *Selected Poems* (Penguin, 1977), 85.
[38] Kipling, 'The English Flag', in *Selected Poems*, 95.

his own question: 'What can he know of Britain, or the world, who only England knows?'

To some extent, the appropriate response to such a question had in fact already been given, in 1963, a year before Powell's speech. C.L.R. James famously transposed Kipling's phrase, asking, in *Beyond a Boundary*, 'What should they know of England who only cricket know?'[39] Notionally a book about cricket, *Beyond a Boundary* is actually an exposition of the political consequences of 'playing the game'. The book is also a response to Henry Newbolt's 1892 poem, 'Vitaï Lampada', with its repeated refrain of 'Play up! Play up! And play the game!' That poem uses cricket as a means of delineating a particular kind of English ethical spirit: a commitment, even in the face of war, to the spirit of fair play and commitment to the team or nation. James proposes a much more nuanced analysis of the overlap between the ideological configuration of cricket when seen from the point of view of the colonized.[40]

Where Powell lamented introspection, James had seen the crucial importance of introspection for the development of historical progress and of modernity as such. He explains this in his 1953 'Notes on *Hamlet*', where he describes Hamlet as the character who struggles with how to live in the great opening to modernity. That opening is profoundly concerned with communication and with the relation of words to actions. Hamlet is 'the precursor in human personality of the supremacy of reason, of rationalism; and the essence of rationalism is the communication of ideas. He needs to communicate',[41] writes James. In this, Hamlet precedes and gives a form to 'the orator who sways the public', but, crucially, for James, knowing oneself – thinking critically at all – stems from the very priority of speaking: 'If Hamlet soliloquised so much, one reason is that he loved to soliloquise. These thronging ideas sprang from the need and possibility and necessity of expressing them.'[42] In this sense, for James, the 'knowing England' of which Kipling and Powell write requires that

---

[39]C.L.R. James, *Beyond a Boundary* (1963; repr. 5-Star, 2000), ix.

[40]For details of the conditions surrounding Kipling's poem – and for an excellent examination of the relation of Kipling to C.L.R. James – see Claire Westall, 'What they knew of nation and empire: Kipling and C.L.R. James', in *Kipling and Beyond*, ed. Caroline Rooney and Kaori Nagai (Palgrave Macmillan, 2010), 165–84.

[41]C.L.R. James, 'Notes on *Hamlet*', in *The C.L.R. James Reader*, ed. Anna Grimshaw (Blackwell, Oxford, 1993), 244–5.

[42]James, 'Notes on *Hamlet*', 245.

one stand outside of England in the first place, and this is a position that neither of those empire-minded individuals could do.

* * *

John Major, by contrast with Powell, strives to place British people in an arena of debate, one where they will certainly have an identity that is based on their specific difference from other nations, but one where they can still talk, as equals and without issuing imperial and imperative orders, to the people of those other nations. That depends upon the maintenance of politics, upon our acceptance that there is inevitably – and, politically, helpfully – a discrepancy between fact and language. It is interesting, further, that in this same speech, Major notes one of the single greatest benefits of British membership of the European Community: 'two generations of peace'. Major's peace here can be set firmly against the Powellite vision of 'the Tiber foaming with blood'. Such Powellite racist violence is the logical corollary of the confusion of fact and linguistic truth, and it has found, in Powell and his contemporary heirs – the Faragist UKIP xenophobes of our time – its prophet and political articulation.

The allusion to Orwell in Major's speech is interesting, especially coming as it does from a Conservative voice. In 'England Your England', Orwell asks what it might be that characterizes English identity. When he catalogues some typical images, he finds a 'diverse chaotic individuality': bitter beer, heavy coins, greener grass than elsewhere, blatant advertising, knobby faces, bad teeth, gentle manners, clogs in Lancashire, lorries on the Great North Road, pin-tables in Soho pubs, and those 'old maids biking to Holy Communion through the mists of the autumn mornings' to which Major would refer.[43] These, Orwell says, are but fragmentary images, certainly; yet they are also '*characteristic* fragments of the English scene'.[44] Like T.S. Eliot in 'The Waste Land', written under the shadow of the Great War, Orwell is finding fragments to shore up against the potential ruin of an England that is once again, in 1941, in a war where, 'As I write, highly civilised human beings are flying overhead, trying to kill me'.[45]

---

[43] Orwell, *Collected Essays*, 57.
[44] Ibid.
[45] Ibid., 56.

When he takes his description of these fragments further, he looks for any kind of common denominator among them, for something to make a dominant image out of the muddle, and he turns to 'the common people'. This will be the cornerstone of Orwell's truth of fact, as it were: the 'real' England behind the official image.[46] Interestingly, however, the thing about the common people is that they are always at odds with the official image: their being highlights a fissure within the reality of England, and some of this is based in their attitude to language. 'In all societies', Orwell writes, 'the common people must live to some extent *against* the existing order. The genuinely popular culture of England is something that goes on beneath the surface, unofficially and more or less frowned upon by the authorities.' These people, he says, 'are inveterate gamblers, drink as much beer as their wages will permit, are devoted to bawdy jokes, and use probably the foulest language in the world'.[47]

It is interesting here that we can find a link between a dissident life (which is also, paradoxically, the life that is most common in England) and a foul tongue. In Orwell's England, it is the ruling classes that always 'govern their tongue' in that they watch how they speak English and, like Sampson and Newbolt, demand a certain conformity in speech, or 'standard' English. At the same time, the common people are themselves less governable *by* the ruling classes as long as they retain their own foul English. In governing their tongues, the ruling class cannot yet govern *by* their tongue, even if this is their undemocratic desire.

This is utterly at odds with the politics of Powell, clearly, as he veered towards the tyrannical intimacy of English word and political deed, but the key thing in that difference is the strikingly similar attitudes to language. For Orwell, there is indeed a category of people called 'the English-speaking' – those who, as we noted earlier here, are 'haunted by the idea of human equality', but it is their unreliable and quasi-anarchic *diversity* – and especially their linguistic diversity – that offers the nation protection against totalitarianism. 'With all its sloth, hypocrisy and

---

[46]In making this appeal to the real England of common people, Orwell is doing something that is completely the opposite of Nigel Farage's assertion that victory in the Brexit referendum was a victory for 'ordinary people, decent people', as my argument will later show.

[47]Orwell, *Collected Essays*, 59. For a further reflection on 'common people', see Alison Light's investigation of her own family history, in *Common People* (Penguin, 2015). There, she remarks (p. xxii) that 'poverty homogenizes, whereas family history humanizes'. Orwell might have said exactly the same.

injustice, the English-speaking civilization is the only obstacle in Hitler's path,' Orwell writes.[48]

The linguistic diversity – differences of accent between Scots and English, Cockney and Yorkshireman, Indian and Trinidadian – can be retained and fully respected, but this does not mean that there is any lack of an overall British identity, Orwell argues. Further, he notes – with a complex and nuanced eye – the attitude of the English to learning foreign languages. This, too, unifies the English speaker and gives her and him an identity that can be set against the difference of foreigners. 'Nearly every Englishman of working-class origin considers it effeminate to pronounce a foreign word correctly,' he writes. This remains the case even after the Great War when English speakers were in close contact with foreigners, and the only result of that, he claims, 'was that they brought back a hatred of all Europeans, except the Germans, whose courage they admired'.[49] There is an innate resistance, in this attitude to foreign languages, 'that repels the tourist and keeps out the invader'.

Oddly, just as Major misquotes Orwell, so also Orwell rests part of his own case on a misquotation. He misquotes the writer that Major wanted to see as a cornerstone of English education: Shakespeare. The misquotation is also strikingly relevant not just for 1941 when Orwell was writing but also for our own historical moment. Further, the misquotation is itself at one remove, for Orwell is quoting (he thinks) Neville Chamberlain quoting (or misquoting) Shakespeare. In all of this, coherence is being stressed over correspondence; alliances triumph silently over tribal divisiveness, and there is an attempt to maintain the possibility of democratic politics over the resolution of conflicts through fundamentalist violence.

Orwell is concluding his essay by arguing that a certain spirit of resistance to Hitler, a Socialist resistance to totalitarian rule, can survive even if Britain is defeated in the war. He recalls that 'a piece of Shakespearean bombast was much quoted at the beginning of the war' and gives us the lines from *King John*: 'Come the four corners of the world in arms / And we shall shock them: naught shall make us rue / If England to herself do rest but true.'[50] (The actual lines in Shakespeare describe not four corners of the world, but three.)

---

[48]Ibid., 107.
[49]Ibid., 65.
[50]Ibid., 109.

What is the meaning of 'truth' in these lines? There is an idea of being 'true to oneself', which broadly translates as being honest in behaviour, making your words match your actions and behaving in an authentic fashion. For England to rest 'true' to itself, its behaviour must match its intrinsic character, so to speak, and the claim is that, as long as this kind of truth persists, England will survive any kind of foreign onslaught or attack. Now, if, as Orwell suggests, the intrinsic character of England is given by its foul-mouthed common people, by those who are dissident with respect to the great official voices of power, then it follows that it is precisely *this* kind of authority – the authority of the *ungoverned* tongue – that will save England. As he puts it, England 'is not being true to herself while the refugees who have sought our shores are penned up in concentration camps, and company directors work out subtle schemes to dodge their Excess Profits Tax'.[51]

This is a message as pertinent today as it was in 1941, but it is one that is also entirely at odds with the kinds of Conservatism advocated by the English nationalism of Powell and of his political successors. Its continuing relevance in our own time demonstrates to what extent that Powellite tendency to English exceptionalism and its intrinsic iniquitous hierarchy persists: the English superior to, and not wishing to be tainted or contaminated by, contact with foreigners, even if they are refugees; within England, the superiority of the wealthy over the poor. The fundamental point here is that, in the end, these are actually questions and issues that are underpinned by a specific attitude to political English: they are language questions, and thus they relate to the claims that politicians may make upon how their language can become deed.

The truth of England, for Orwell, is not found in the official institutions, like the House of Lords, but rather it is to be found 'in the fields and the streets, in the factories and the armed forces, in the four-ale bar and the suburban back garden'. The truth to be found in England, here, is not that of the Bible, because such a Powellite truth is one that eschews the foreign tongue (the speech of the refugee, the foul mouth and 'improper English' of the commoner) and that condones the tax avoider in ways that ensure ever-increasing economic divisions and inequalities. But equality itself, of course – we remember – is, for Orwell, precisely the ghost that haunts England, and whose voice must come back from beyond

---

[51]Ibid.

the grave if England is to continue to survive. If we are to find 'truth' as some essential element in England, it is to be found in the ungoverned diversity of voices, including those of the foreigner: it is to be found in the commonly shared and in the commoner, not in the exception hero, the St George of English nationalism. Orwell, for one, would have stressed the simple fact that George was Turkish.

* * *

In Chapter 3, where I addressed what I called 'Fundamentalist English', I drew out the mode of thinking that related the *English* language specifically to truth, by extension suggesting that the English-speaking peoples had a privileged relation to truth as such. There, the King James Bible – the Authorized Version – is deemed to be authoritative precisely because it is an English-language version. The implicit claim is that God spoke or thought in English, and that the words in which the Bible were originally written – Hebrew, Aramaic, Akkadian and so on – were all some kind of coded deviation from a tacit and underlying *ur*-text, and King James initiated the project to recover that truth-telling text, that originary statement of the way of the world, as if it lay like the sheet of a palimpsest under the cover of the visible and audible foreign language. At issue here is a special kind of 'correspondence', a correspondence between an imagined God and the English-speaking person.

Such thinking persists in the minds of politicians from very different persuasions. George Orwell, for instance, found a spirit of socialism – specifically English socialism – in an ethics that derives from a theological hinterland. When he considers what Hitler is essentially trying to do, he finds that 'it is precisely the idea of human equality – the "Jewish" or "Judaeo-Christian" idea of equality – that Hitler came into the world to destroy'. Against this, Orwell argues that 'The whole English-speaking world is haunted by the idea of human equality' and that it is 'from the English-speaking culture' that 'a society of free equal human beings will ultimately arise'.[52] From a completely opposite political point of view, Enoch Powell rehearsed his related claim that 'our own English tongue' is 'the tongue made for telling the truth in'.[53]

---

[52]George Orwell, *The Lion and the Unicorn*, reprinted in Orwell, *Collected Essays*, 106.
[53]Enoch Powell, speech to Royal Society of St George, delivered on 22 April 1964, in *Freedom and Reality*, 256.

These two – Orwell and Powell – obviously have different accounts of 'the truth', yet both derive those accounts from a specific understanding of Englishness, an Englishness that has its roots in a supposed intimacy between the English language and the word of God in the Authorized Version of the Bible. What better place, then, to begin a consideration of truth and the profane – in the sense of the 'outsider', or what George Herbert called the 'outlandish' – in political English from a specific biblical instance in which truth is called explicitly into question, and called into question for explicitly political reasons?[54]

John's is the Gospel that explicitly related God to language: 'In the beginning was the Word, and the Word was with God, and the Word was God' (John 1:1). It is in this Gospel that the question of truth is raised in it most poignant and extreme moment. According to John 18:37, Christ stood before Pilate and stated that he came 'into the world, that I should bear witness to the truth. Every bone that is of the truth heareth my voice.' The next verse has Pilate responding with my key question here: 'Pilate saith unto him, What is truth?' John's Gospel – the Gospel that is obsessed with issues of language – is alone in making much of the question of truth in this scene. In this account Pilate is obviously torn and tormented, and the source of the torment lies in the political predicament in which he finds himself. This is a genuine politicization of truth, and a politicization of 'the Word' that, for John, is at the source of all existence.

On the one hand, in the political context in which Christ faces Pilate – with a specific land and population living under political occupation by the forces of a foreign Roman military body – Pilate clearly wants to release Christ, finding no legal fault in him, and he insists repeatedly that Christ is human, stating explicitly 'Behold the man!' (19:5). However, he is put into a real predicament when he hears the response of the Jews in his audience. They cry out in reply: 'If thou lets this man go, thou are not Caesar's friend: whosoever maketh himself a king speaketh against Caesar' (19:12). We have here an insertion of philosophical issues of truth into the dynamics and contingencies of a political situation. There arises thereby a substantial question concerning the authority of the word, of specific languages, and of the contest of truths in such a political situation. The Jewish people, paradoxically for a people under

---

[54]See George Herbert, *Outlandish Proverbs* (1640). 'Outlandish' means 'foreign', from lands outside of England, and languages outside of English.

occupation, remind Pilate of his own political allegiances to Caesar and to the laws of Rome, even here.

It is when faced with this dilemma that Pilate hands Christ over to be crucified, and he then writes the title that will be placed on the cross. That title is a name, a proper name accompanied by a specific kind of authority and literal 'entitlement': INRI or 'Jesus of Nazareth The King of the Jews'. Pilate is making a name – and entitling – Christ. For the avoidance of all doubts, the title is written three times, according to John: in Hebrew, Greek and Latin. Confronted with it, the 'chief priests of the Jews' say to Pilate that he must not write that Christ *is* the King of the Jews, and that he should write instead 'that he said, I am King of the Jews'. To which Pilate replies, 'What I have written I have written' (19.19-22), refusing to change his text while yet also permitting the crucifixion to go ahead.

Pilate is caught trying to reconcile and regulate the competing claims of politics – Caesar's claim on legal authority – against the claims of philosophy and writing – a claim on linguistic legitimacy. He does this, thereby raising philosophical questions of truth, in a context that is thoroughly enmeshed in political crisis and turmoil. In this scene in John's account, truth becomes a linguistic matter, but it is set in a context that explicitly puts the word of an alleged God, a transcendent word (the word that, for John, is at the start of everything and the start of all existence and that even is constitutive of God), against the political word, the word (and world) that is governed by Caesar and Caesarism, a Judea under Rome. This is a good instance of how something that is claimed as a substantive fact becomes merely a contingent observation, and the contingency depends entirely upon the linguistic context into which the claimed fact is inserted.

It is not for nothing that Nietzsche, who would explain the nature of truth and lying in a non-moral sense, took Pilate's words 'Behold the Man' for his own autobiographical writing, *Ecce Homo*. Nietzsche's argument regarding truth is that it is essentially a matter of linguistic conformity to specific culturally agreed norms. That is to say, truth is first a matter of linguistic propositions; and second, a linguistic proposition passes for true as and when it finds agreement as the way in which speakers describe things. This is a median position between truth-correspondence and truth-consistency; the consistency here is the consistency with which words, meanings and values are agreed among a community. It is also the philosophical version of my claims that, in politics, truth-as-fact becomes contingent and depends not upon empirical realities but rather upon linguistic contexts. Further, the establishment of a linguistic context is, in fact, the establishment also of a community or a polity that will share that language and accept its ideological norms *as if* they were facts.

The biblical problem is that we have, in the political conflict of a land under occupation by a foreign force, a contest between different and even mutually exclusive sets of agreed cultural norms. The result of this – for a secular society – is that truth is always enmeshed in politics or that it is a matter of judgement within a polity, and, further, such judgements are based upon a politicization of the very language in which the truth is being claimed or proclaimed. As I indicated already, a liar, according to this, is a kind of linguistic dissident not a moral failure.

The issue at stake in John's Gospel account regarding Pilate and truth is one of identity, and of a claim to authority. Pilate is caught between, on the one hand, some absolute version of truth – that Christ is a man, *ecce homo* – and on the other hand, an absolute version of political authority, the due given to Caesar as a matter of secular law. The political situation is also one of crucially contested authorities. The fact is that the Romans are an occupying army in Judea, and that fact suggests that truth can be validated or 'authorized' and rendered authoritative, in the final instance, by might and by violence. That is to say, if Caesar fails to be the superior power by words or by money – if his language-game is resisted in Judea in this specific case – then he can always turn to physical force and violence, and it is this that Pilate's audience knows when they turn against him and demand Christ's crucifixion and the liberation of Barabbas.

Pilate hovers uncertainly, then, between divergent accounts of what might constitute truth. There is a truth that is enforced, by violence if need be, and that is derived from political power, and there is truth as a linguistic matter: 'What I have written I have written.' It is only this latter that is genuinely rhetorical, and only this that is also underpinned by a demand for democracy. Further, we might also claim that it is only this latter that is *genuinely* political, precisely because it does not rest its claims, in the final analysis, upon the exercise of violence and power.

For Pilate, Caesar's power is a power that can eschew the niceties of political rhetoric, because Caesar's head is on the coins that permit the society to function economically. That simple fact might recall for us not only my arguments about the film of *The King's English* in Chapter 3 but also the observations about the primacy of money in the claims for political validation made by Odey, Farage and Rees-Mogg in this chapter. Pilate's immediate concern, as shown here and also in the other Gospel accounts, is to find a way to exculpate what he is experiencing as his own guilt or complicity in an action that he wants to disown but that his political position requires that he adopt. When he hands Christ over for crucifixion, he is at pains (in all the accounts) to say that he is simply fulfilling the will of the people.[55] He washes his hands – literally, according to Matthew – of the responsibility.

It is not always noted, however, that in doing this, Pilate is actually echoing the rhetorical manoeuvre of Christ himself. When Pilate asks Christ if he is 'the king of the Jews', Christ's response is always the same: those are 'your words, not mine'. There is here a specific rhetorical mode at work, in which both Christ and Pilate seek to distance themselves from the consequences of their words – effectively to behave as if it is the voice of the other that speaks the words that they themselves eschew – and to divest themselves of guilt or culpability in what is about to happen as a result of their encounter. The symbolic expression of this is in the account given by Matthew 27:24: 'When Pilate saw that he could prevail nothing, but that rather a tumult was made, he took water, and washed his hands before the multitude, saying, I am innocent of the blood of this just person: see ye to it.'

The encounter is also fully and thoroughly political: it stems from Christ's earlier preaching, as described in Luke, 20:22-25, when he is asked, 'Is it lawful for us to give tribute unto Caesar, or no?' Lying behind this is an invitation to Christ to reveal himself as a political insurgent and insurrectionist, with the corresponding hint that, if he must be forced to deny this, then the necessity of the denial itself indicates that there must be some element of truth in it. The parallel today is when someone asks, 'Should we withhold our taxes from the State?' Christ – again like a contemporary politician trying not to alienate wealthy tax-avoiders – gives an evasive answer by offering a kind of parabolic thinking. His response is, 'Shew me a penny. Whose image and superscription hath it?'

---

[55]The textual references here are to Mark 15:15, where Pilate is 'willing to content the people'; and to Luke 23:24, where Pilate 'gave sentence that it should be as they [the people, with their "loud voices" (23:23)] required'.

When they answer 'Caesar's', Christ gives the well-known reply, as if by the logical demonstration of a truth, 'Render therefore unto Caesar the things which be Caesar's, and unto God the things which be God's.' In this way, he says two things at once and throws responsibility for further action onto his listeners: if you think you should pay taxes to Caesar, complying thereby with the truth of political power, then do so, but also attend to a different order of truth and power, that which allegedly transcends the secular and belongs to 'the word', to that 'truth' to which Christ says he has come to bear witness. Politics arises here precisely when there is a potential conflict between the two positions, between the (locally) legal and the (transcendent) legitimate. The parable throws the predicament back to the people for them to find or make their own resolution, but the resolution is always enmeshed in politics. The most basic 'Yes' or 'No', in all moments of decision, are instances of political statement.

In all of these accounts, however, something fundamental is laid bare. Truth can be variously described. I do not mean by this simply that there are four different accounts of the life and death of Christ in the four Gospels. Rather, I mean that truth is not just contingent upon but also 'conditioned' by its relation to politics, language and absolutism. If we were to remain simply with the first of these options – that is, that there exist four divergent accounts of the life and death of Christ – we fall into either relativism (it all depends on your point of view; do you prefer John to Mark, Matthew over Luke) or into the belief that there does actually exist a fundamental essence of the truth – the facts of the case – in relation to which all the linguistic accounts are attempts, with varying levels of success, at accurate description. In this case, then, we always end up with the same thing: the truth of the fact (what actually happened historically) set against the truth of the language used to describe and recount the fact (what constitutes authority and legitimacy in the various accounts). The fact retains all material primacy, and language is an immaterial second-order of being, always set at a remove from historical or material existence. If that is so, then we are saying that language is, at best, an 'airy nothing', and that it is incapable of provoking material action. Language becomes politically irrelevant when it is set against the brute facts of reality; and the logical corollary of this is that power trumps authority.

If, however, we attend to the conditionality of truth, we are acknowledging that the truth itself is dependent upon politics, by which

I mean to say that some accounts are more 'authoritative' and are regarded as carrying more weight entirely because of the political issues in play in any given situation. What Christ tries to do with this latter is to pit the power of God against the power of Caesar, as it were. That is, he is claiming a *kind* of political power and is ascribing it to a king of a realm that no one can actually see and that does not exist in any material terms: a realm without money, and thus without counterfeit, and – according to the logic – therefore also without dissimulation.

5 WORDS, DEEDS AND DEMOCRACY

Using his favoured medium of communication, Donald Trump has repeatedly told his followers, via a series of tweets, that climate change is a hoax. On 6 November 2012, long before his successful bid for the US presidency, he tweeted that 'The concept of global warming was created by and for the Chinese in order to make U.S. manufacturing non-competitive'. In this specific tweet, he makes a claim that rests on no substantive empirical evidence. It is and was a simple unwarranted assertion, and, further, it is and was clearly untrue. Trump's aim, however, was not to alert people to a truth that could be universally acknowledged. Rather, his aim was, first, to establish a tribal allegiance against a specific and identifiable enemy. China was the enemy, and US manufacturing was the friend, the tribe whose allegiance he sought.

The route to success in this operation is by repeated assertion. Repetition generates easy familiarity, reaching a point where even the most irrational of claims will stop having any shock value and will start to be treated as standard or normative. This is how cliché works, for example, and, prior to the rhetorical deployment of cliché, it worked in the language of proverbs. Proverbial knowledge is akin to cliché, and both will eventually deviate – or, more precisely, degenerate – into 'common sense' (which is often neither genuinely 'common' nor constitutive of rational 'sense'). Repetition enables the production of ideological speech whose purpose is to arrest critical (or indeed any) thinking.

Before the followers on twitter would repeat the assertion – and thus start to believe it or to 'side with' its speaker – Trump himself would have to repeat it several times, in order to start emptying it of meaning and to reduce it to the status of 'what gets taken for granted' – or 'common sense' – by his tribe. Thus, through the years between 2012 and his eventual election to the presidency, he returned again and again to his theme. He lodged the following series of tweets between 2013 and 2014: 'Snowing in Texas and Louisiana, record setting freezing temperatures throughout the country and beyond. Global warming is an expensive hoax!' 'This very expensive GLOBAL WARMING bullshit has got to stop. Our planet is freezing, record low temps, and our GW scientists are stuck in ice.' 'NBC News just called it the great freeze – coldest weather in years. Is our country still spending money on the GLOBAL WARMING HOAX?' 'Ice storm rolls from Texas to Tennessee – I'm in Los Angeles and it's freezing. Global warming is a total, and very expensive, hoax!'

With extraordinarily paradoxical chutzpah, Trump changes the political climate of opinion by deriding the very possibility of climate change itself in all of this. Through his medium of the abbreviated shorthand of Twitter, he tries to establish a climate of opinion that makes it normative to debunk climate change or to assert that it is a specific weapon being deployed by the Chinese in order to damage his tribe, the US manufacturers and working-class individuals whom he is courting.

We have dealt with the issue of truth in relation to this in my previous chapter here. With this specific example, I want to consider the relation of words to deeds, the ways in which the establishment of tribal ideologies or common-sense language and rhetoric can work to elevate a bogus description of reality into an actual political reality. We know this most immediately from theological myth, perhaps most clearly manifest in the Old Testament of the Christian Bible. There, in Genesis, 1:3, we find the extraordinary claim that 'God said, Let there be light; and there was light'. This is the extreme form in which word becomes deed or in which a statement about reality becomes constitutive of the reality itself. It may be mythical, and obviously not true in any meaningful sense of that word; yet it is rhetorically very powerful, and it works to establish a tribal allegiance among those who will proclaim themselves to be Christian.

Such linguistic fundamentalism has a political counterpart, and, as we might expect in this alignment with religious fundamentalism, it is always authoritarian and potentially totalitarian. Trump's insistence regarding climate change is one such example. There are many others, of course, and, historically, they have been associated with dictatorship, aptly enough. A dictator is, literally, one whose words or speech lays down what must pass for historical reality.

One of the many errors that Trump makes in my specific example, of course, is to confuse climate with weather. Weather, we might say, is the episodic event (like 'it is snowing today'), whereas climate is much more long-term and describes the conditions within which it becomes normative to expect snow, say, or sun, at specific periods of the year. We might say that weather constitutes something like the episodic nature of a deed, while climate constitutes an underlying set of linguistic norms or descriptions within which the deed makes sense and passes as normal, uneventful, unremarkable. What Trump is doing is trying to establish a specific mood or climate within which we will expect certain deeds to become possible.

Another way of putting this – and one that would be familiar to students of literature, criticism or linguistics – derives from the linguistic propositions of Ferdinand de Saussure at the start of the twentieth century. Saussure made a distinction between *langue* and *parole*. *Parole* was any individual statement or speech-act, whereas *langue* describes the fundamental codes of language that makes any specific speech-act possible. In this, *langue* is a kind of underlying set of laws and grammatical norms that make it possible for individuals to utter individual *paroles* in a meaningful communication. In my argument here, *langue* is the political climate within which individual *paroles*, or weather-events and political enactments, make sense and can therefore be accepted non-problematically.

The normative *langue* of English indicates that a meaningful sentence must contain a main verb. Often, there will be a subject of that verb, and there may be an object or some other complement of the verb. Thus, for example, 'Eat' would constitute a sentence, whereas 'Beef' does not. Likewise 'I eat' is also a sentence, where 'I' is the subject of the verb 'to eat'. We might have 'I eat beef' or 'I eat hungrily', but 'Beef spectacles computer' is not a meaningful sentence, because it does not conform to the rules of the *langue*. This does not mean that we cannot say 'Beef spectacles computer', of course (I have just said it); it simply indicates that if we do say it, it does not constitute a statement that operates according to the usual rules of English. It may be poetry, for example; it may be a deliberate and surreal deviation from the norms; or it may be trying to inaugurate a new form of speech. Within this – and even when the language operates in accordance with the usual rules – it is possible to generate a political climate in which certain deeds become inevitable.

A historical example from the UK takes us back to the extraordinary year-long miners' strike of 1984. This strike was controversial in many ways. I want here to concentrate attention on one ostensibly minor yet very specific detail, and the detail in question focuses on one word: 'drift'.

The miners' strike began on 5 March 1984, when miners at Yorkshire's Cortonwood colliery were told that their pit would close. This, however, was to be the first of a whole series of closures planned by the then Tory government of Margaret Thatcher. Knowing that her Tory predecessor as Prime Minister, Ted Heath, had been defeated by the miners in 1974 and had lost power as a result, Thatcher had prepared tactically to ensure that her government would 'win' this particular battle, a battle that was instrumental in the longer-term strategy of weakening trade union collectivism. Stocks of coal had been steadily built up, to ensure that the miners would have to be on strike for many months before the effects of the strike would be felt and before the country needed more coal production.

The strike lasted for a year, until 5 March 1985, when the miners returned officially to the pits. Their defeat was brought about partly through a war of attrition, and the attrition was focused on the insistent and ostensibly neutral and innocent use of one word: 'drift'. The surreptitious yet insistent insertion of the phrase 'the drift back to work' took a word and made it a political reality. One key tactic deployed by the government was to make a series of claims, throughout the strike, that it was nothing like as solid as the National Union of Mineworkers claimed. The phrase was instrumental in establishing this as a normative belief, and then as a fact. Fundamentally, the government was trying to drive a wedge between the NUM leadership and the membership, and they appealed to the members over the heads of Arthur Scargill and Mick McGahey (who was leader of the Scottish National Union of Mineworkers).

As in any strike, there were workers who wanted to continue to work. This was perhaps exacerbated in 1984 by the fact that Arthur Scargill refused to hold a national ballot that might give added political legitimacy to the strike; and this meant that even some unionized miners would carry on working. The Thatcher government generated a level of antipathy to Scargill himself, and cabinet ministers frequently described him as comparable to Hitler, in messages that were reported – and thus repeated to the point of becoming commonplace – by the national press and other news media outlets.[1] Famously, Margaret Thatcher

---

[1] See Seumas Milne, *The Enemy Within*, 4th edn (Verso, 2014), 9, 13 and passim.

herself referred to Scargill as 'the enemy within', explicitly comparing him thereby to the Argentinian junta ('the enemy without') whom she had defeated in the Malvinas/Falklands conflict of 1982. References to him as a terrorist or gangster were given credence through repetition, not only in Conservative-supporting media but also even in some news media normally aligned with working-class interests, such as the *Daily Mirror*.[2]

Such a climate of opinion made it possible for the government to support what was essentially State-endorsed violence carried out by the police. The violence, we might say, was the weather-event made comprehensible (and thereby ostensibly justified) by the frenzied climate, and, combined with political manipulation of national media (including the BBC), it was thus that police violence became not just acceptable but even admired and supported. The government brought police in to the operation, to ensure that non-striking miners would be able to cross picket lines. While the confrontations between miners and police started off in an uncontroversial manner – with both sides describing the confrontations as good-natured, full of banter, and with some low-level pushing and shoving – they turned utterly brutal at Orgreave on 18 June 1984. As is now clear, the 'Battle of Orgreave' involved straightforward politicization of the police force on the part of the government of the day and gave permission to use violent means to break the strike.

When the strike persisted despite this, the government then turned more insistently to softer power, the power of rhetoric. Now, it was the deployment not of the police or of straightforward physical violence that mattered, but rather it would be the persuasive power of language and of 'the message' that would be called into play. The task for the government was to make everyone believe – before the strike was actually lost by the miners – that it was all over. Instead of reporting simply that some miners had continued to work, they started to talk of something that they called 'the drift back to work'. The strategic aim was to turn a statement into a reality: *fiat lux, et facta est lux*.

The key semantic thing about 'drifting' is that it is something beyond individual control. The government's repeated assertions – themselves repeated faithfully by the official media – that there was a 'drift back to

---

[2]Milne, *The Enemy Within*, 31ff.

work' indicated that this was something more powerful than the will of any individual miner. Additionally, any miner who had remained at work became evidence of the power of this alleged drift, for they were counted as miners *returning* to work as part of the irresistible and unstoppable drifting movement. Miners were being carried, like so much flotsam and jetsam, by currents that were naturally occurring and beyond anyone's control. The language rendered the miners passive, and encouraged the belief that there was a momentum behind an alleged return to work. The force of nature – water, rivers, the sea itself or anything else that might drift – was determining events.

Furthermore, 'drifting' leaves room for inaccuracy and vagueness. It was not necessary for actual numbers of miners working or returning to work to be verified; it was simply enough to indicate and to garner support for the image of a wave that gets bigger, inexorably, before resting back at the calm of the shoreline. Thus, when the *Observer* newspaper analysed the actual figures that the Coal Board and government were advancing in their claims about the 'drift back to work', they found that the calculations were completely erroneous and misleading. Such a fact could not counter the image of the drift, for the simple reason that the alleged drift needed no actual numbers in any case.[3]

The effect of this was massive. It took what the government wanted to be the reality – what, for them *ought* to be the case – and made it reality – or what *is* the case. Word became deed. The political English of the government became the only language that 'made sense', the only words that were in touch with deeds – even if they were not, in fact, describing the reality of deeds at all but were simply asserting a wish. The climate of opinion was sufficiently changed – by the use of a rhetoric that itself appealed to forces of nature – to bring about the reality that the government wanted to be the case.

Trump's language about climate change does the same thing. There is a further development, however, in recent times. Trump knows that, if he makes a wild claim, the very wildness of it will draw attention, and it will be reported. Once it is reported, Trump and his supporters can then comment on the media report, and, in this way, what starts out as a wild claim finds itself established as part of the mainstream discourse. Instead of people discussing the sanity of Donald Trump and whether he has lost

---

[3] See Bill Schwarz and Alan Fountain, 'The role of the media', in *Digging Deeper: Issues in the Miners' Strike*, ed. Huw Beynon (Verso, 1985), 123–38.

touch with empirical realities, a state of affairs comes about in which the claims that he makes are taken 'seriously but not literally'.[4]

The relation of words to deeds – that way in which wishing that something is the case might have the effect, simply via words, of making something come about – needs further analysis here. When does word become action? This question has a serious political purchase. At one extreme, for instance, a criminal might seek to defend himself by suggesting that his violent action is a mode of 'self-expression' and is thus protected under laws governing freedom of speech. Less extreme is the vexed issue of freedom of speech when a close alignment is made between, for example, defamatory language and violence against the person described by that language.

So it comes about that the relation between political language and the enactment of a political deed needs further clarification. As the historical case of the UK miners' strike of 1984 shows, the effects can be massive. That strike was instrumental in a substantial political revolution that broke the power of collective action and established instead a polity in which the state had a relation only with private individuals. One of its effects was the normalization of a social, cultural and political agenda of a generalized 'privatization of all interests', whose political effects remain vibrant generations later.[5]

* * *

In 1955, J.L. Austin gave the 'William James Lectures' at Harvard. James Urmson and Marina Sbisà edited the lectures, as *How to Do Things with Words*. Austin stated that his initial idea for the lectures derived from work that he was doing in 1939, and, in his characteristically slow and methodical fashion, he developed the ideas further as a series of lectures on 'Words and Deeds', given between 1952 and 1954 in Oxford. The lectures proposed a very specific mode in which words actually constituted deeds, under the heading of the performative speech-act. When someone says, for example, 'I name this ship "The President"', then the speech itself

---

[4] This is the phrase used, famously, by Salena Zeto, 'Taking Trump seriously, not literally', *Atlantic*, 23 September 2016, available at: https://www.theatlantic.com/politics/archive/2016/09/trump-makes-his-case-in-pittsburgh/501335/ (accessed 20 March 2018).

[5] For more on this, see my essay 'The privatization of human interests: Or, how transparency breeds conformity', in *Transparency, Society and Subjectivity*, ed. Emmanuel Alloa and Dieter Thomä (Palgrave Macmillan, 2018), 283–304.

is not just a description of what the speaker is doing, it constitutes the actual action itself. Famously, Austin himself starts out in his lectures with a seemingly straightforward opposition between performatives and constatives (as he initially calls other modes of speech) but ends up by arguing that there is something of the performative in every constative and something of the constative in every performative.[6]

Although Austin's opposition breaks down, he nonetheless indicates something that is of crucial importance in considering the political dimension of words and of speaking itself. It is possible to *do something* just by *saying something*. In the case of the biblical *fiat*, we have (as I have pointed out above) the extremist and basic character of this exposed as a dictatorial and extravagantly authoritarian move. In saying *fiat lux* the biblical god authorizes and initiates something, brings something about, merely by speaking. To believe that '*fiat lux, et facta est lux*' is a true description of an event, however, is to subscribe to the climate in which the words themselves occur. You need faith to subscribe to the faith that is being called for in demanding belief that what the statement says is empirically true.

In what follows here, I am more interested in those instances that are much less extreme, instances in which we can see that words are being used to create a climate in which some things that might usually be considered as politically unpalatable and even literally unspeakable can become not just spoken but also received as valid or true. One way into this will be through a brief consideration of some contemporary issues around free speech on university campuses. This has become a contested issue in recent times, especially given the liberal idea of the university as itself a kind of protected space for the most open and free dialogue and debate. Policies of 'no-platforming', constructions of 'safe spaces' and the like have become problematic for those who might advocate complete and total freedom of expression (even and especially when those policies are willfully and mischievously misrepresented in populist media). That is why this issue becomes a useful way into the wider political scenario in which word can provoke or become deed.

Frank Furedi – a very well-known sociology commentator and former leader of the Revolutionary Community Party of the 1970s and 1980s – has intervened in the debates around so-called 'safe spaces' and 'no

---

[6]This is analysed in meticulous detail in J. Hillis Miller, *Speech Acts in Literature* (Stanford University Press, 2001), 6–62.

platform' policies on university campuses. His fundamental argument is that the sector and our contemporary society have engendered a culture of infantilism. In my terms here, the climate is that of the nursery, as it were, and it is as if the only permissible 'weather' in such a climate is that associated with shelter, security and the comfort blanket. (I stress that this is Furedi's position, not my own.) In short, Furedi's view is that we should acknowledge that a university is not a child's playground, that those who attend or otherwise engage in the work of a university are mature adults, and that we should basically therefore all grow up. We should have learned one fabled saying from our childhood: 'sticks and stones will break my bones, but words will never hurt me', and, as responsible adults, we should now behave with that lesson firmly in mind.

A more substantial element in his case is that 'controversy' is now marked with an entirely negative value because it potentially jeopardizes the reputation of a University brand. Consequently, anything that might be suspected of being controversial now has to be placed under the register of risk, and risk management is there in order to calm and indeed even eradicate controversy as such. Risk management will evacuate controversial statements or speech of its controversial content, through various institutional and managerial means and mechanisms. What, though, is the risk in question in this mentality? Simply stated, it is the risk that something bad will happen either as a result of a controversial speech, or that the speech itself will be a negative event, that it will constitute something bad for someone even as it is being uttered. Risk management avoids this potential controversial disruption essentially by either banning the speech, banning the speaker from campus or so circumscribing what can be said that the speaker ends up speaking essentially only to those who already know and agree with the content of the speech. The speaker speaks to herself or himself: free speech is protected, as long as it is not heard. This is, for Furedi, obviously ridiculous and a travesty of what a university should be about.[7]

For libertarians such as Dennis Hayes and Kathryn Ecclestone, Furedi's descriptions of our contemporary university predicaments resonate

---

[7]See Frank Furedi, *What's Happened to the University?* (Routledge, 2017), 89–106. Some libertarians hold similar views. Many such libertarians (often former Revolutionary Communist Party colleagues of Furedi), associated with the online journal, *Spiked*, find themselves in uneasy alignment with the political far right, who know exactly how to exploit the good intentions of the liberal.

soundly. These latter suggest that it is not so much the nursery that has colonized the space of the university but rather the sick-bay. For these, there is a dangerous rise in what they call 'therapeutic education', according to which education has ceded place to emotional support. This first stage in an educational revolution moves on to a further development in which individuals are celebrated precisely because of their emotional difficulties, which must be paraded in an admirably transparent show of vulnerable identity. While we might see this as a crucial element in celebrity culture, these thinkers instead see that it has permeated everyday culture, such that 'emotional vulnerability' has become an indispensable element of a student's identity. The contemporary ideologies of 'therapeutic education' demand that such vulnerability must be noted, indulged and respected, they argue, and this remains the case even if such an attitude deprives the individual student of being exposed to anything that might be new thinking, a disruptions of norms and so on.[8]

Behind all of this, of course, lurks the argument that I have been exposing throughout these pages, regarding the relative weight that one gives in political debate to logos and pathos, reason and feeling. Furedi, perhaps inadvertently, adds a further issue. In describing the University today as an institution giving way to infantilism, he opens the question of the status of the child or infant as such in political discourse. 'Infant' derives etymologically from *infans*, meaning non-speaking. The infant, in these terms, must prioritize pathos entirely over logos, for the simple reason that the infant does not yet have a shared language within which to express its views. The only language the infant has is that of the body: cries, laughter, contortions forced by physical condition and so on. The infantilization of politics is much more significant than the alleged infantilism of the university institution, for it replaces the politics of reason with the politics of the body – and this leads eventually to only two things: violence and far-right extremism.[9]

The positions outlined by Furedi, Hayes and Ecclestone make sense as defences of completely unconstrained free speech. At the same time, the positions work only to the extent that these thinkers consider only moments of inclement weather, as it were, while disregarding the climate in which such speeches may be freely made. It is one thing to defend

---

[8]See, for a good example of their work, Kathryn Ecclestone and Dennis Hayes, *The Dangerous Rise of Therapeutic Education* (Routledge, 2008).
[9]I explore political silence, non-speaking, in Chapter 7.

someone's right to make an anti-Semitic comment, for example, under a generally libertarian attitude to freedom of speech. It is, however, another thing entirely to act as if such a speech is harmless in a social atmosphere of a generalized climate of permitted racism, say. When one considers the linguistic climate, one can see that there is good reason to moderate one's 'first amendment absolutism' (the phrase that Christopher Hitchens once used to describe his own position), the kind of utter endorsement of completely free speaking in any and all circumstances.

Politics, in fact, depends upon our subscription to the view that speaking might change things. Above all, I speak to my political opponents in order to change *them*, to get them to change their minds or attitudes regarding specific issues. If words did not change things in the political sphere, then we would be in danger of resolving differences simply by violence, by the essentials of bodily force, like the frustrated toddler. Politics is the name we give to those activities that eschew violence in the name of working out what might be the best social arrangements for our polities.

Within this, speeches contribute to the making of a climate. When Enoch Powell repeatedly addressed immigration, he was doing something that is itself, at one level, entirely politically neutral: he is discussing an issue that is of political importance. However, when he *insistently repeated* that address in a way that saw immigration only and purely in negative terms, and even if immigration was not the primary issue, he was making a climate. Once that climate is established, racists can find that their racist speech – each single racist comment, uttered in any and every situation – gains a credibility and legitimacy. Things previously considered unsayable enter mainstream conversation as non-controversial or, if controversial then at least positions that must be respected and addressed. Once this – 'normalization' – is achieved, then it is not too great a distance to the point where words become acts.

For a good example, we can ask, utterly legitimately, what is the relation between the prevailing political language around Brexit, say, and the murder of a pro-Remain MP, Jo Cox, by Thomas Mair. As he shot and stabbed her, Mair repeatedly shouted 'Britain First!', a slogan of the neo-fascist far right in the UK. The shock of this murder, in the middle of a political campaign, was followed by the further shock that no political voice made the connection between the murder and the language of the political campaign explicit. In a conspiracy of silence around the matter, it was as if it was somehow bad manners, the height of impropriety, to do so. A political murder is accepted but mediated as 'anything other than politics'; calling it out as the result of perverted political language is not so accepted. This was not the silence of the infant but the silence of complicity. In refusing to make the connection between political language and murderous deed here explicit, the political class failed to take seriously the very logic of democratic politics. That logic suggests that words should indeed shape behaviour. In this case, the behaviour – murder – was provoked and enabled by the climate of far-right nationalist and racist political English. The murder indicates how much the political climate has changed, in that such fundamentalist language has gained traction. To fail to call this out is itself a mark either of cowardice or of complicity with the perverse climate that is now costing the lives of politicians and others.

* * *

In a different environment in the United States, Steven Levitsky and Daniel Ziblatt draw attention to the rhetoric of Newt Gingrich. In 1978, Gingrich attempted to secure political office, having previously failed twice to do so. In this third attempt, he discovered a new ruthlessness. Levitsky and Ziblatt write that, when Gingrich met with some young voters in June 1978, he started 'wooing them with a blunter, more cutthroat vision of politics than they were accustomed to'. He 'warned the young Republicans to stop using "Boy Scout words, which would be great around the campfire, but are lousy in politics"'. Instead, he started himself to call upon a new language, the language of war: 'What we really need are people who are willing to stand up in a slug-fest.'[10] As this position started to gain ground, through repetition, Gingrich created an audience, and then turned to the media. 'Taking advantage of a new media technology, C-SPAN, Gingrich "used adjectives like rocks," deliberately employing over-the-top rhetoric.'[11]

'Using adjectives like rocks' cuts to the quick of what is at stake in this. It is something that the political right, especially (though, obviously, not exclusively), has learned to do. It is important to stress here that I am

---

[10] Levitsky and Ziblatt, *How Democracies Die*, 146–7.
[11] Ibid., 168. Levitsky and Ziblatt are quoting from Ronald Brownstein, *The Second Civil War: How Extreme Partisanship Has Paralyzed Washington and Polarized America* (Penguin, 2007), 142.

not referring simply to the tradition of political insult (with which I will deal in the next chapter). I am referring instead to how it is that some politicians manage to use words to do things – not simply to persuade or argue, but, in using words like rocks, to effect material change.

Trump's establishment of an atmosphere or climate that condones violence is a clear case in point. Levitsky and Ziblatt list a few examples: 'If you see somebody getting ready to throw a tomato, knock the crap out of them, would ya? Seriously. Just knock the hell out of them'; 'I'd like to punch him in the face'; 'In the good old days, they'd rip him out of that seat so fast'; 'We had some people, some rough guys like we have right in here. And they started punching back. It was a beautiful thing.'[12] These examples come from platform speeches all made within a roughly four-week period during the election campaign. They were followed by a speech in August 2016 in which Trump 'warned' his audience that, if Hillary Clinton were to be elected, she would work to revoke the right to bear arms. At this point, he more or less openly incited assassination: 'If she gets to pick her judges, nothing you can do, folks. ... Although maybe the Second Amendment people – maybe there is. I don't know.'[13]

Political speeches such as these worked to endorse the legitimacy of violence within political argument and debate. They combined with Trump's insistence – shared and repeated by many of his supporters – that the mainstream media peddled only 'fake news' to produce one of the least savoury moments in US political campaigning in recent times. After Trump had been elected, there were several congressional elections in the following year, 2017. In Montana, Greg Gianforte stood, and was endorsed by Trump personally. Gianforte's team was unhappy with the way in which the UK's *Guardian* newspaper had been presenting the candidate and his campaign. When Ben Jacobs, a Guardian political reporter, approached Gianforte with a question about Republican Party health-care policies (specifically Trump's desire to abandon Obamacare), Gianforte attacked him physically, shouting 'I'm sick and tired of you guys. ... Get the hell outa here' as he body-slammed Jacobs to the floor, smashing his spectacles. Gianforte's campaign manager, Shane Scanlon, identified Jacobs as 'a liberal reporter' and aligned that description with the further adjective 'aggressive'. Gianforte subsequently entered a guilty

---

[12]Levitsky and Ziblatt, *How Democracies Die*, 63–4.
[13]Ibid., 64.

plea to the charge of 'misdemeanor assault' – and was indeed found to be guilty. He was also successfully elected. The break into physical violence – that bad weather moment, emerging from the climate of verbal violence established by Trump – became no barrier to democratic election.

In the UK context, the 2016 referendum regarding European Union membership took place, and the result, announced on 25 June 2016, yielded a small majority of the voters (but only 37 per cent of the total electorate) for leaving the European Union. The latter stages of the Leave campaign had focused heavily on the question of immigration, with a repeated mantra that the people of the UK should 'take back control' of the UK's national borders. The Leave argument was that the conditions of daily life for people in the UK had deteriorated because of immigration. Membership of the European Union entailed endorsement of the principle of free movement of European Union citizens across all internal national borders, and this, according to the Leave campaign, meant that 'we' could not control an influx of immigrants coming to the European Union. (In fact, even within the rules governing free movement of people, the UK did in fact have very substantial legal controls over immigration. The simple fact of the matter was that successive governments, both Labour and Conservative, failed to exercise their rights to that control.)

Throughout the campaign, Leave permitted a further blurring of distinctions between European Union immigrants and non-European Union immigrants. The campaign ran a number of stories suggesting that it was possible that the entire 77 million-strong population of Turkey (not a European Union member) would arrive in the UK unless the UK left the European Union. As this idea gained traction, Nigel Farage (at that time leader of the UK Independence Party) unveiled a billboard poster depicting hundreds of Syrian refugees, mostly non-white, fleeing from war. The by-line on the billboard said 'Breaking Point: the EU has failed us all' and added the words 'We must break free of the EU and take back control of our borders'.[14]

By this point, a climate had been created in which a white nativist English exceptionalism was constructed as a specific model of English identity, and it depended upon the opposition of the white English to virtually all 'foreigners'. In short, the campaign had found its focus in

---

[14]See reports (and image) at: https://www.theguardian.com/politics/2016/jun/16/nigel-farage-defends-ukip-breaking-point-poster-queue-of-migrants (accessed 21 February 2018).

a climate of legitimized racism, or, alternatively expressed, racism had found a way of expressing itself as a legitimate political position, without having to acknowledge its own internal negative ideology. The racist could express herself or himself not in explicitly racist terms (which would require an explicit self-identification as racist) but rather in terms of expressing a pure English identity based on the assumption of an autonomous control of 'our' geographical borders. In this way, racism became not just permitted but almost respectable, based as it was in a supposedly deep patriotism and demand for self-defence against foreign invasion.

For the purposes of my present argument, the most significant thing here is not that the Brexit vote legitimized racism, important though that most certainly is. The most significant thing for the specifics of my argument is what happens, after this verbal climate is established. In the months immediately following the Brexit vote, racist 'hate-crimes', involving direct violence against individuals (many of them non-white UK citizens) rocketed in number. The national figures, released by the UK's Home Office, revealed a 41 per cent rise in the month immediately following the vote. Some regional police forces reported a 100 per cent rise. The crimes included events such as an arson attack on a family home, racist graffiti being sprayed onto cultural centres, physical attacks on European Union nationals who were living and working in the UK.[15]

The racist climate of the language around the Brexit campaign created the ideal atmosphere in which the hard rain of incidents of criminal racism could fall heavily and insistently. None of this has helped to arrest the seeming determination of some to follow through on the referendum vote, and take the UK out of the European Union. As with the case of Gianforte, the climate has changed. Political rhetoric – 'politicized English' with its associated 'politicized Englishness' – has done this and is instrumental in legitimizing actions and deeds that the speakers of the political words would otherwise disown. But climate change, in this arena as in others, is human-made, and the political speakers and agents here must accept their responsibilities for making that change. They probably

---

[15] See, for example, reports at: http://www.bbc.co.uk/news/uk-38976087 (accessed 21 February 2018); http://www.independent.co.uk/news/uk/crime/hate-crimes-eu-referendum-spike-brexit-terror-attacks-police-home-office-europeans-xenophobia-a8004716.html (accessed 21 February 2018) and http://www.aljazeera.com/news/2017/10/hate-crimes-rise-brexit-vote-attacks-171018110119902.html (accessed 21 February 2018).

will not: the language, they will say, has 'drifted'; the new political centre has 'shifted to the right', as if of its own volition.

* * *

In the case of the United States, we might regard the Constitution and its twenty-seven Amendments as having similar status to a theological text. The Constitution is commonly revered as the founding political statement of 'our forefathers'. Like the Bible, it is subject to endless interpretation, a kind of Talmudic Midrash, through which generations of judges and scholars attempt to understand the 'real' meaning and intention of the words of the text itself. As a 'founding document', it is, indeed, 'fundamentalist'; simultaneously, it is subject to legal and hermeneutic 'construction'.

The Second Amendment is of special interest in this context. The text of the Amendment, while always retaining the same words, exists with a number of different punctuations. Jefferson signed off a text that has one comma, thus: 'A well regulated militia being necessary to the security of a free state, the right of the people to keep and bear arms shall not be infringed.' I draw attention to the comma here because it has been at the root of a legal debate over the meaning of the Amendment as a whole, and the resolution of that debate determines whether it is individuals who have the right to bear arms or whether the right is what is described as the 'collective right', which therefore does not refer to specific individuals but only to individuals forming part of a 'well regulated militia'.[16]

Given the history of gun-crime and the debates over gun control in the United States, this comma becomes significant. In the other versions of the text, where there are multiple commas, the punctuation becomes even more troubling for any simple and straightforward univocal sense. For literally thousands of people, these tiny punctuation points determine matters of life and death, when individuals are shot and killed

---

[16] I should draw attention here – partly against my own case – to Adam Freedman, 'Clause and effect', *The New York Times*, 16 December 2017, available at: http://www.nytimes.com/2007/12/16/opinion/16freedman.html (accessed 22 February 2018). Freedman outlines the disputed legal readings of the text, all dependent on the use of the comma, before pointing out that 'there could scarcely be worse place to search for the framers' original intent than their use of commas', given the lax and indeterminate use of all punctuation in the eighteenth century. The fact remains, however, that the commas have indeed been at the centre of jurisprudential argument.

by other individuals who carry – and then use – arms. This is a directly political issue, in which words and their interpretation come face to face with acts and deeds. Furthermore, the position of the gun lobby, especially the National Rifle Association, which funds large numbers of politicians (mostly, though not exclusively, Republicans), makes this a central element in American political life. In this, it relates our question of words and deeds to the politics of democracy in a jurisdiction that identifies itself as a cornerstone of democracy as such.

The comma and – even more importantly – the meaning of the phrase 'the right of the people' both sit at the core of this concern. For the National Rifle Association, the right to bear arms *as an individual* – and thus as an individual member 'of the people' – is of paramount importance to their understanding of US democracy. On NRATV, the television station run and operated by the NRA, individuals mount their claims for the legitimacy of bearing arms – specifically, guns – as a central element of their individual American identity. This identity is underpinned not by politics, but rather – the claim always is in the NRA's statements – the identity is underpinned and given by God.

Dan Bongino, one of the 'ordinary individuals' presenting on NRATV is clear. Your rights, he argues, 'were granted to you by God' and are merely *protected* by the political arrangements of the State. He undermines the power of politics almost completely in this and compounds that view further when he adds, 'Government grants you nothing. Government protects rights you already have.'[17] For Dom Raso, who also presents on the TV station, the right to bear arms is not only inalienable but also, again, part of what it means to be an American citizen. Raso introduces himself in four descriptors: 'I'm a veteran, a business owner, an NRA member, and a Christian.' This identity, he argues (somewhat tautologically), is protected by 'being an American'.

Raso then recasts these four personal characteristics as 'freedoms', and they are all interconnected, so that 'if one freedom falls, all freedoms will fall'. That statement is repeated, its importance signalled by appearing also in writing on the screen. Rhetorical repetition then reinforces the message, and it is a message whose content indicates that Raso – as an American – is a fighter. 'We don't just fight for our second amendment. We fight for our flag; we fight for our gun rights; we fight for free speech;

---

[17]See https://www.nratv.com/home/video/dan-bongino-truth-matters (accessed 21 February 2018).

we fight for our freedom of religion. We fight [pause] for our American values. And we fight to keep America the greatest nation ever known to man.'[18] Like Bongino, Raso also claims that these freedoms have been given to 'us' by God.

The political links established in the rhetoric have a simple determined meaning. Given that these four 'freedoms' are allegedly inextricably linked, Raso's logic indicates that if you don't carry a gun, you can't be a Christian or a business owner. Capitalism (being a business owner) is tied firmly to religion (being a Christian) and to the potential for violence (bringing a gun to your fight, struggles – and, indeed, to your daily business affairs). Further, these all link to being an American, now as an identity that is tied to war with other nations (being a veteran). This is Christian fundamentalism as a continuation of the medieval Crusades, carried through in the name of individual acquisition of wealth, by violence if needs be.

Bongino's most elemental claim is that he stands for truth against opinion, which he characterizes as a weapon of the far-left. Like any fundamentalist, he needs a transcendent source for that truth. Both he and Raso claim this fundamentalism in a Christian theology. For these, it is as if 'the forefathers' who wrote the Constitution, and then entered its Second Amendment, were kin to the patriarchs of biblical scholarship. Yet, one of the key arguments made by the NRA depends not upon biblical scholarship or textual exegesis; rather, it depends upon the lexicon of Donald Trump, whose presidential campaign the NRA had helped bankroll with at least $21 million.[19] Its key argument is that citizens and politicians who advocate some form of gun control are trying to 'weaponize the First Amendment against the Second'. This message is repeated often on NRATV. It gets its central standing from Wayne Lapierre, Executive Vice President and CEO of the NRA, who, in turn, is repeating the rhetorical tropes of Donald Trump.

---

[18]See https://www.nratv.com/series/commentators/episode/commentators-season-7-episode-9-all-freedoms-are-connected (accessed 21 February 2018).

[19]Some reports give a higher figure, up to $30 million. Following the Marjorie Stoneman Douglas high school multiple shooting and murder of seventeen school pupils on 14 February 2018, Michael Hiltzik revealed something of the extent to which the NRA's massive political lobbying operation skews politics. See his report: http://www.latimes.com/business/hiltzik/la-fi-hiltzik-nra-politicians-20180215-story.html (accessed 21 February 2018).

Lapierre opens his own NRATV briefing with an address 'to every dishonest member of the failing American news media', telling them 'let me explain why you've never been less trusted, less credible, or less respected'. This is a straightforward riff on Trump's determination to undermine news media, with his repeated mantra on 'fake news'. To Lapierre, it seems that all the media needed to do 'was to get the facts right. About our guns. And our freedom', he says, in a rhetorical flourish that identifies freedom itself with the gun. But, he claims, the media didn't listen. 'Instead you weaponized the First Amendment against the Second.' Freedom of speech (guaranteed by the First Amendment) must therefore be 'disarmed' when it is used to criticize those who read the Second as an endorsement of gun culture. Against this, according to Lapierre, the NRA is 'freedom's safest place'. He, along with Dana Loesch (Special Assistant to the NRA's Executive Vice President for Public Communication), issues quite explicitly threatening videos against many named individuals and against the news media and political establishment. Dana Loesch features in one video on NRATV about to set fire to *The New York Times*. These threats of violence, of course, come backed with guns.

In all of this, the climate of a permitted violence is being generated and bolstered by a continuous maintenance of a high level of threats to engage in violent action. Indeed, it is more than a permitted violence that is at issue here: it is a legitimized violence. At times, it is almost as if American identity depends upon the propensity to fight, armed with a gun. Given this, it becomes all the more 'ordinary' that the many mass-killings that occur in the United States are committed by 'ordinary' individuals.

The position I describe here is not unique to the United States, of course. There have been similar constructions of the political climate in other jurisdictions, and many of them are jurisdictions founded upon revolutions that have involved straightforward violence. Mao famously argued, in 1938, that 'Every Communist must grasp this truth: "Political power grows out of the barrel of a gun"', adding that 'Our principle is: the Party controls the gun'.[20] When Mussolini assumed power in Italy, he invented the slogan, 'libro e moschetto, fascista perfetto' (a book and a musket makes the perfect fascist), which then mutated into a prescribed literary education in schools that led to the chanting of 'credere, obbedire,

---

[20]Mao Tse-Tung, 'Problems of war and strategy', available at: http://collections.mun.ca/PDFs/radical/ProblemsofWarandStrategy.pdf (accessed 21 February 2018).

combattere' (believe, obey, fight).[21] More recently, in 1981, Sinn Féin adopted a political strategy in which they argued that 'with a ballot paper in this hand, and an Armalite in the other' they could take power.[22] In all these cases, political rhetoric is being deployed in ways that invite the explicit eschewing of political debate, and its replacement with violence as a means of resolving disputes.

Of course, many will take the view that the turn to violence is a legitimate political strategy in certain circumstances. However, the relevant point here is that, in jurisdictions that describe themselves as democracies precisely because they do not legitimize such violence, we are now in a place where a climate has been created that makes such violence unexceptional. It has become part of the accepted lingua franca.

* * *

In his serial assault on what he calls 'fake news', Donald Trump presents himself, by implied contrast, as 'authentic'. Charles Lindholm writes that 'there are two overlapping modes for characterizing any entity as authentic: genealogical or historical (*origin*) and identity or correspondence (*content*)'. In this context authentic individuals are 'original, real, and pure; they are what they purport to be … their essence and appearance are one'.[23] In anthropological research, such authenticity is often aligned with a rejection of sophistication – or at least a rejection of sophistry and of the appurtenances of 'culture'. Indeed, so-called 'primitive' individuals, including the rural peasant, become figures who can be 'imagined and portrayed as representative of coherent and pristine' modes of being. Imagined as being 'close to the paradisiacal Garden of Eden … they were regarded as being in contact with mysterious and primordial spiritual forces no longer perceptible to modern humanity'.[24]

---

[21]See the documentary *Giovinezza! Il fascismo e I giovani*, available at: http://www.raistoria.rai.it/articoli-programma-puntate/giovinezza-il-fascismo-e-i-giovani/25223/default.aspx (accessed 22 February 2018) and Valeria della Vale e Vanni Gandolfo, *Me ne frego! Il fascismo e la lingua italiana*, available at: https://www.youtube.com/watch?v=A7G-hnVVDiU (accessed 22 February 2018).

[22]Richard English, *Armed Struggle: The History of the IRA* (Oxford University Press, 2004), 224–5.

[23]Charles Lindholm, *Culture and Authenticity* (Blackwell, Oxford, 2008), 2.

[24]Lindholm, *Culture and Authenticity*, 5.

This, in some ways, helps explain how it is that Trump was such a subject of identification for the rural poor in rustbelt states in the US presidential elections in 2016. It is not at all the case that the rural poor are in any way lacking in culture, but the climate that was generated during the campaign set the self-described 'ordinary Joe and Jane' against establishment 'elites', or 'country' against 'Washington', and it was this that Trump exploited. He lacked sophistication; he was uncultured, and, above all, he 'told it as it is'. His appeal was never to the intellect but to the supposedly originary materiality of reality, as manifest on the working body. For this reason (among others) his obvious misogyny did not count against him in the eyes of many voters.

When he tried to degrade and denigrate a female journalist, Megyn Kelly, Trump's language was very specific: 'You could see there was blood coming out of her eyes, blood coming out of her whatever. In my opinion, she was off base.'[25] The 'whatever' was a half 'wherever'. The soundtrack gives 'whadderever', and it is prefaced by a significant pause. Whether the reference was – as Trump subsequently claimed – to Kelly's nose or rather, as seemed evident at the time, to menstruation, the point is that his primary reference was physical. He appealed to the body as the final arbiter of value.

In this context, it matters little whether one regards menstruation positively or negatively; it matters not at all whether one thinks that women should assume public roles with authority or not. The key thing, for Trump, is that his language sustains the idea that an individual's worth not only is related directly to the body but is written on it. In blood. The language sustains the ideology that suggests an individual's worth is related directly to genetic factors that are physical and essentialist. In such a context, even to claim menstruation as a positive is already to be operating within an ideological climate set by Trump's terms. The ideology of this is clear: authenticity is seen in the physical body, violence, the 'fight' of the NRA, the 'punch in the face', menstrual or other blood that flowed or was spilt in Trump's campaign.

In peddling the idea that he was 'telling it like it is', Trump plays a language-game that is central to virtually all populist movements. Populism, however, is not intrinsically democratic. Indeed, in many

---

[25]Philip Rucker, report on 8 August 2015, available at: https://www.washingtonpost.com/news/post-politics/wp/2015/08/07/trump-says-foxs-megyn-kelly-had-blood-coming-out-of-her-wherever/?utm_term=.58685684027e (accessed 21 February 2018).

ways, it is a subversion of democracy, and one that is common to far-right political language routines. Central to it is an unstated proposition. 'Telling it like it is' is identified, certainly and openly, with 'being realistic' but not at all with 'being true' or speaking truth. The implication is that he who is realistic in this way is unlike the regular politician, the establishment elitist who speaks the language of the political class. Thus, the realist can claim to be on the side of 'the people' and can figure the regular or established politician as being 'out of touch'. One major unstated element here is that the realist, being 'in touch' with realities, has a stronger sense of the material and physical conditions of life than the more cerebral, intellectual, rhetorically sophisticated elite politician.

It is not only the case that the body is set against the mind here; it is that pathos is completely prioritized over logos. The consequence is profound. Beneath that ideological preference for the force of the body over the ostensible immaterial value of reason, something yet deeper is happening: truth itself is set against reality. While the democrat pledges allegiance to truth in the sense that she or he relies on verbal argument and reason to arrive at the better decisions, the populist, by contrast, appeals to a 'reality' that will not countenance truth but that prefers to attend to the primacy of feelings, both physical and emotional.

These material and physical conditions of life (including the emotions) are related directly to the human body. It is obviously an attractive proposition to imply that, if you vote for me, your body will be the site of a more pleasurable existence than if you vote for the elitist. What does the elitist know of my discomforts, sitting comfortably as she or he does in the relaxed talking-shop of a parliament or Congress? The populist, in short, tells me not that she or he 'understands' me; rather she or he physically and sympathetically touches my arm or hand while telling me that she or he 'feels my pain'.[26] In some more crude cases, as with Vladimir Putin, the body of the politician is itself put on ostentatious display, be it in the arena of judo (Putin is a very accomplished judoka) or in the figure of the president riding horseback, bare-breasted, in the outdoors, or as he surfaces from the Black Sea bearing lost ancient amphorae. Figurations of

---

[26]It was Bill Clinton who made much of the claim that 'I feel your pain', when he was being heckled by Bob Rafsky during the 1992 presidential campaign. I wrote about this in more detail in Chapter 6. For the exchange between Rafsky and Clinton, see the report in *The New York Times*, 28 March 1992, available at: http://www.nytimes.com/1992/03/28/us/1992-campaign-verbatim-heckler-stirs-clinton-anger-excerpts-exchange.html?mcubz=0

the body, such as these, are also intimately tied to religious iconography, especially in representations of the body in pain and suffering.

This takes the question of truth in politics into a clear new dimension. As I argued in Chapter 4, the politician is extremely concerned not primarily or simply to make empirical truth claims but rather to foster a group allegiance, to persuade a listener to come to the politician's side of the argument and to forge a community of individuals who will support her or him, to become one of her or his 'insiders'. My argument here indicates that one task of the politician is to convert word to deed, to 'make reality' or construct the truth. It now follows that, for the populist who will 'feel my pain', the task in hand is to address the hard realities of the material condition of my body; and that reality is mortality as such, or my fundamental human condition. Address this, in however indirect a fashion, and the populist politician will secure my *belief* in her or his legitimacy as a representative of my real conditions of life.

For Aristotle and the ancient world, truth was eudemonic. It was regarded as intrinsically therapeutic to gain knowledge, and, as knowing things 'healed' the pain occasioned by ignorance, knowing the truth made us feel better. However, as Hans Blumenberg has pointed out, something happens to the conception of truth in modernity. Through the eighteenth century, broadly, we start to measure truth not in terms of the amount of pleasure it gives us but rather in how hard or austere it is. The modern age ushers in a climate in which 'the separation between cognitive achievement and the production of happiness' diverge, and a 'lack of consideration for happiness becomes the stigma of truth itself, a homage to its absolutism'.[27] This is part of the price we pay in order to make the claim that 'knowledge is power'. It is also what governs the climate in which we start to accept, non-controversially, the idea that truth is always harsh, hard to face and resistant to our demand for happiness and pleasure – especially bodily pleasure.

Within modern capital, the body is identified more and more as the site of labour. It is thus marked (especially within modern Christian cultures that subscribe to the myth of a 'fall' from nature) by the marks of that labour: sweat, pain, fatigue, blood and the scars of use. There is thus, within capitalist modernity, an intrinsic division between the values that we ascribe to the worker-by-hand and the worker-by-brain. The

---

[27]Hans Blumenberg, *The Legitimacy of the Modern Age* (1966; trans. Robert M. Wallace; MIT Press, Cambridge, MA, 1983), 404.

latter is forever condemned to justify her or his existence as a 'labouring' individual and is forever condemned to fail to do so. As an 'expert', the 'intellectual' is set apart from the truth of labour, living in her or his comfortable and bloodless ivory tower, and is seen as divorced from the material concerns of everyday living. The intellectual is 'merely' academic, and that which is academic is seen as having a purely theoretical and not a material justification for existence. Mao had a recipe for dealing with this problem: he called it a 'Great Proletarian Cultural Revolution' in 1966. The disaster was structured around a rejection of any and all forms of intellectual expertise, in the interests of restoring Mao's initial Revolution to its supposedly ideologically pure roots in the primacy of the labouring body.

Shockingly, the 'realist' politician in our time follows this – while disavowing it, of course – and she or he focuses attention on that body and, in doing so, stakes an unconscious claim upon truth as such. This is no longer an empirical truth but a fully tribalized account of what passes for truth. Crucially, it disengages from the intellect, and, at the extremes, it disengages from thinking itself. Instead, it turns to the primacy of the gut, the gut feeling, the 'instinct', and the body that seeks to assuage the pain of its intrinsic mortality. In the United States, it may not endorse a Maoist Cultural Revolution of course, but, in the name of the 'great proletariat', now recast as 'the people', it prioritizes the NRA account of reality: fighting.

Given that it eschews thinking and the work of the intellect, this fundamentalist position must also never permit of a change of mind. The logic here points to a prioritization of the politician's *sincerity* or ostensible *authenticity* over her or his grasp on reality. That authenticity is primal, bodily and physical, even bloody. It explains Trump's concern about the size of his penis, his interest in menstruation and, completely aligned with this, his support for the NRA. As with Mao (or in the Soviet context, Stalin; in the Nazi context, Hitler), however, politics becomes reduced to the cult of personality. One definition of 'personality' in political terms is not just 'words supplanting deeds', but, even more troublingly, it is 'the name becoming the deed'. The identity of the politician in this becomes sacrosanct, but, more importantly, it also provides the foundation for a politics built around names and identity as such: the most profound and fundamentalist form of identity-politics.

We have come, in our own neologisms in politics, to accept this as almost normal. This is why we 'brand' or identify political allies or opponents by those names: Marxist, Stalinist, Maoist are well known, but, ostensibly less devastating through fundamentally the same, Thatcherite, Blairite and so on. Such political labelling or name-calling is always based upon a tacit claim for ideological purity, and, in turn, that is based upon fundamentalist claims to truth. Fundamentalism is certainly a political position, but it is anathema to democracy, for it aims to arrest any argument, dialogue, debate – or even political conversation. All that matters, in this, is the identity of the citizen: how 'authentic' is your Marxism, or your Thatcherism, and so on.

* * *

Truth and power become the two forces that are now placed in a kind of dialectical opposition to each other. The opposition can be clearly stated. It is the opposition of straightforward brute force against the evidential and discursive claims of verbal authority: violence against speech. From this we derive the Quakerish claim that there is always a certain critical legitimacy and even heroism accorded to those who will 'speak truth to power', or use words to counter and undermine violence and brutal power. However, given also that we know that power is underwritten by the threat of violence, 'free speech' is itself always intrinsically under threat, and especially so when it is a free speech spoken against the demands of power. The threat extends usually also to the speaker.[28]

The practice of politics, we might say, is the organized confounding of these two things: power and authority. The politician seeks to be able to exert material and historical power through the authority of her or his arguments in words and through debate. This sounds like an ideal, but it is flawed precisely because of the mixing of power and authority, almost as if these were the same thing or as if there was a seamless continuity between them that makes them indistinguishable from each other. If or when the politician gains assent to their argument, then we can say that those arguments and that point of view have gained their legitimacy. That legitimacy, however, equates only to the securing of authority: their argument or perspective is now one that has acquired an authoritative standing and even agreement among participants or speakers in a community. However, politics demands more than such assent: the

---

[28]See Timothy Garton Ash, *Free Speech: Ten Principles for a Connected World* (Atlantic Books, 2016), especially chapter 3, 'Knowledge', for an extended consideration of this specific point.

politician seeks not just the intrinsic authority afforded to an argument, but instead the material power to exercise that authority *over* others in a community or polity. Rhetoric may be the means, but power is the end.

That is to say, the purpose of standard political rhetoric is to effect a slide between agreement or assent on the one hand and the exercising of power on the other hand. Political rhetoric attempts to establish a seamless continuity between word and deed.[29] In its most extreme form, this is the dictatorial tyranny that allows one powerful speaker to state that things *are* so because he or she *says* they are so. At the much less extreme and more mundane or everyday level, what we have here is a description of parliamentary or congressional practice, in which participants give their voices or votes to a specific argument within a chamber that is dedicated to the power of the word. It follows that parliamentary democracy is *always* intrinsically jeopardized by the shadow of tyranny, and that, for those who might want to extend democracy and to give voices to all, the confounding of power with authority yields a serious problem.

In the maintenance of democracy, we must always be sure that authority and power are two separate orders, and the corollary of that is that power will always be subjected to authority and must bow before the logic that is inscribed within verbal authority or argument. In classical terms, *ergon* or deed must always remain subservient to *logos*, the logic that is inscribed in words and argument. Dictatorial tyranny follows when *ergon* is merged with *logos*, such that power cannot be subjected again to authority, for authority has now been circumscribed within power itself.

The last step in the sequence above – in which authority slips into the exercise of power – is potentially contentious, for it need not be based upon any truth of fact: it is based simply on rhetorical persuasion and the power of the word to present facts in terms of interpretations of facts. The politician's rhetoric is a specific *inflection* of facts, and what she or he has secured is merely an agreement with that inflection. The facts of the case might differ still, for these facts are of an entirely different order of being. The facts are historical and necessary; the inflected presentation of them is merely contingent.

What, further, of those who remain unpersuaded by the politician's case or rhetorical argumentation? It is here, indeed, that the real

---

[29]See Hans-Georg Gadamer, '*Logos* and *Ergon* in Plato's *Lysis*', in his *Dialogue and Dialectic* (trans. P. Christopher Smith; Yale University Press, 1980) for a superb philosophical analysis of this.

and substantial consequence of the slippage between two orders of truth-telling is to be found. Those who remain unpersuaded resist the politician's interpretation of the empirical facts of the case and thus remain committed to the facts-as-such, seeking to hold to an account of the truth of fact over the truth of linguistic proposition. The crowds at Donald Trump's inauguration really were pretty small: that is the empirical fact – and, having noted that fact, I will remain resistant to any mere 'interpretation' that proposes that there may be 'alternative facts' of the matter. Consequently, I will resist Kellyanne Conway and Sean Spicer when they try to present an interpretation as a fact: in doing this, they are behaving as if the truth of their own linguistic proposition is utterly and entirely at one with truth of fact. They thus confuse authority with power and choose to exercise power instead of retaining or trying to establish their authority. This is one among many reasons why Trump's presidency jeopardizes democracy and continually threatens to veer towards tyranny. The problem is that Trump is but the extreme of the current climatic norm.

Famously if apocryphally, George Washington said that he could not tell a lie, thereby initiating the myth that the US President cannot be the speaker of lies and that the White House should be a bastion of honesty and probity. In the latter half of the twentieth century, however, this was very obviously put to the test in numerous cases. We might consider the first of these to be Watergate, which led to the resignation of Nixon before he could be impeached; and his problem was not so much the crime (bad though that was) but the cover-up, which Nixon and others sustained by dishonesty in their words and deeds. Richard Nixon had misled the American people and had betrayed the mythic sanctity of the White House. What is important in this is not so much that they lost control and grasp of empirical realities (indeed, they had this in spades, for they had committed the misdemeanours); rather what is important is that they lost control of the words and their meanings. The barrier between insider and outsider was broken, and Nixon's nickname as 'Tricky Dicky' – as someone who was not fundamentally sincere or authentic in what he said – became understood as the 'real' Nixon.

Consequently, the White House had to be purged of any such stain on that original Washingtonian ideal, an ideal based on the control of language. Gerald Ford stepped in as a more or less transitional President, before the election of Jimmy Carter, a President who put his Christian religion and moral uprightness at the core of his thought and actions, ostensibly realigning the White House with a probity that is grounded in theology. However, in the subsequent elections, we arrived at Ronald Reagan, a one-time B-movie actor: a man whose entire *profession* was therefore given over to dissimulation, a form of lying.[30] These are the real precursors of Donald Trump, a man who seems constitutionally incapable of telling the truth in any normal sense of that term, and whose presidency seems to be a polar opposite of that Washingtonian myth. Where Washington could not tell a lie, Trump seems to be incapable of telling the truth.

However, one great and, perhaps, absolutely fundamental element in the election of Trump to the presidency was that he was thought by numbers of American people to 'tell it like it is', and he was thought to be sincere in doing so and sincere in his claim to be on the side of the blue-collar working class in the rustbelt states. The emphasis on sincerity in politicians – that is to say, the emphasis on the consistency theory of truth in which the world-as-such is degraded in importance – can lead us to a state of affairs in which any appeal to fact will be ignored. The corollary of this is not just that truth-as-fact is lost but also that reason has a less central and less important place in political argument than emotion.

Further, since many reasonable people, attuned to the fact that politicians' claims are not usually based in a recounting of 'truth-as-fact', it is obvious that 'telling it like it is' is considered to be revealing that which usually goes unsaid. What goes unsaid, in turn, is that which is disreputable or scandalous, and thus the logic follows that the politician who is characterized as 'telling it like it is' is usually the one who says the most outrageous and taboo things. They can bolster and underpin their claim on 'sincerity' by a complete 'ungoverning' of the tongue, a complete ban on any form of restraint, etiquette or respect for established protocol. Profanity sits enthroned at the centre of the White House.

---

[30] A major factor in deciding this election was the attitudes of both the candidates to the use of military force in the resolution of international political conflicts. It constituted the first question posed to both candidates during the TV debate, when Marvin Stone, editor of *US News and World Report* asked the first question, on Reagan being 'all too quick to advocate the use of muscle' while Carter was seen to prevaricate on these issues. See debate at: https://www.youtube.com/watch?v=tWEm6g0iQNI (accessed 22 February 2018), uploaded to the web courtesy of the Ronald Reagan Presidential Library.

6 PROFANITY AND FREE SPEECH

In his extensive and substantial defence of the fundamental principles of free speech, Timothy Garton Ash notes a specific nuance regarding the relation between 'having rights' and 'what it might be right to do'. He argues that 'A right to say it does not mean that it is right to say it', and, further, 'a right to offend does not entail a duty to offend'.[1] Arguments over free speech in our time have often attended to the issue of offence, and many have taken the ostensibly definitive line that the freedom to speak out about anything should not be constrained by the fear of giving offence. In its extreme form, the degrees of offence given and taken become a measure of the absoluteness of the freedom, a kind of homage paid to the principle governing free speech itself.

Political language is rife with offensiveness, and, unlike the shamed and self-accusing Claudius in *Hamlet*, many politicians often positively seem to enjoy the fact that 'my offence is rank'.[2] There is a long and often amusing history of profanities and insults throughout the history of political debate and rhetoric. It is certainly anything but the case that political rhetoric observes the niceties of *délicatesse*, or the decorous proprieties of Jane Austen's sitting rooms. As James Ball reminds us, the US context gives numerous examples of such insults. During the US presidential election of 1800, for example, supporters of John Adams

---

[1] Ash, *Free Speech*, 79. See also Stefan Collini, *That's Offensive!* (Seagull Books, Kolkata, 2011).

[2] Shakespeare, *Hamlet*, 3:3. Claudius's offence is 'rank' because, having 'the primal eldest curse upon't, / a brother's murder', it recalls the biblical story of Cain and Abel. Political fratricide usually simply means attacking one's own side; and a good deal of political linguistic offence is reserved for this. It is especially prevalent on the political left, where the charge of being a 'splitter' is frequently made.

stated that 'a Jefferson presidency would mean' that 'murder, robbery, rape, adultery and incest will be openly taught and practiced'. In response, Jefferson's supporters labelled Adams not just as a 'gross hypocrite' but also as a 'hermaphrodite', with clear malign intent behind the description.[3] In more recent times, the writer and commentator Gore Vidal described Ronald Reagan as 'a triumph of the embalmer's art', and there have been numerous references to Silvio Berlusconi resembling a waxwork dummy, following his many cosmetic bodily modifications.

In modern history at least, the language of political rhetoric in the UK has been every bit as 'robust', to put it politely. Disraeli said that Robert Peel had a smile that 'is like the silver fittings on a coffin'. When Sir John Simon changed his party affiliation for a second time, David Lloyd George said that 'he has crossed the floor twice, each time leaving behind a trail of slime'. Churchill described Attlee as 'a sheep in sheep's clothing' and as 'a modest man with plenty to be modest about'. He joked that 'An empty taxi arrived at 10 Downing St, and when the door was opened, Attlee got out'. Attlee himself said that 'Democracy means government by discussion, but it is only effective if you can stop the people talking'. His Labour colleague and great orator, Nye Bevan, famously said that 'No amount of cajolery, and no attempts at ethical or social seduction, can eradicate from my heart a deep and burning hatred of the Tory party. So far as I am concerned, they are lower than vermin.' In relation to Churchill, Bevan welcomed the 'opportunity of pricking the bloated bladder of lies with the poniard of truth'.

More recently, Clive James said that Margaret Thatcher 'sounded like the Book of Revelations read out over a railway station public address system by a headmistress of a certain age wearing calico knickers'. Clement Freud called her 'Attila the Hen'. Ian Paisley called her 'Jezebel', bringing us closer to obscenity and profanity by implying that the Prime Minister (whose own background was in Methodism) was akin to a whore. Within this particular insult, there lies a mode of religious sectarianism or, more precisely, a religious exceptionalism that permitted Paisley to figure any and all who were not of his own churchly tribe as being intrinsically of the devil's party. As with much political insult, sexual innuendo was a determinant of the linguistic climate. The British clown-politician, Boris Johnson, has been a keen player in 'lowering the tone' of political debate, though he gets away

---

[3]James Ball, *Post-Truth: How Bullshit Conquered the World* (Biteback, 2017), 17.

with this through the careful dropping of the occasional classical allusion or the introduction of an archaic term. He calls Jeremy Corbyn a 'mutton-headed old mugwump' or an 'Islington herbivore', and then makes his way on to straightforward obscenity when he accuses Recep Tayyip Erdoğan of being a 'wankerer' who has sex with a goat.

Profane obscenity is perhaps most explicit in the language of Silvio Berlusconi who, when asked his views on Angela Merkel, said that she was 'an unfuckable lard-arse'. I have already referred to Trump's comments about Megyn Kelly, after she gave him a difficult interview: 'She starts asking me all sorts of ridiculous questions. And, you know, you could see there was blood coming out of her eyes, blood coming out of her wherever.'[4] Of Rosie O'Donnell, the comedian and LGBT activist opposed to Trump's politics, Trump said that 'she is a disgusting person, a disgusting creature. She's a mean-spirited, unattractive woman, with a pig-face. I really want some of her money, from that big fat ass.'[5]

Clearly, by the time we arrive at this kind of insult, or at the similar offensiveness in France of the philosopher Alain Badiou calling Nicolas Sarkozy 'Rat-man', the routine misogynistic remarks of Donald Trump, and the routine sly slurs of a European far right that seeks to mobilize racism through attacks on foreigners, we have gone far beyond what seems to be the more or less legitimate hurly-burly of a political to-and-fro. Berlusconi's statement about Angel Merkel is shocking, but the real shock, of course, is that no one is any more shocked by his making it. What was once unsayable has become here a part of the now utterly degraded lexicon in which Berlusconi conducts his political business. That lexicon plays on the closeness of word to deed that I described in my previous chapter here, and it is menacing in its fundamental violence and misogyny.

Such language, in its obscene profanity, is clearly not intended to facilitate reasoned debate. On the contrary, the profanity is instrumental in establishing a tribal divisiveness that precludes the possibility of there being a meeting-ground on which argument can take place. We have seen the by now well-documented shift from logos to pathos, but this

---

[4]See report at: https://www.washingtonpost.com/news/post-politics/wp/2015/08/07/trump-says-foxs-megyn-kelly-had-blood-coming-out-of-her-wherever/?utm_term=.70cd20 59ff3a (accessed 12 March 2018).

[5]Available at: https://www.youtube.com/watch?v=x0Kcx25WCg4 (accessed 12 March 2018).

goes a step further. The rational word (*logos*) cedes place to the priorities of force (*energeia* or *ergon*), including now linguistic force, and the onlooker or auditor is simply being invited either to join in the profanity or to close the door against it. This is, at root, the validation of the political strategy of winning by force and violence. Such a politics, giving high value to profanity in this way, is a threat to democracy and to the rational debate – logos – that is supposed to underpin a democratic polity.

At the core of this is a particular construction of the individual in terms of tribal identity: the affiliation to a single cause, being 'one of us', in Thatcher's divisive formulation. 'Commitment Politics' or CP, if I can coin that term (hinting at its opposition to and reversal of the PC or 'politically correct'[6]), is based upon a divisiveness that explicitly sets people in opposition to each other. It is now as if participants are speaking different languages even, and, if you want to talk to Berlusconi, say, you need to speak his kind of profanity.

I have adverted in the preceding chapter here to how Trump gained his success through his claims upon authenticity and 'telling it like it is'. Faced with this, Hillary Clinton had a serious political problem. If she applied the principles of rational debate, she simply confirmed Trump's characterization of her as being of the elite and on the side of a corrupt establishment, and thus inauthentic – 'crooked'. If she argued on Trump's terms, and used his kind of insults, she would be seen as a second-order imitation of Trump, and thus, again, she would be seen as 'inauthentic'. Trump's linguistic strategy placed her in a position where all she could aim to do was to minimize losses while trying to hang on to the basic principles of democratic engagement.

In its intrinsic structure, Trumpian insult eventually breeds within political discourse a specific form of nativism that suspects and distrusts anything that is foreign or 'other' on the grounds that it is elitist, and thus opposed to 'the people' in whatever specific identity the politician aims to give to them. To borrow a term from Amartya Sen, it 'miniaturizes' the individual to the 'singular classification' of an identity that is predicated on a single one of the many identifying characteristics that properly make up any individual, and it then reduces 'the people' to this specific form.

---

[6] 'Political correctness', of course, is a favourite bugbear of the political right. It is true that PC may bring about unforeseen issues for liberals, but the proper reply to the right is simple: 'If you think political correctness is bad, take a brief look at political wrongness.'

In Trump's case, the identity is 'American', set against 'Washingtonian'. In the UK during the same politically turbulent year of 2016, it was 'English' rather than 'European', or even 'British'. In that specific jurisdiction, 'political English' required a full politicization of the language itself, and one that claimed an identity between the purity of that language and authentic human existence and membership of 'the people'. That may in itself go some way towards explaining the vulgar tone of much of the campaigning. It certainly helps explain how it comes about that anyone who questioned or disagreed with the result of the 2016 European Union referendum becomes identified as an 'enemy of the people'. The phrase, of course, has itself a somewhat menacing history, given its use in the political murder of opponents in the French Revolution, Stalinism and Maoism.

* * *

Sen stresses that identities are extremely important. However, my identity is plural: 'I can be, at the same time, an Asian, an Indian citizen, a Bengali with Bangladeshi ancestry, an American or British resident, an economist, a dabbler in philosophy, an author, a Sanskritist, a strong believer in secularism and democracy, a man, a feminist, a heterosexual, a defender of gay and lesbian rights, with a nonreligious lifestyle, from a Hindu background, a non-Brahmin, and a non-believer in an afterlife' and so on, and on. This yields the possibility of multiple kinds of affiliations, with individuals whose own multiple identities overlap with at least one aspect of my own. Some of these, of course, seem to be politically trivial, but even the most trivial can become of political import. Sen gives the example of 'people who wear size 8 shoes'. That ostensibly neutral category becomes a *political* identity if, for example, 'size 8 shoes become extremely difficult to find', as they once were in some Communist regimes, and, at this point, wearers of size 8 shoes have 'a shared predicament' that 'can give reason enough for solidarity and identity'.[7]

Political problems – including the tendency to violence – arise when, instead of acknowledging the provisionality of these differing priorities, 'my' identity is given by one characteristic, to the exclusion of others. In such a moment, 'identity can ... kill – and kill with abandon. A strong – and exclusive – sense of belonging to one group can in many

---

[7]Amartya Sen, *Identity and Violence* (Penguin, 2006), 19, 26.

cases carry with it the perception of distance and divergence from other groups. Within-group solidarity can help to feed between-group discord.' Further 'violence is fomented by the imposition of singular and belligerent identities on gullible people, championed by proficient artisans of terror'.[8]

A good example of this is to be found in the US presidential campaign in 2016. Donald Trump sought corroboration from 'the people' by identifying Hillary Clinton as someone opposed to their interests. In doing this, he characterized her as one whose identity lay firmly with a political 'Establishment' that he described as a congeries of crooks and criminals. Trump and his erstwhile security adviser and campaign supporter Michael Flynn orchestrated chants of 'lock her up', describing Trump's completely legitimate rival for the presidency not as an opponent, but as an adversary and as 'crooked Hillary'.

While 'crooked' itself is not a profane term, the description of Clinton in these criminal terms is nonetheless abusive, and, with the hints of jailing Hillary Clinton – a jailing that was enthusiastically mimed by Trump's supporters pretending to be handcuffed at his rallies – it seemed to come close to straight endorsement of political violence. However, for the present argument about political rhetoric, the most important thing about it is that it is indeed linked, in fact, with a fundamental idea of profanity. The word 'profane' derives from a Latinate root: *fanum* signifies a 'temple'. The profane were those who had to stand before the temple because they were not entitled to enter. Profanity, in this sense, is directly related to the tribalism of the 'singular identity' described by Sen, and, in some political cases – as with Trump's description of Hillary Clinton as 'crooked' – this is a singular and belligerent identity, being championed by Trump.

The campaign, in its populist rhetoric, actually sought to turn the temple – the Establishment – inside out. Those outside – the profane – would be the new insiders. The previous insider would now be placed in a different 'inside': the jail where she was to do her time. The linguistic project imagines jailing Hillary Clinton, or at the very least constraining her 'within' a temple or Establishment that Trump's language sought to delegitimize entirely. Those 'outside' were to become the new insiders; those prepared to be profane in their language would now become the

---

[8] Sen, *Identity and Violence*, 102.

new insiders banishing propriety to the outside of political power and 'jailing' it there.[9]

The power of profanity can veer from the merely amusing to the utterly violently menacing and, as Sen points out, the resulting tribalism yields a very narrow view of identity that can kill.

In extreme circumstances – more extreme, at first glance, than those prevailing in contemporary US politics – tribalism such as this has led to people being locked inside their temples before the temples are set alight and burned. Perhaps the most well-documented such atrocity is that which occurred in Oradour-sur-Glane on 10 June 1944. The Nazis locked the men of the village in barns where they were shot in the legs before the barns were set alight, and the women and children were locked in the village church, which was then also set alight. The same violence has been repeated in numerous cases of ethnic conflict – based upon the politics of identity and tribalism – across the world in more recent times.

Oradour was, clearly, a determinedly vicious and preconceived act. It rested upon overt and naked aggression and violence, and this violence was itself founded upon an extremist nationalist and racist ideology. Innocent individuals suffered directly as a consequence of this utterly unconcealed ethnic and tribal violence. Obviously, in many ways the very point of politics as an activity is that it usually works to try to avoid such violence in the first place. However, as Clausewitz famously informed us, the distance between politics and war is not absolute.

Clausewitz bases his thinking on a fundamental observation that 'war is an act of violence intended to compel our opponent to fulfill our will', and it is this statement that leads eventually to the more well-known proposition that 'war is nothing but a continuation of political intercourse, with a mixture of other means'.[10] If we concede this essential continuity between war and politics, it might also be illuminating to consider whether certain political arrangements, including those grounded in conflicts between classes, say, might be profitably considered in terms of war and violence. It will turn out that, in some instances, there

---

[9]The profane is identifiable with the outsider, even the foreigner, in this; and, in the case of Trump, the question – at the time of writing – is focused on whether there was an actual foreigner, Putin, pulling the political strings during the campaign, and since. In turning the US Establishment inside out, through this literal profanity, has Trump brought a Russian President into the heart of the White House?

[10]Carl von Clausewitz, *On War*, ed. Anatol Rapoport (Penguin, 1982), 101, 402.

is an argument readily available that suggests that there may even be a continuity between the extremes of something like Oradour on the one hand and more ostensibly mundane tragedies on the other hand.

It is instructive to consider a recent tragedy in the UK in these terms. When Grenfell Tower in London burnt to the ground in 2017, a serious issue of social class-division, based often on ethnic allegiance, was revealed. The borough in which Grenfell sat is one where there is a clear division between the wealthy and the disadvantaged, the latter group being housed in Grenfell with a disproportionately high number of individuals of non-British origin, many of them disempowered by their status as immigrants, both legal and illegal. The division is quasi-tribal.

Seventy-one of these people died, and their deaths were a consequence, most immediately, of the fact that the local council and the tenant management company appear to have provided inadequate fire-safety building materials and conditions. While it is obviously crude and misleading to suggest that there is a parallel between Oradour and Granfell – and, for the avoidance of doubt, that is not what I suggest here – it is nonetheless the case that the atrocity and the tragedy each have their appropriate political mentality as a predetermining circumstance. In Oradour, that mentality is laid bare, open and aggressively direct in the act of premeditated violence. In the case of Grenfell, this is not what happens; yet, if we consider Clausewitz seriously, then we can see that the two events exist on a spectrum. The spectrum can be described variously: it goes from war at one end to politics at the other; it goes from violent action against 'othered' individuals all the way through to its seeming opposite in discursive description of individuals whose class-position deprives them of cultural and political legitimacy and authority; it goes from direct aggression to covert discrimination that cannot be openly acknowledged.

Behind this, further, there lies a political strategy deriving from the Conservative housing policies of the Thatcher years, which were designed to reduce council provision of housing and to prioritize its privatization instead. The most significant issue for present purposes is that the political strategy of privatization during the 1980s was cast in the political language of human and political rights. The Thatcher government devised a policy that they called 'the Right to Buy'. It was designed to 'permit' council housing tenants to buy the house in which they lived, but 'permission' became recast as an issue of fundamental 'rights'. The effect was to degrade the very idea of the council house and, by corollary metonymic consequence, its occupants. These were people who did not avail of their rights, as it were. They were thus not fully Thatcherite citizens. When I indicate that Grenfell is one consequence of this, I mean to point out that the tragedy there was not simply a product of 'nature' and not a natural disaster; rather, it had a political substratum that rested on political language.

We can think of the kind of tribalism in question here – both in its immediately visible conscious forms (Oradour) and also its less immediately visible and determined form (Grenfell) – as a phenomenon based in a kind of nativist isolationism. It says, 'speak my language, or else I will not just ignore you but seek to silence you.' It says, 'I will give authority only to my lexicon and, unless you speak this, you are a foreigner, and, as such, your language lacks legitimacy here.' It says, further, 'your lack of linguistic legitimacy implies your lack of legality, and so you will be deemed to be a criminal threat to "us", to those who speak "my language" and who thus show that they are legally entitled to presence and to legitimate representation here, members of my tribe.' Profanity – and its close partner, obscenity – can engender tribalism and can establish the conditions for violence. We should note and stress that, where Oradour was the direct and conscious enactment of such violence, Grenfell was not; but the point is that the political English of the 1980s – essentially a language that 'profaned' those not committed to the politics of privatization – established the material conditions that made Grenfell not only possible but, in the end, actual.

Given that it depends upon tribalism, profanity also works – at the political level – through the elaboration of a sympathy between speaker and audience. We know this, in a less tendentious fashion, through the work of thinkers such as Drew Westen. Westen makes the case for a psychological understanding of political situations, by acknowledging that people tend to make political choices – especially with regard to voting – not on purely rational grounds but rather with preferences that are driven by emotion. In some ways, this carries into the political realm what we already know from economics.

The economic ideology of market fundamentalism is one that we know to be fatally flawed because it rests on the false assumption that all consumers and citizens are rational free-choice individuals. This empirical fact has not impeded the progress of market-fundamentalist economics towards ideological supremacy in recent times, such that many citizens now regard it in many situations as utterly normative and natural. Citizens, now identifying themselves primarily as consumers, are shaped by emotion every bit as much as by reason: we buy things not because it makes good economic sense to do so, but because of many other factors. Among those factors is the determination to identify ourselves as particular types of individual, as members of a tribe. I buy Nike footwear, say, not because it makes economic sense to do so (I cannot afford it), but because I want to be 'like' other people who have those trainers. This is a matter of claiming identity. I support Xi Jinping's claim to be Chinese President-for-life, say, or I vote Trump, Brexit, Erdoğan, Orbán, Putin (to give the most recent obvious political examples), not because I have made a rational political decision but because I want to be of the relevant tribes.

At its extreme, the priorities of nativism that underpin this mentality leads to an isolation that comes close to solipsism. I begin by identifying with a large tribe ('Trump supporters', say), but within the tribe, there are sub-groups with whom I feel a closer affiliation ('Second Amendment Absolutist Trump supporters'), and then, within this, a yet smaller circle ('Christian Fundamentalist Evangelical Second Amendment Absolutist Trump supporters') and so on in ever-narrowing spirals. Eventually, my identity is nothing more than my identity with myself as an absolute particular. This kind of thinking goes hand in hand with a form of violence that we know as 'aggressive individualism'. In such a political regime, based upon this aggressive and exclusivist individualism, all social life becomes reduced to a more or less violent set of confrontations between the private 'me' and those whom I identify as foreigners or individuals from other tribes. This – a politics based on a fundamentalist aggressive and acquisitive individualism, perhaps better known as 'resentment fuelled by greed' – is unpleasant and difficult to acknowledge for those who generate such a politics, so they mediate it and make it sound respectable by labelling it instead as 'competition' or 'competitiveness'.

Amartya Sen calls this kind of individualism a mode of 'miniaturization' of people. He makes a distinction between, on the one hand, a kind of hierarchy of identity in which the multiple identities of each individual can all be subsumed under one, 'the presumption that people can be uniquely categorized based on religion or culture' (xiv), say. Against this is that rich diversity that accepts 'the plurality of our affiliations' (xiv) and that maintains an identity based upon what he calls being 'diversely different' (xiv) from each other.

There are two opposed political philosophies available to us in regard to this. The first is one that accepts such narrowing and miniaturization, which might better be described as a diminution of the individual and a diminishing of our selfhood as such. The second is one that acknowledges the fact of tribalism and its basis in sympathy, but that seeks nonetheless to eschew such diminishment and to embrace a more edifying expansion of selfhood.

* * *

The easiest way to illustrate this difference and what is at stake in it is to consider so-called 'culturally specific' judgements, sometimes thought of as a mode of 'culturally sensitive' relativism. A specific society or group stones to death a woman accused of adultery, say. In response, I judge this as an act of barbarism and condemn it in the most extreme terms, perhaps laced with profanities or obscenities as a mode of insult or political attack (the very term, 'barbarism', is itself such an insult, based on a degrading of the language of those whom I condemn). The miniaturist tells me that I have every right to judge the stoning community, but that I must do so only through a profound sympathy for and identification with the specific behavioural standards of that community. I must understand and speak the language of their tribe; I have no right to judge it as from my own values, the values of my own tribal affiliation or identity. If we leave it at this, then two things follow: (1) I narrow the range of my possible judgements by focusing them simply and completely within the specific bounds of that community or tribe, silencing my own language (rendering it literally 'profane' and placing it outside of legitimacy), and (2) women continue to be stoned to death in that community for alleged adultery. I have, as it were, rendered myself 'profane', my language and its possible political interventions or judgements silenced.

The more edifying response goes, instead, in a different manner, and not one that is simply and completely opposed to the tribe's norms. It is not a simple or straightforward rejection of the stoning tribe: this is not a Samuel Huntington 'clash of civilizations' thesis, with the absolutism of a kind of determinate war between cultures in which one is completely 'profane' and the other regarded as self-evidently valid. In the edifying response, I begin, instead, by acknowledging the standards of the community in question, and I understand that, within the norms that govern those standards, stoning is appropriate. However, I continue to expand the basis for my judgement, and I now make a further judgement, a judgement of the standards of the tribe itself, among whose norms are the legitimacy of stoning a woman to death for alleged adultery.

In response, therefore, I try to open the door to a possible exchange of views, such that the tribe can expand their own horizons and call their own initial judgements and norms into question, while I, too, join in debate and seek to widen my own lexicon. In this, three things follow: (1) I extend the range of possible judgements and give them a wider ground, a more expansive selfhood from which to make a judgement; (2) I broaden the social group to make a 'diversely different' basis for a social and political relation between 'my' tribe and the tribe of stoners and (3) women may no longer be so casually stoned for alleged adultery. In this, then, profanity is circumvented: none are left outside the temple, or parliament; violence edges towards political legitimacies and authority vested in language.

We usually refer to this second route, historically, as 'progress'. Even within a single polity, such edifying judgements are positive, and that is for the simple reason that they allow us to live the world differently from how the historical tradition states that it 'must' be lived, or how we have always done things. The edifying route of diverse difference enables the escape from coercion by past norms and the opening of genuinely secular change. It is such progress that allows us, for example, to jettison the death penalty for criminal activity or to ensure that women have the right to vote or to allow working-class people to live with dignity or to criticize the poster in the window of the boarding house that says 'no blacks, no Irish, no dogs'. These are all things that 'our tribe' used to permit, without difficulty, but the expansive judgements of such norms, and a refusal simply to accept those norms as being 'acceptable' in their own polities, have enabled us to progress in terms of civility. In short, this diverse difference widens the vocabulary and the available lexicon of meanings, for everyone who is engaged in the polity.

This problem and this confrontation between diminishing and expansive judgement, we might say, is at the basis of an identity-politics that has increasingly become normative in our times. When languages cannot coincide at all, thanks to the priorities of tribal affiliation, then the very possibility of political debate is threatened.

* * *

Tribalism persists in political English, notwithstanding this threat. It manifests itself not under the negative significations of exclusivity and tribalism but rather in the positive validation of a 'jargon of authenticity'.[11] Authenticity, in modern and contemporary politics, is aligned with a specific mode of individualism. The authentic person is the one who distinguishes herself or himself from social norms, and who does so in a manner that is based upon supposedly being true-to-oneself, as we have seen. However, there is more to this; for it is not always enough to be true-to-oneself and thus to present an utterly consistent analysis of politics. It is also important that, in being thus true-to-oneself, one is also more directly in contact with the allegedly 'natural' condition of life: an ostensibly innocent bio-political existence, as it were. Authenticity in politics sometimes means the complete eschewing of political guile, and a claim for a romantic and prelapsarian condition of being in tune with a natural order of things. In this, the politician is simply finding legitimacy in something that transcends the messiness of political artifice, and presents as 'Mr Normal'.

This was the ill-fated position of François Hollande, former President of France, in his attempt to distinguish himself from Nicolas 'bling-bling' Sarkozy. Hollande rapidly became re-titled (by Arnaud Montebourg) as 'Flanby', comparing him to a kind of jelly that wobbles in all directions but that eventually resumes its initial shape. The closest English translation would refer to the character of 'Mr Wobblyman' in Enid Blyton's *Noddy* novels for children. In trying to claim 'normality' for himself, Hollande instead attracted a whole series of insulting names: 'Guimauve le conquérant' (Marshmallow the Conqueror), coined by Guillaume Bachelay (himself from Normandy) in a corruption of Guillaume le conquérant; 'fraise des bois'; 'Monsieur you're joking' and so on.[12]

In the English context, Jeremy Corbyn, Labour's unlikely leader, is another such 'authentic' politician. Corbyn is seen to be authentic precisely because he does not rest his judgement on consensually shared

---

[11] See Theodor Adorno, *The Jargon of Authenticity* (1964; trans. Knut Tarkowski and Frederic Will; Northwestern University Press, Evanston, 1973). Adorno argues, among other things, that the idea of an authentic (existentialist) self is based upon an error. The idiom of authentic being depends upon the false idea that, in looking inward, a subject can transparently reveal herself to herself and can make existential choices regarding action based upon that selfhood. Such a position is flawed because it presupposes a division between the self and the world as its founding principle, and, for Adorno, there is no such division possible.

[12] See Michel Revol, 'De Flanby a Pépère', *Le Point*, 10 avril 2013, available at: http://www.lepoint.fr/politique/de-flanby-a-pepere-tous-les-surnoms-d-hollande-10-04-2013-1653042_20.php (accessed 21 March 2018) for a long list.

ideas or statements regarding the truth of how the world is. By turning away from that, and towards his own internally preferred descriptions of the world, based as it is upon the primacy of his own desires, experiences or unconscious – all of which yield his specific mode of political analysis – he is thought to be relying fundamentally upon an authentic being. Moreover, in this case – and very unlike the supposed authenticity of Donald Trump – Corbyn rests a good deal of his political appeal on the implication that in his authenticity he is not simply being consistent with long-held personal belief but actually with the condition of nature itself. It is not for nothing that the presentation of Corbyn made much of his commitment to his garden allotment. His self-presentation as rather scruffy – uncomfortable in suit and tie – goes hand in hand with his self-presentation as 'natural' and deeply in intimate contact with the natural order of things.

Corbyn is 'not stylish', as the editorial team at the fashion magazine *GQ* agreed, even as they worked out how to present him on the front cover of their January/February 2018 edition.[13] He refused to wear the kind of suit that would be the norm for the magazine and was 'adamant that he wouldn't wear anything other than a Marks and Spencer suit'. The editor of *GQ*, himself a Tory supporter, noted that, in the shoot for the cover, 'there is an "air of authenticity" around Mr Corbyn.'[14] Such 'authenticity' has not always played well, however.

Corbyn's predecessor as a left-wing leader of Labour was Michael Foot. Foot was one of the greatest political orators of the modern era: extraordinarily well-read, with a rhetorical brilliance in phrase-making, including some very biting – and wittily funny – descriptions of his opponents. The morning after Foot died, James Naughtie described him on the BBC as perhaps 'the last of a breed, preserving a grand style of political rhetoric that has all but gone'.[15] His rhetoric owed a great deal to his interest in literary Romanticism and its revolutionary potential. One of his pamphlets was *Byron and the Bomb*;[16] his satirical oratory owes much to his interest in Jonathan Swift just as much as in Nye Bevan; his sense of

---

[13] See http://www.gq-magazine.co.uk/article/jeremy-corbyn-gq-video-documentary (accessed 21 March 2018).

[14] See https://news.sky.com/story/gq-editor-jeremy-corbyn-photoshoot-was-torture-11151403 (accessed 21 March 2018).

[15] See https://www.youtube.com/watch?v=C0ykxM3w2MU (accessed 21 March 2018).

[16] Michael Foot, *Byron and the Bomb* (University College Cardiff Press, Cardiff, 1983).

benevolence is a 'debt of honour' paid to Hazlitt. In the popular political imagination, however, none of this persists. Instead, the legacy relates to Foot's body and physical appearance. The infamous so-called donkey jacket that he wore when he attended the memorial service at the Cenotaph now stands in a cabinet in Manchester's People's History Museum. Although it was, in fact, a rather expensive coat, its iconic fame rests on the fact that Foot was attacked when he wore it by the right-wing populist press that alleged that, through its supposed scruffiness, Foot disrespected the war dead. The cartoons that dogged him presented him as Wurzel Gummidge, a dishevelled tramp-figure from a TV series for children.

The historical shift here is itself instructive. In the days of Foot, authenticity in oratory involved a high degree of culture: acquired knowledge. His political standing was high precisely because of his interest in literary culture and history, and he learned from figures whose politics he did not obviously share, such as Disraeli, for example. Corbyn's authenticity depends very little on this kind of authentic literate culture; rather it depends upon a primary appeal to nature itself, as in the modesty of an ordinary life that includes the making of jam from the fruits of his allotment. Culture itself is now the site of a contestation for authenticity, even within the political left.

Meanwhile, in the United States, Donald Trump presents himself differently, yet also with a claim to authenticity. It is precisely because he has seemingly never read a book nor made a pot of jam or worked the soil, that he pierces through an allegedly ideological description of the world that the Establishment holds to be true and accurate, the 'ordinary everyday' world. That is to say, in short, he posits the authenticity of his own inner self against a material reality or world that he now describes as ideological to the extent that this reality is supposedly merely a construct – the *cultural construct* – of a dominant or established tribe. Culture, in this case, is precisely the enemy. His language, deriving from his authentic inner being, is now set against the 'fake news' that constitutes the actual and material conditions of the world. Those conditions are now described as inauthentic, and they are inauthentic because they are merely cultural.

As some writers have indicated, one possible critique of authenticity as a political principle is that it can easily be aligned with the antisocial personality disorders of narcissism.[17] Yet the political effect is different,

---

[17] See Christopher Lasch, *The Culture of Narcissism* (Norton, New York, 1979).

precisely because the jargon of authenticity does not isolate its speaker at all; rather, it recruits the audience as members of the tribe. In this, as these cases show, it is not just reason that is demoted, but culture too is seen as the enemy of the primacy of the body and its supposedly unmediated and immediate feelings or intimate sensations.

Further, since many reasonable people, attuned to the fact that politicians' claims are not usually based in a recounting of 'truth-as-fact', it is obvious that 'telling it like it is' is considered to be revealing that which usually goes unsaid. What goes unsaid, in turn, is that which is disreputable or scandalous, and thus the logic follows that the politician who is characterized as 'telling it like it is' is usually the one who says the most outrageous and taboo things. This is the cornerstone of profanity's political rise and triumph in our times.

The 'revelation' that Trump sexually harassed women as an everyday occurrence and thanks to his celebrity status therefore did him absolutely no harm at all. The same can be said for the fact that he mocked a respected reporter's physical disability. These events bolstered, underpinned and even extended his claim on 'sincerity' by a complete 'ungoverning' of the tongue, a complete and wilful ignoring of any form of restraint, etiquette or respect for established protocol. This mode of authenticity is brutal in its assault upon culture as such.

Apocryphally, Göring was alleged to say that 'when I hear the word culture, I reach for my gun'. The phrase is itself a fictional one, from Hanns Johst's Nazi play, *Schlageter* (a homage to Albert Leo Schlageter, whose death the Nazis celebrated as a proleptic martyrdom to their cause). Trump and his acolytes, thanks to the disregard of this kind of culture, would not recognize the aesthetic root for the celebrated saying, but they might more or less echo it and say, 'When I hear the word culture, I reach for the NRA.'

The cliché is that a politician campaigns in poetry but governs in prose, but, in recent times, we have seen this changing to a position where a politician campaigns in profanity and governs by obscenity.

* * *

We are now at the position, then, where we can acknowledge the full force of Arendt's arguments regarding the relative disregard that political language might have for truth. In our time, we have learned – with often damaging consequences – to prioritize sincerity or a feigned sincere authenticity over any allegiance to the facts of the world as it is. That is to say, we have prioritized our wish to be insiders, so to speak, to be 'one of us' or 'Thatcher's children' in the UK, say, and the successful politician is she or he who proclaims – in all sincerity and credibility – their determination to open the door to the insides of power for the profane among and within us to enter. The politician who wins is the populist who tells us that, by following her or his tribal view, we will be able to 'take back control' of our lives.

This goes some way towards explaining the logic behind the work of Drew Westen, who has argued – via his work in psychology – that what motivates people to vote as they do is emotion and not (or not primarily) reason. We vote in alignment with fantasy, as it were. The famous 'left-behind' – another description of the profane, those who stand *pro-fanum* – cannot acknowledge the fact that they are indeed left behind, for that is too humiliating, and thus they align themselves precisely with those who have left them behind in the first place, often the right wing.

It might indeed be argued that the people who are really those 'left behind' are those who retain some idea or ideal of political realities in which the politician wants to claim that she or he does respect the truth of fact. In our time, that is a position that is entirely démodé, as it were. Instead, our politics is governed not just by emotion but also and even primarily by tribal affiliation based upon the emotions, and, in turn, those emotions are valued in terms of their supposed authenticity and sincerity, and measured by the profanity of the politician's celebration of that which is taboo, even embarrassing. A politician weeping alongside the afflicted in a tragedy, for example, is worth many more votes than the detached politician who reveals via reasoned argument that the truth behind the tragedy is political corruption.

Such a state of affairs requires that emotion itself be prioritized and privileged as the key determinant of all political value. Its clearest formulation might be in the phrase associated with Bill Clinton during his 1992 presidential campaign in the United States. It was a phrase that he would utter twice, during an extremely heated discussion when Bob Rafsky was vigorously heckling him at a campaign meeting in New York City. Professionally, Rafsky had been a senior Vice President of a New York Public Relations organization, but he left this position in 1989 to devote time and energy to ActUp (the AIDS Coalition to Unleash Power), and he was himself an AIDS patient. Rafsky challenged Clinton to 'declare war on AIDS', and Clinton replied, saying, 'I'm listening. ... I know how it hurts. I've got friends who've died of AIDS.' Rafsky heckles again, suggesting that Clinton's motivations are related to his personal ambition, and it is in response to this that Clinton utters the phrase with which he became firmly associated during the rest of his campaign and even after. He said that 'I'm trying to do something about it', referring to the entire political situation, in which Rafsky had claimed that government were ignoring people and that they were dying of neglect. 'I feel your pain,' said Clinton. 'I feel your pain', he repeated, 'but if you want to attack me personally you're no better than Jerry Brown and all the rest of these people who say whatever sounds good at the moment.[18] 'I feel your pain' becomes a classic formulation that signals the importance of empathy in contemporary political rhetoric.

The exchange between Clinton and Rafsky combines Clinton's claim that he is empathetic towards those who are in need of political assistance with his claim that he is utterly consistent politically, as Clinton distinguishes himself from other politicians who change what they say depending on audience. Against this, he claims that 'The reason I'm still in public life is because I've kept my commitments. That's why I'm still here. That's why I'm still standing here.' Clearly angered, Clinton goes on to make his claims in a vernacular, where decorum disappears and profanity – albeit mild – enters: 'I'm sick and tired of all these people ... making snotty-nose remarks about how I haven't done anything in my life and it's all driven by ambition. That's bull, and I'm tired of it.'

Recall again here the etymology of 'profanity'. To be 'profane' is to stand before a sanctuary or consecrated place, but to be therefore outside of it. When Clinton, in this example, lapses into vernacular profanity, describing his opponents as people who speak bullshit, he is aligning himself with Rafsky, as one standing outside of the hallowed temple of political power – the White House – but inviting Rafsky to stand with him such that, through the intimate relation and identification of each with the other gained through their joint empathy, the profane itself *becomes* the sacred, and the outsider steps into that circle of consecrated power, the White House itself. The point here is that the profanity becomes

---

[18]See the report in *The New York Times*, 28 March 1992, available at: http://www.nytimes.com/1992/03/28/us/1992-campaign-verbatim-heckler-stirs-clinton-anger-excerpts-exchange.html?mcubz=0. Brown was one of Clinton's rivals for the Democratic nomination in 1992.

emblematic of an affinity and an empathy that will not just establish a tribal support for Clinton but will also itself embody the change that Rafsky and Clinton desire. Historically, the degeneration in political rhetoric here is that Clinton's 'sympathy' becomes, with the passing of time, Trump's tribalism. Where Clinton retained some semblance of what Sen would call diverse difference, Trump eschews it entirely, and, correspondingly, the rhetoric becomes all the more extreme in its profanity.

* * *

Profanity, in general, appears to be routinely normalized in contemporary political discourse, perhaps especially in English. There are examples in other languages, of course. Here, however, my concern is primarily with a generalized profanity in English. The reason for this emphasis is that – as I showed in Chapter 3 – the English language has claimed a specific relation to a fundamental (and fundamentalist) truth, gleaned from a self-proclaimed theological source. As I elaborated on that in Chapter 4, that is also related to a sociopolitical structure that generates 'insiders' or elites against outsiders. It is this that I will explore here in more detail, for it relates directly to issues of truth and of the loss of faith that we are witnessing in politics worldwide.

In the preface to his history of the Brexit campaign in the UK, *All Out War*, Tim Shipman notes that 'British politics can be a profane business. Many MPs and their aides swear like troopers, and the rhythms of their speech often require expletival emphasis'. Shipman's book is indeed pretty full of swearing, despite the fact that 'I have censored these efforts where the profanity is simply used as punctuation – not least because the spin doctors from both main campaigns asked me to spare their mothers' blushes – but where it is essential to the emotion of the sentence I have left it in. Be warned,' he writes.[19]

This is the kind of language that becomes the key characteristic of the fictional Malcolm Tucker, the spin-doctor in Armando Ianucci's TV series *The Thick of It* and in the major comic political film *In the Loop*. Political profanity is what generates Tucker as a character, and, indeed, it more or less constitutes the totality of his character.

---

[19] Tim Shipman, *All Out War* (rev. and updated edn; William Collins, 2017), xxv. I will consider censorship in the next chapter.

Malcolm Tucker is above all a walking personification of profanity as such.[20] Many suggested that he was based on the real-life Alastair Campbell, though Campbell himself disputed this, notwithstanding his own acknowledgement that he has a well-earned reputation for plain speaking and forthrightness.[21] Indeed, Campbell has had to depend on that reputation in order to sustain the claim that he did not 'sex-up' (and thus falsify) the famous 'dodgy dossier' that supposedly justified Blair's martial intervention in Iraq. He has always held to the claim that, throughout, he and Blair acted honestly: 'there was no lying, there was no deceit,' he said on the occasion of the publication of the Chilcot Report, hoping that Chilcot would put the allegations of dishonesty to bed for the final time.[22]

Once again, it looks as if sincerity and a certain kind of 'plain-speaking' – a language that veers straightforwardly into simple profanity – are intimately linked in political English. Andrew Rawnsley describes how Campbell addressed his first lobby briefing with journalists in the Blair administration of 1997 with the words 'Explain to me just why I should waste my time with a load of wankers like you'.[23] Tucker speaks the opening words of Armando Ianucci's film *In the Loop*, and they resemble extremely closely those spoken by Campbell in that exchange. Tucker walks into 10 Downing Street, muttering 'Good morning, my little chicks and cocks' to no one in particular. Indoors, passing a colleague, he makes small talk by asking how his football team played at the weekend, and the pleasant and sociable response is met with a dismissive and not so very *sotto voce* 'wanker' from Tucker.

The film proper begins with Tucker listening to a tape of Simon Foster (played by Tom Hollander), a government minister. Foster has stated,

---

[20] Peter Capaldi, the actor who played the role of Malcolm Tucker, has noted that if he forgot his lines at any time, he just inserted some more swearing until he remembered them. See the report and interview, available at: http://www.dailyrecord.co.uk/entertainment/celebrity/thick-star-peter-capaldi-people-1039750

[21] See Alastair Campbell, 'Was I offended by this brutal spinmeister? No. I was bored', *The Guardian*, 24 March 2009, available at: https://www.theguardian.com/commentisfree/2009/mar/24/in-the-loop-alastair-campbell

[22] Alastair Campbell, 'Now Chilcot says it too: We did not "sex up" intelligence in the WMD dossier', *The Guardian*, 6 July 2016, available at: https://www.theguardian.com/commentisfree/2016/jul/06/chilcot-we-did-not-sex-up-wmd-dossier

[23] Andrew Rawnsley, 'When the spinning had to stop', *Observer*, 18 June 2000, available at: https://www.theguardian.com/politics/2000/jun/18/labour.tonyblair

in a radio interview with the real-life broadcaster Eddie Mair, that as far as the UK government is concerned, 'war is unforeseeable'. At this point, Tucker immediately flies off the handle and sets out to roast Foster. On the way, he calls a newspaper, advising them not to run the story of Foster's statement that 'war is unforeseeable'. At this point, the status of truth and lies is raised, and it will become a central element in the film's narrative. It is clear that the editor on the other end of Tucker's phone plans to run the story and equally clear that he rests its validity on the simple empirical fact that Foster said what he said, and what everyone heard. Tucker, however, is having none of this: 'You might have heard him say that but he did not say it. And that's a fact', and he follows this by threatening to expose some sexual peccadillo committed by the editor at a recent political event.

The truth of fact becomes subject to an entirely different set or prerogatives. This is not quite the realm of 'alternative facts', but it is certainly a claim that 'facts' are subject to the contexts in which they are spoken and described. Facts become contingent upon their contexts, and their very essence is thus opened to manipulation by the deft use of language to change the frame of those contexts. When the frame in question is explicitly related to taboo matters – such as illicit sexual infidelity – then the entire context is shaped by profanity and obscenity. The sanctity of factual reality as the ground for truth becomes simply the terrain on which linguistic play – whose extreme form is the development and extension of profane metaphor – can be built. That is to say, the description of the world becomes a platform for a play in language, almost a form of perverse poetry.

Tucker, in fact, is like a modern manifestation of what classical English Literature once identified as the 'metaphysical poets'. These poets flourished in the seventeenth century, with extravagant displays of wordplay, wild and extended metaphor, and unlikely – even perverse – images and presentations. When Samuel Johnson wrote his biography of Abraham Cowley in 1777, he noted Cowley's association with several other seventeenth-century writers who seemed to share many characteristic poetic tropes. These – 'metaphysicals' – revelled in 'a combination of dissimilar images, or discovery of occult resemblances in things apparently unlike'. They were poets who, for Johnson, never achieved anything of the sublime, but what they lacked there was that 'they endeavoured to supply by hyperbole; their amplification had no limits; they left not only reason but fancy behind them; and produced combinations of confused magnificence, that not only could not be credited, but could not be imagined'.[24]

For the somewhat austere Samuel Johnson, this was not something to be celebrated, because Johnson began from the premise that 'the basis of all excellence is truth'.[25] Johnson did not especially value the novelty of this new poetic language because he thought that it deviated too far from nature and from the natural as such. The 'unnatural' condition of their extended metaphors, or 'conceits', led them to produce thoughts that are 'not obvious but neither are they just', and in this they veer towards what Johnson explicitly calls a kind of perversity.[26]

In all of this, Johnson was extending further the criticism of the metaphysical poets made initially by John Dryden, the first official English Poet Laureate. Dryden's complaint about these poets was that their outlandish metaphors 'perplex the minds of the fair sex with nice speculations of philosophy'. In short, the problem for both Dryden and Johnson was that the poets eschewed 'telling it like it is', thereby losing touch with feelings (especially with feelings of love), preferring instead to revel in the play of language for its own sake. That play, in which they deliberately extended metaphors to a point where they broke with any link to empirical realities, was one that drove them from the material conditions of life. Although they concentrated their criticism on matters of love poetry, Dryden and Johnson could easily have been saying the same thing about politics, and the divergence of language-games from empirical contact with real readers.

Dryden's position as Poet Laureate was a position of political significance. Indeed, while it remains so in our time, it is true to say that in Dryden's case, this was a matter of some greater substance. His religious conversion, to Roman Catholicism, precluded him from taking the Oath of Allegiance under the Protestant William III, and this led to his dismissal from the office in 1689. That religious belief was intimately tied to a political position, and Dryden found himself at odds with the prevailing orthodoxy. Having been a key insider, he now stood 'outside the temple', as it were: profane and no longer of the elect or elite. In fact his own poetry had often verged on profanity itself, in its satires and lampoons of fellow poets. One major example is 'MacFlecknoe', his satire

---

[24] Samuel Johnson, *Lives of the Poets*, vol. 1 (Oxford University Press, 1968), 14–15.
[25] Johnson, *Lives of the Poets*, 4.
[26] Ibid., 5.

on Thomas Shadwell, the 'True Blue Protestant Poet', on whom he lavishes fake praise, 'celebrating' Shadwell as one 'confirm'd in full stupidity', who 'never deviates into sense'. On the occasion in the poem when Shadwell is to be crowned as the 'emperor of dunces', Dryden tells us that 'From dusty shops neglected authors come, / Martyrs of pies, and reliques of the Bum'.[27] Those lines indicate that the poetry of Shadwell and his admirers should be used as toilet paper (relics of the bum), or for lining the trays on which pies are baked (martyrs of pies).

Malcolm Tucker would appreciate this satire, though he would find it mild. He would also enjoy the metaphysical conceit, the extended metaphor that takes him further and further into profanity, perversity and obscenity. He starts from a simple simile: 'Don't try to be funny. You're about as funny as a blind toddler in a fucking minefield.' He moves on to think of the human body in a manner that distantly recalls Nazism: 'I'll sell off your fucking flayed skin as a sleeping bag'. He personalizes the insult: 'I'm listening. I'm fucking all ears. I'm fucking Andrew Marr here.' In this, he takes a cliché ('I'm all ears') and enlivens it or quickens its pulse by the gratuitous reference to the real-life Andrew Marr (a political TV presenter and interviewer who does have protruding ears). He heads for violence: 'You get sarcastic with me again, and I'll stuff so much cotton wool down your throat it'll come out your arse like the wee tail of a playboy bunny.' He mocks the youth of a US intern: 'His briefing notes were written in alphabetti-spaghetti, and when I left him I nearly fell over his fucking umbilical cord.' He goes for hyperbole: 'Are you sure you're working as hard as me, because I'm sweating spinal fluid here. I'm a fucking husk.'[28]

The comedy in the case of Tucker derives from the fact that his language spirals further and further from reality, as if the language itself determines how far he can go in extending an unlikely metaphor. Often, the extension takes him not just into the realm of the implausible but into the realm of that which usually goes unsaid: the unspeakable, which, in turn, becomes the profane and the taboo. We have become somewhat used to political profanity in recent times, and, indeed, it is this that, for many, dramatizes an alleged decay in political rhetoric. Yet, as we have seen above, a moment's research will show that this is far from the case: profanity and bad-mouthing have been with us in politics for a long time.

---

[27]John Dryden, 'MacFlecknoe', in *The Poems and Fables of John Dtyden*, ed. James Kinsley (Oxford University Press, 1970), 240.
[28]All of these examples are taken from Ianucci's film, *In the Loop*.

It is noteworthy that, as with Tucker, a good deal of rhetorical profanity in politics turns to issues of the body. The examples above from Berlusconi, Boris Johnson, Trump and others make that clear. More importantly, the rhetoric turns on revealing the parts of the body that are usually unseen, and the insults and taunts revert to matters dealing with defecation or genital functions (and alleged dysfunctions). The point of this is not to 'humanize' an opponent but rather to stigmatize her or him, to suggest that their slick appearance is all for show and that, underneath, they are dirty, untrustworthy and (in some cases) of the devil's party. The profanity plays on titillation, on the undermining of piety and on the revelation of 'truth' about the body of the opponent: a truth that is undeniable because it is utterly material, even if usually covered and hidden from view. It should perhaps not have been so shocking, after all, that Donald Trump and Marco Rubio traded taunts about the size of Trump's penis.

There can be no doubt that the tradition of political *insult* can be hugely entertaining and amusing, but in most cases, as with Malcolm Tucker, the comedy arises from the unreality of the descriptions. The substantive question is how serious such profanity and obscenities become in political discourse, and, even more fundamentally, how they affect political activity. Specifically, the question is one that invites us to consider language and its relation to tribalism, and to what I might call the empathy of the profane. What this means, put very simply, is that we should consider how it is that political 'insiders' deploy profanity to establish a supposed affinity with the 'outsiders' as a tactic in claiming that their elitist views are actually a proper reflection of the non-elect, those who consider themselves to be 'ordinary people', those 'outside'.

Nigel Farage laid bare what underlies this in his reaction to the victory of those who had campaigned to exclude the UK from the European Union. He stated then that this was 'a victory for real people, a victory for ordinary people, a victory for decent people'. At that same moment, Farage's friend and political associate, Crispin Odey, a financial investor and Brexit supporter worth over £400 million (or member of the same political and linguistic tribe), was making £220 million from betting on the currency markets.[29] It is unclear how Farage might reconcile his claims about 'ordinary people' winning in the light of this.

---

[29]Shipman, *All Out War*, 433, 441.

More recently, the prominent far-right Conservative MP, Jacob Rees-Mogg, has attacked former Conservative Prime Minister, John Major, in the wake of Major's speeches arguing against Brexit. According to Jacob Rees-Mogg, John Major is part of the European elite, and, clearly, in saying this, Rees-Mogg is demarcating tribal allegiances and affiliations, in which he is contrasting himself with Major's 'elitist' tribe. John Major grew up poor in two rented rooms in Brixton, the son of a trapeze artist and music-hall entertainer who eventually made a living for the Major family by selling garden gnomes. Major left his state school at sixteen, with three 'O'-level qualifications, and worked as a clerk before gaining qualifications in banking through studies at night school, spending some time unemployed. Jacob Rees-Mogg is the son of a former editor of *The Times* newspaper and was brought up in a country estate with an extravagantly large house and some 250 acres of land. He went to private education in Eton College before going to Oxford University, and he has amassed a personal fortune estimated to reach over £100 million.[30] Major: elite? Rees-Mogg: anti-Establishment? The fundamental point here is that 'elite' has now become a term of abuse, a term that is less spoken and more 'spat out'. The so-called elite have become the new profane, as it were, and populism wants not just to kick the elites out of the temple but also to expel anything formerly associated with elitism: culture, knowledge, curiosity, reason, education, concern for the public general good.

In the two cases here: Farage's 'ordinary people' against Crispin Odey; Rees-Mogg against the obviously caricatured 'elitist' John Major, we find a very peculiar situation. It is this populist and anti-democratic alignment of the actual elites – the tribe of Rees-Mogg, Odey, Farage – with the 'profane' outsider or 'ordinary people' that needs exploration now. As we will see, the answer returns us to the specifics of English itself but with the establishment of a profound intimacy between English-as-such and politics-as-such. The result is that 'English' will be seen to be political through and through.

---

[30]See Nesrine Malik, '"Elite" is now a meaning less insult that's used to silence criticism', available at: https://www.theguardian.com/commentisfree/2018/mar/07/liberal-elite-populism-brexit-elitist (accessed 12 March 2018).

7 REMNANTS OF DISSENT: FREE SPEECH, POLITICAL SILENCE AND GUILT

Most political democracies have, as one of the key cornerstones that sustain the polity, a commitment to the principles of free speech. In this closing chapter, I want to consider a little what this might mean in material fact when considered under the rubric of a politicized English. There are numerous questions that lurk underneath the cliché regarding our valuing of free speech. For a simple example, what is the meaning of the adjective 'free' here? Does it refer to the speech itself, or to the speaker? In most usages, there is a curious slippage between the two, to the point where it is as if qualifying speech as 'free' is exactly the same as granting freedom, political and otherwise, to a citizen. If any and all speeches are 'free', then how come some are more legitimate than others, in that they gain a readier audience while other speeches go more or less unheard and unattended to? Are some of these 'free speeches' more valued or more valuable than others, and if so, is the 'free' in question related to an *economy* that essentially gives a value – and, in some cases, a price – to some speeches? What is the cost of a 'free' speech? What is the 'price' of citizenship in a polity?

This is of increasing importance in a contemporary climate in which a growing culture of intolerance veers towards the political silencing of dissent, and where the political far right deploy the liberal priorities of free speech in order to preach what Viktor Orbán in Hungary has characterized as a mode of 'illiberal democracy'. In the speech where Orbán first gave details of what he meant by this, he noted in passing that the very mention of such a thing would be 'categorised as blasphemy by the liberal world'. As 'blasphemy' is, literally, 'profane talk', he was thus embracing what I described earlier as a kind of literal profanity.¹ The far-right politics of one such as Orbán perverts the fundamentals of democratic liberalism, but it does so by using the very tools that gird the structures of that democratic liberalism in the first place. In the extremes to which this sometimes goes, the first result is the silencing of dissent (often via terror and fear-mongering), but the second is worse, for it silences by murder as in the case of many political assassinations worldwide, but also in the everyday situations in which, for example, a serving British MP, Jo Cox, can be shot and stabbed to death in the street by Thomas Mair, a far-right activist.

The questions over the meaning of free speech, especially in an age of growing intolerance, are basic for any polity that would be democratic. Some individuals, within democracies as much as within tyrannies or authoritarian States, discover the real price of speaking out: like Jo Cox, they are sometimes killed. The price of their free speech was their life itself. After the Marjory Stoneman Douglas high school shooting on 14 February 2018 in the United States, the National Rifle Association – predictably – argued their usual case that the only thing that stops a bad guy with a gun is a good guy with a gun. Leave aside for the moment the simple fact that what this really means is that, as far as the NRA is concerned, it is better to sell two guns than to sell just one, thus further boosting the market in guns. Let us concentrate instead on the expressly *political* rhetoric of the NRA.

The NRA equates the Second Amendment, in their construal of it, to be a fundamental principle of American freedom. It constitutes a single part of the identity of America and of its citizens, according to

---

¹See Viktor Orbán, 'Speech at the 25th Bálványos Summer Free University and Student Camp', 26 July 2014, available at: http://www.kormany.hu/en/the-prime-minister/the-prime-minister-s-speeches/prime-minister-viktor-orban-s-speech-at-the-25th-balvanyos-summer-free-university-and-student-camp (accessed 14 March 2018). Two things are worth noting here: (1) Orbán does not use the term 'illiberal democracy', but rather describes what he calls the desirability of 'the illiberal state' which, though illiberal or non-liberal, remains a democracy; (2) the entire speech is based on a fundamentalist view of the nation state as the fount of all values and policy. In respect of this latter, Orbán consistently stresses his claim that Hungary and Europe are 'Christian', and that this is under a supposed threat from Islam. He might be well advised to consider that Islam gave Europe much of what now passes for contemporary culture and civilization, including maths, science, medicine, philosophy and art.

NRA propaganda, and it thus becomes a key means of expressing that identity. To carry a gun is a fundamental mode of self-expression as 'an American' according to this: it is a fundamental characteristic of identity. When he was campaigning for election to the US Senate, Judge Roy Moore pulled a gun from his pocket on stage and waved it around, to show his commitment to the Second Amendment, as part of his claims for legitimacy as the Republican candidate. This goes along with his ritual arriving at polling stations on horseback, wearing a cowboy-style Stetson: all contribute to his political identity and seek tribal affiliation to it from his audience.[2]

Further, and following logically from their specific constructions and cultural associations, the NRA defend the Second Amendment as something that is akin to the First Amendment and almost umbilically connected to it. Both these freedoms – the freedom of speech and the freedom to bear arms – are of a piece to the NRA and their members or supporters. After the shooting at Marjory Stoneman Douglas, Donald Trump stalled over any substantial move towards proper gun control. Students then pointed out that it is thus a simple matter of doing the maths to find what Trump – a man whose value system seems to be encoded by markets – regards as the price of a school student's life. Simply divide the sum of up to $30 million that the NRA donated to Trump in his campaign by the number of school students killed by guns since his campaign started, and you'll get the price of each life that was eradicated in the 'defence' of the Second Amendment and its freedom of self-expression. In a politics that has been financialized in this way, with an intimacy, and even an identity, between government and commercial business – and the United States is not really unusual in this regard – 'free' speech can be marketed and, indeed, is very readily marketed and financialized.

In what follows, I want to explore the consequences of this, and also to consider the political importance of 'speaking out' or 'speaking truth to power': that is, I'll examine the actual relation between First and Second Amendments in practice. But I also want to explore the question of political silence, including the silence that is sometimes the result of the political intolerance of free speech. A useful way to do this is to consider the conditions governing free speech when it is under threat, as

---

[2]See, for example, report at: http://abcnews.go.com/Politics/video/ala-senate-candidate-pulls-gun-campaign-rally-50097240 (accessed 14 March 2018).

it was during the twelve years of Nazi rule in Germany, 1933–45. Perhaps surprisingly, it is the institution of the university – and the correlate of free speech, academic freedom – that becomes central to this, as I will show here.

* * *

When the American military forces arrived in Heidelberg at the end of the war in 1945, they composed a 'White List' of individuals who, they believed, had demonstrated enough personal and political integrity over the preceding twelve years to occupy, now, some key leadership positions for the rehabilitation of a post-Nazi Germany. One name on the White List was that of Karl Jaspers, who – along with his Jewish wife, Gertrud – had remained in Germany and had nonetheless survived the years of Nazi rule.

Those years had been neither easy nor straightforward, of course. First, Jaspers had watched in horror as his former friend, Martin Heidegger, became Rector of Freiburg University in 1933 and promptly denounced 'the much lauded "academic freedom"' calling it a principle that would henceforth be 'expelled from the German university'. This was the very freedom that had been the cornerstone of Jaspers's 1923 text, *Die Idee der Universität*, where he wrote that the university 'derives its autonomy – respected even by the state – from an imperishable idea of supranational, world-wide character: academic freedom'. Such freedom 'is a privilege which entails the obligation to teach truth, in defiance of anyone outside or inside the university who wishes to curtail it'.[3]

Then, on 26 January 1937, the Nazi authorities had passed the 'German Law Concerning Civil Servants' (*Deutsches Beamtengesetz*), known colloquially as the Civil Service Act. This Act extended the requirements of the 1933 'Law on the Restoration of the Professional Civil Service', which had barred 'non-Aryans' from employment in the civil service. Now, in 1937, the new requirement added that not only civil servants themselves but also their spouses had to be 'citizens' with the status of

---

[3] See Martin Heidegger, 'Self-assertion of the German University', available at: http://la.utexas.edu/users/hcleaver/330T/350kPEEHeideggerSelf-Assertion.pdf and also at: https://archive.org/details/MartinHeidegger-TheSelfAssertionOfTheGermanUniversity1933 (accessed 21 August 2018); Karl Jaspers, *The Idea of the University*, ed. Karl W. Deutsch, with Preface by O.L. Zangwill; trans. H.A.T. Reiche and H.F. Vanderschmidt (Peter Owen, 1960), 19.

Reichsbürger if they were to retain their position.[4] While Gertrud Jaspers might be a 'subject' or *Staatsbürger*, she could not, as a Jew, become a citizen. The enforcement of this law, carried out under the aegis of Ernst Krieck as Rector of Heidelberg, became instrumental as a pretext under which Karl Jaspers would be forcibly 'retired' from his position in the University of Heidelberg. Finally in this cumulative weakening of Jaspers's position, he would also be barred from all forms of publication in Germany, with effect from 1938.

Thus it was that Jaspers was officially, formally, and effectively silenced at the hands of the Nazi state. His silencing might have been legal (that is, in accordance with the law of the Nazi state) but it was hardly legitimate (that is to say, it was not justifiable in the transcendent terms governing academic or, indeed, any other freedom).[5] This silence, however, has a complicated status, even beyond the fundamental philosophical question regarding the conflict between what is legal and what is legitimate. The silence is politically enforced and thus constitutes an oppression of Jaspers's freedom to speak and to associate with both his fellow intellectuals and with the general public.[6] Simultaneously, however, it may also have been something that was, no doubt incidentally and serendipitously, instrumental in keeping him alive through the twelve years. After all, those who spoke out against the regime and who dissented openly were not safe.

The troubling question that follows is this: Did the silence – or the simple fact that Jaspers accepted the imposition of such silence without dissenting from it openly, assertively and loudly – constitute any form of tacit complicity with the regime? Did the failure openly to dissent place him in a position where he was at least tacitly complicit with the regime's actions, and thus partly implicated in the atrocities that the

---

[4]See, for example, Maria Georgiadou, *Constanti Carathéodory: Mathematics and Politics in Turbulent Times* (Springer-Verlag, Berlin, Heidelberg, New York, 2004), 341, for the effect of this on university academics.

[5]One outcome emerging from the Nuremberg Trials after the war was the ratification of the principle that national laws could be subservient to international law, especially in relation to laws concerning human rights. See Philippe Sands, *East West Street* (Weidenfeld & Nicolson, 2016), for an outstanding account of the legal history around this.

[6]Jaspers saw freedom of association as a fundamental condition for the establishing of academic freedom. He writes, 'In order to do the work of the university successfully, there must be communication of thinking men. Scholars must communicate with one another, teachers with their students, and the students among themselves. ... Here is the living core of university life,' *Idea*, 51.

regime committed? Does there exist a position of respectable *neutrality* in a silence that hovers between complicity and dissent, or is the division between dissent and political complicity with terror absolute? Under what conditions is silence – willing or enforced – itself a mode of political speech?

This question clearly haunted Jaspers. In 1946, on his return to full legal rehabilitation, he republished *Die Idee der Universität*, and spoke (alongside Julien Benda and other celebrated figures) on 'the spirit of Europe' at the inaugural *Rencontre International de Genève*, where he pondered the question of the relations between the intellectual and the polity, the function of the intellectual in relation to politics.[7] Most significantly for this present argument, he also gave a series of lectures in Heidelberg, to be published as *Die Schuldfrage*. With help from his former student, Hannah Arendt, the text appeared in English via New York's Dial Press in 1947 as *The Question of German Guilt*. Right at the start of this text, he addresses directly the question and status of politicized silence.

Initially, Jaspers considers the question of silence under the ostensibly neutral terms of the kind of academic freedom that he had placed at the centre of his idea of the University. What, he asks, does political power want? Does it want 'free research, a region free from its immediate influence', or would it prefer to control and delimit the bounds of thought and research – ideologically to determine results in advance and skew 'research' to ensure the production of such results, results that would serve the primary purpose of endorsing existing political power? 'Before 1933 we had permission to think and talk freely, and now we have it again,' he writes. This renewal is clearly a positive.

We should note that it raises an issue that is pressing again in our own time: to what extent should research be conditioned and determined by governments, and, by extension, to what extent should the freedom to present research results be conditioned by the money that sits behind governmental power? These are questions about the relation of government to knowledge and about the ways in which the communication of knowledge – via teaching and persuasion of various rhetorical kinds – ought to avoid being indebted to the commercial

---

[7]For more detail on the context of this return to public life – and its relation to the University as institution – see the introductory chapter of my study, *The New Treason of the Intellectuals* (Manchester University Press, 2018).

concerns associated with the exploitation of that knowledge. We will consider this more fully in the pages that follow.

Meanwhile, in 1946, it does not follow for Jaspers that talk should be or even could be completely unconstrained, given his open acknowledgement that 'all thought and research depend on the political situation' and that 'talking about all things as we like and please is license, anyhow'. Speaking out, even now in 1946's opening of a period of catharsis, requires what he calls 'political tact' that will circumscribe what we can and should say or discuss. As he puts it, 'Though it may be painful and not an ideal situation, political tact may at times exact silence on certain questions and facts everywhere in the world, in the interest of the most propitious solution.'[8] This is a position akin to that which, as I pointed out at the opening of my previous chapter, is well encapsulated in Timothy Garton Ash's observation that 'a right to say it does not mean that it is right to say it.'[9] Within political English, how does a silence such as this operate? How do we evaluate 'free speech' in this kind of zero condition?

There is available to us, however, a re-configuration of Timothy Garton Ash's proposition, one that proposes a different inflection. His formulation implicitly raises the unstated question of when it is right to say it: 'under what conditions is it *incumbent* on an individual to exercise the right to free speech, in order to defend freedom of speech and of assembly?' Does a political English find its proper realization only when it is spoken aloud, or are there circumstances in which the silence will be more politically effective?

Jaspers's statement suggests that his silence during the twelve years should be construed not as complicity – that is, not as constituting assent to the regime and the atrocities it was committing and about which he knew – but instead as a matter of 'political tact'. That stance not only excuses the silence but also removes it from the realms of neutrality and instead positively weaponizes it: it is as if silence is to be construed as a deliberate political tactic that was instrumental in seeking 'the most propitious solution' to the predicament of living with and alongside

---

[8] Karl Jaspers, *The Question of German Guilt* (1947; trans. E.B. Ashton; Capricorn Books, 1961), 9.

[9] Ash, *Free Speech*, 79. We might add here that Milton makes a similar distinction in his sonnet 'I did but prompt the age to quit their cloggs', where he makes his celebrated distinction between 'licence and libertie', the latter being engaged to truth while the former, if it is indulged, leads to 'waste of wealth and loss of blood'. See John Milton, *Poems*, ed. B.A. Wright (J.M. Dent, 1976), 80.

Nazism and – purely by the fact of living with it and surviving it – thus finding oneself potentially complicit in atrocity.

Further, Jaspers here also implies that talk itself is somehow cheap, that it constitutes license instead of liberty when it becomes talk about 'all things' and when it is essentially self-indulgent, or as he puts it, 'talking about all things as we like and please'. Political tact actually *requires* silence in some situations, if the best political goal – that of liberty from tyrannical authoritarianism – is to be achieved. This latter observation raises a further issue regarding 'the economics of free speech'. Crudely put, does 'free' speech actually have a price?

Shakespeare had considered this, in *Hamlet*. When the Ghost first appears, it maintains a silence, despite Horatio's repeated pleading with it to speak. When Hamlet hears of the Ghost's presence, he bids Horatio and Marcellus to 'Let it be tenable in your silence still', to 'Give it an understanding, but no tongue'. Then, the following night, when Hamlet himself meets with the Ghost, he notes that 'It will not speak'. The Ghost would address Hamlet alone, and Hamlet withdraws to a sequestered and secret spot with the Ghost to hear what might be said, as if in some clandestine or underground political meeting – which is what this meeting actually is, given that it prompts a regicide.

Hamlet knows that this speech and hearing may cost him dear, but argues, 'what should be the fear? / I do not set my life at a pin's fee'. As the Ghost also knows, freely speaking out – in the political rottenness that constitutes the regime in the state of Denmark – will entail a price, and that price is a matter of life and death. Having heard what the Ghost reveals about the political atrocity of his murder, Hamlet then immediately demands a tactful silence from his colleagues, Horatio and Marcellus, making them swear to 'Never make known what you have seen tonight'. Silence here is a deliberate political counsel. It also enters into an economy of speech or political expression: speech withheld, or 'saved up', is eventually repaid by the explosion of self-expression in the expense and expenditure of physical violence.

This is not how we usually view such matters. Dissent – especially dissent from the norms and rules of a political regime – is usually evidenced not by silence but by the very positive act of speaking out, loudly, bravely, defiantly and heroically in an assertion of the expressly political values of free speech and of critique. The eloquent David faces down the Goliath of political power and violence, as it were. Dissent is not usually tacit but characterized by what the cliché calls 'speaking truth to power'. Dissent thus sides with the explicit statement of truth and is set up in (literally) *explicit* opposition to a raw and brutal power which, by implication, finds its basis in lies and in the coercive demand for complicity in lies among those over whom crude power is exercised.

Dissent questions the legality of power by asserting the legitimacy of truth-telling – and doing so aloud. In this, we might say that 'dissent' is the expression of reason against power. This is not the political conversion of word into deed; rather it is the expression of word *against* deed in a very fundamental sense. It pits the intellectual against the politician. That is not a simple opposition, however: it simply is an acknowledgement that the intellectual (or, in exemplary form, the academic) is answerable to a different structural regime of power from that which is enjoyed by the politician. The intellectual's primary relation is to legitimacy and not to legality. In turn, this is a fundamental definition of the operation of academic freedom.

We should recall here that it is academic freedom that Heidegger would expel from the German University under Nazism, and we should also note the contemporary recurrence of this motif. The clearest example of that recurrence is perhaps to be found in Hungary, where Viktor Orbán's government has exercised repressive force over the operations of the Central European University. The assault against the Central European University has two relevant key elements here. Firstly, Orbán's self-described 'illiberal democracy' has little time for dissent, responding to criticism either by direct or legislative violence, such as the jailing of critics and opponents (a tactic widely used elsewhere by far-right politicians, such as Erdoğan in Turkey). Secondly, it is important that the Central European University is largely funded by George Soros, who is Jewish; and, when Orbán attempts to justify his use of force against the University, his language suavely deploys classic anti-Semitic tropes.

It is not so much that we are reliving the political times of the 1930s and witnessing a revival of Nazism in all this; the question is whether we have ever really escaped from it and moved on at all. The Anglophone world – and its university institution – is not immune from this.

Academic freedom is not entirely identical with free speech but is intimately related to it. Further, it follows from the definition I have just offered that the exercise of academic freedom is intrinsically a political expression, an expression of a thought that has a purchase, however directly or indirectly, upon a polity. In 1988, Kenneth Baker's 'Education Reform Act' proposed, among other things, the formal abolition of academic tenure. This step constitutes a move that intrinsically jeopardizes the academic's security and places it at risk. To counter this, the Act rehearsed a support for academic freedom. In Section 202 (2) (a) of the Act, we find the determination that 'academic staff have freedom within the law to question and test received wisdom, and to put forward new ideas and controversial or unpopular opinions, without placing themselves in jeopardy of losing their jobs or privileges they may have at their institutions'.[10]

This wording explicitly contravenes the principles of academic freedom enshrined in the UNESCO declaration of November 1997 (section VI, A, 27), which states that

> Higher-education teaching personnel are entitled to the maintaining of academic freedom, that is to say, the right, without constriction by prescribed doctrine, to freedom of teaching and discussion, freedom in carrying out research and disseminating and publishing the results thereof, freedom to express freely their opinion about the institution or system in which they work, freedom from institutional censorship and freedom to participate in professional or representative academic bodies. All higher-education teaching personnel should have the right to fulfil their functions without discrimination of any kind and without fear of repression by the state or any other source.[11]

The difference is clear: the UK's definition of academic freedom is not only restrictive and constraining, but it is also explicitly politicized in the 1988 Act. The key is the insertion of the phrase 'within the law', set against UNESCO's open phrasing 'without constriction by prescribed doctrine' and 'without discrimination of any kind and without fear of repression by the state or any other source'. The Baker Act allows academic freedom to operate only under the sign of legal prescription, which structurally undermines the very function of the intellectual who exercises her or his freedom by calling existing legal prescription into question, and by placing thought and expression under the sign of legitimacy instead. The circumscription of academic freedom by its subjugation to the laws of

---

[10]See text of the relevant section of the Act, available at: http://www.legislation.gov.uk/ukpga/1988/40/section/202 (accessed 22 March 2018).

[11]See http://portal.unesco.org/en/ev.php-URL_ID=13144&URL_DO=DO_TOPIC&URL_SECTION=201.html (accessed 22 March 2018).

the state thus undermines the principle precisely at the moment when it claims to endorse it.

This is precisely the thing that Heidegger did when he 'expelled' the principle of academic freedom from the German institution. Nazi politics was explicit regarding this. There is a question now hovering over the UK's position on this, for it seems as if the 1988 Act tacitly expels the principle, through the politicization of expressions made under the rubric of 'research' or 'teaching'. In seemingly endorsing the academic freedom that involves speaking truth to power, the Baker Act actually silences precisely such speech. It 'seems' to endorse academic freedom, but, as Hamlet might say, 'Seems? I know not seems'. The wording of the Act produces a potential legalistic minefield and a clear predicament for anyone engaging in any research or teaching carried out in and through the medium of the English institution, including the institution as the home of 'English' as a specific discipline. The Act, in placing legitimacy in a position subservient to legality, serves not to encourage academic freedom at all. In fact, the quiet coercion involved in this linguistic slippage – legality trumping legitimacy – jeopardizes the academic who thinks and expresses herself according to what is legitimate, for the law now requires conformity with legal precepts as a condition of communication at all. What if the academic action of 'thinking legitimately' leads us to a position where we would question existing laws? In short, a government does not need to become as crude as the Nazis were to secure this kind of arrangement.

* * *

One recent thinker within English literary and cultural studies who was utterly explicit about the responsibility of the intellectual to dissent by speaking out was Edward Said. In his 1993 Reith Lectures, published as *Representations of the Intellectual*, Said describes the intellectual as being intrinsically charged with a special responsibility. The intellectual 'is an individual endowed with a faculty for representing, embodying, articulating a message, a view, an attitude, philosophy or opinion to, as well as for, a public'. The intellectual's function 'is publically to raise embarrassing questions, to confront orthodoxy and dogma (rather than to produce them) ... to be someone who cannot easily be co-opted by governments or corporations'. The intellectual must speak out on behalf of others who are silenced in various ways, to represent the forgotten.

It follows, for Said, that silence or, worse, being silenced is not an acceptable option, because 'There is no such thing as a private intellectual'.[12] Silence, by definition, implies holding things privately within the self, and being silenced implies being constrained thus to hold back that which could or should be spoken aloud.

According to this account, Jaspers stands in an awkward position. There was no doubt that Jews, Romani, homosexuals and others (including critical intellectuals) were being persecuted and then systematically murdered by a particular regime, such murder being the clearest expression of its politics. There was equally no doubt that these people were also being then 'forgotten' by many or most of the regimes of international politics. It is one thing not to raise arms, in violent deeds, against this, but is it not the case that the failure even to *speak* against this constitutes not just appeasement but, worse, complicit support for it? In considering this question under the general rubric of guilt, Jaspers invites the question of whether what we might call 'political silence' was a tactic governed primarily by ostensibly justifiable self-preservation (and ask yourself 'what would I have done?') or whether it contained, within its intrinsic nature, an indirect assent to – and thus complicity with – the regime whose guilt regarding deeds the silent philosopher or intellectual must inevitably share. If he salvages the respectability of such silence, can we go further and claim this kind of tactful reticence as itself a mode of dissent? Must it be the case that dissent should always speak out?

The Question of German Guilt answers this in a complicated, even convoluted fashion. Jaspers distinguishes four types of guilt: criminal, moral, political and metaphysical. At one extreme, criminal guilt belongs to those who directly committed crimes in the Nazi atrocities, and the Nuremberg courts will adjudicate, with all due propriety, on their crimes. At the other extreme lies metaphysical guilt, a guilt shared indiscriminately by everyone as a condition of our human existence as such, akin to what Cioran would call *L'Inconvénient d'être né*,[13] a guilt suggestive of theological notions of 'original sin'. Between these lies moral guilt, which arises from the responsibility that I have for all my deeds, even if I was 'just following orders', and so this still refers to actual

---

[12]Edward Said, *Representations of the Intellectual* (Vintage, 1994), 9.

[13]E.M. Cioran, *L'Inconvénient d'être né* (nrf, Gallimard, Paris, 1973). Cioran, who spent the years 1933–5 in Berlin, expressed sympathy not only with Hitler and the Nazi movement but also with totalitarian movements and with fascism elsewhere across Europe.

material acts. It is the category of 'political guilt' deriving from that fact that 'Everybody is co-responsible for the way he is governed' – that is, for the legitimacy of the regime under which we live – that becomes the most pressing guilt-question for Jaspers.[14]

This convoluted schema allows Jaspers to identify – and to limit or circumscribe – his own guilt. It also essentially exculpates him and his silence almost completely. He is neither criminally nor morally guilty (both of which involve active deeds) and thus cannot be charged with complicity in the atrocities. He is metaphysically guilty, but then so is everyone, German or not, Nazi or not – so this hardly counts as a distinguishing trait.

'Political guilt' is what pins him and his fellow Germans down, because they allowed Nazi power to rule the state. This is an odd guilt, for it fails to individualize, and holds an anonymous mass responsible for the politics of the state.[15] The schema permits Jaspers to acknowledge a guilt-without-complicity, in which 'political guilt' is certainly shared while he nonetheless avoids being complicit with the atrocities to which guilt can be ascribed. However, although ostensibly evading complicity, this does not yet fully elevate his silence-as-political-tact to the status of dissent.[16] Can such silence therefore be a mode of political language, a kind of 'political rhetoric in absentia', as it were? How might silence 'communicate' itself as an expressly political act, and one that has a clear ideological perspective and impetus?

The question remains and can be simply stated: Can silence within a totalitarian or authoritarian regime become a mode of dissent, or must it imply simple and uncomplicated unspoken complicity with the regime? Does an individual have a responsibility to speak out at all times, or can she or he reserve a right to silence without thereby inculpating themselves? To put this another way: if free speech is a constituent element of being a citizen in a democratic polity, does it follow that one must *always and*

---

[14]Jaspers, *Question*, 31.

[15]Hannah Arendt would find this unacceptable, because, as she insistently notes, guilt always individualizes. See, for example, *Responsibility and Judgment*, ed. Jerome Kohn (Schocken Books, New York, 2003), 21, 28–30 and especially 147–58.

[16]Interestingly, Oskar Gröning, known as the 'accountant of Auschwitz', invoked the sophistry of this schema (without reference to Jaspers) as recently as 2015, when he defended himself by acknowledging his moral guilt but denying criminal guilt over his activities in the war. I consider his case in detail in my *Complicity* (Rowman & Littlefield, New York and London, 2016).

everywhere be such a citizen? Can one exercise the right to free speech by withholding such speech? More forcefully put, can there be no private life, no realm of silence within which one might withdraw from the prescriptions and proscriptions of being a 'total citizen'? The status of silence here invites us to consider more carefully the fundamentals of language itself, especially in terms of 'self-expression', in relation to dissent and complicity. This is all the more important in the age of a confessional culture, which more or less demands total transparency as a cultural and personal norm and which ostensibly celebrates self-expression as a means of escaping from all kinds of unhealthy psychoanalytical repressions of the self.

* * *

Another intellectual who remained in Nazi Germany was Wilhelm Furtwängler, musician and conductor. Unlike Jaspers, Furtwängler was anything but silenced: the Nazis were only too happy to celebrate him and wanted to use his international prestige to give respectability to the regime. Furtwängler's refusal of taciturnity was not via the spoken word but via music. He employed Jewish musicians, refused to sign correspondence with the obligatory 'Heil Hitler', and did not give the Nazi salute. However, he did not openly speak out directly against Nazi rule: his 'dissent' was, essentially, a lack of assent.[17] His music, he claimed, was itself intrinsically a defiance of the regime: aesthetics transcending – and allegedly overcoming – politics and history. Music here operates as a radical and critical foreign language within the regime, a language that – Furtwängler claims – cannot be accommodated and domesticated by the Nazis.

In 1951, Furtwängler opened the newly re-inaugurated Bayreuth Festival by conducting Beethoven's Ninth Symphony. The programme choices here – both the Beethoven and Furtwängler as its conductor – were controversial. The Festival itself had been banned in 1945, fundamentally because of the association of Bayreuth with Wagner's

---

[17]In 1933, at the start of the regime, he did in fact write an article for the *Frankfurter Allgemeine Zeitung*, stating his opposition to discrimination between Jews and non-Jews. Goebbels replied to the article, linking the quality of art to the 'necessity' that it 'surges forth from the people', the *Volkstum* or 'will of the people'. See Audrey Roncigli, 'Wilhelm Furtwängler, une illusion face au nazisme', *Guerres mondiales et conflits contemporains*, 227 (juillet 2007), 75–93.

music, and the further association of both with the anti-Semitism of the Nazis. As was well known, Bayreuth was a key festival for Hitler himself. To reopen with Beethoven's Ninth – a symphony associated with an entirely different politics – was an important gesture, indicating the desire to re-found the German state, post-war, on an entirely different and renewed political footing. This was so, notwithstanding Wagner's own acknowledged indebtedness to Beethoven.

Why Furtwängler as conductor? Furtwängler's survival through the Nazi period had many causes, of course. One of them relates to his ideas regarding the political language of music. He was part of a tradition of musical interpretation that regarded music in rather pure aestheticist terms; and, in this respect, his critical mode runs parallel with the emerging modes of American New Criticism in literary study. The music cannot be paraphrased; it makes sense according to its own internal logic and structure or form. Consequently, the music cannot be 'translated' into a simple linguistic statement.

Ostensibly, therefore, this is seemingly a determination for political neutrality. However, as Neil Gregor points out, 'there was … a clear ideological script' lying behind this. 'The inherited values of musical idealism, with their positing of a canon of timelessly perfect musical works whose meanings were not contingent upon time or place, had at their centre the notion of an incontrovertibly superior Austro-German musical tradition, the veneration of which formed a centrepiece of German cultural nationalism.'[18] It is partly as a result of his critical stance here that Furtwängler managed to negotiate his way through the Nazi years. On the one hand, music speaks, and its message is clear; on the other hand, no one can articulate the message in terms other than those already expressed in the music itself. Furtwängler speaks without speaking out, as it were.

In *Taking Sides*, Ronald Harwood's 1995 play about Furtwängler and the post-war de-Nazification procedures, the character of Major Edward Arnold confronts Furtwängler with some of his recorded statements during the twelve years, including especially disparaging comments about Jewish people: 'Jewish musicians lack a genuine affinity with *our* music', or 'Jewish penpushers should be removed from the Jewish press.' Furtwängler replies that, simply in order to survive, he had, first of all,

---

[18]Neil Gregor, 'Beethoven, Bayreuth and the Origins of the Federal Republic of Germany', *The English Historical Review*, 126:521 (August 2011), 845.

to use the approved language of the Nazis whenever he was required to speak directly. When he said what he said about Jews, he indicates the necessity of what Jaspers would have called 'political tact': 'It depends on the circumstances, to whom one was speaking. ... I used their language, of course I did, everyone did.' He argues that the Nazis controlled the language, via control of the press, adding: 'They regarded any action of dissent, however small, as a criticism of the state, tantamount to high treason.' Such treason, for the Nazis, could be discerned in the failure to speak the approved lexicon.

Furtwängler's fundamental claim is that 'his' language, the language through which he essentially expressed his very subjectivity – the language of music, standing now opposed to the linguistic norms of the Nazi regime – is the one language to which he was essentially always faithful, and that it was in the expressions made in musical language that we find his real and basic dissent from the regime. 'I know that a single performance of a great masterpiece was a stronger and more vital negation of the spirit of Buchenwald and Auschwitz than words,' he says. 'Human beings are free wherever Wagner and Beethoven are played. Music transported them to regions where the torturers and murderers could do them no harm.' Music, here, operates with the same authority – and, crucially, legitimacy – as does the concept of academic freedom in the University for Jaspers: it transcends the bounds and bonds of nationality that are structured by a specific national language and the politically controlled norms – including the legal statutes – that such a national language establishes. It takes the listener and composer outside of a nation to regions elsewhere, and it appeals to that transcendent supra-national or international condition as the basis for its authority and autonomy.

This argument indicates that it is complicity with a *language* – and above all with a language that is a marker of national identity and thus a specifically *politicised language* – that establishes guilt and responsibility for the norms that the language articulates as 'truths'. Clearly, silence will complicate this. Spoken dissent is, perhaps rather fundamentally, an attempt to change a political condition by changing a language, with all that such an act of translation might entail.

What does 'complicity with a language' – and especially with a 'political language' – actually mean in practice? In simple terms, it means speaking in accordance with the norms that govern communication in that language. My insertion of 'norms' here indicates that the language is not merely a mode of communication but also a mode of 'communion' –

the making of identity – with others who share the norms and normative value-systems that pass as legitimate, even comprehensible, within that language. Further, such norms of communication constitute, at least tacitly, the grounds for establishing 'the truth' for the speakers of the language in question, and, in turn, that truth constitutes their shared identity.

The claim for identification among – and between – speakers is, in fact, the construction of a shared complicity in holding to the normative values in question. This is tantamount to saying that a language constitutes a nation, which is not hugely removed from Wittgenstein's observation that 'to imagine a language is to imagine a form of life'.[19] It is precisely what governs the speech by Viktor Orbán with which I opened this chapter. For him, questions about political globalization and the so-called global race miss the essence of contemporary politics: 'there is a more important race underway. … there is a race going on to develop a state that is capable of making a nation successful.'[20] Regardless of our political position regarding nationalism, there remain significant issues underlying this, relating to the morality or otherwise of both dissent and complicity.

From the foregoing, it seems clear that we usually consider two interlinked elements as being central to dissent: speaking out and truth. As I have already pointed out above, these two are intimately linked by Nietzsche, when he considered 'Truth and Lying in an Extra-Moral Sense' in 1873. For Nietzsche, what passes as 'true' is nothing more than a matter of linguistic convention and conformity with other speakers of a given language in a given language community. To put this much more crudely than Nietzsche might have intended, 'truth' is 'nationalized' as and when we consider 'the nation' to be identified with its dominant language or, indeed, whenever we identify the core of the intentional self with a specific national language.

Nietzsche was unsentimental about truth, and happy to confront the moral pieties usually surrounding it. Truth-telling presupposes a social existence, and that social existence depends on us regulating our intrinsic demand for individual superiority over others with the demands of peaceful coexistence. The truth, in these circumstances, is primarily simply a matter of linguistic convention and agreement. We agree on

---

[19]Wittgenstein, *Philosophical Investigations*, 8, §19.
[20]Orbán, 'Speech'.

'a binding designation' for things, and we pass over *in silence* anything that might disrupt the social condition of peaceful existence. In this way, we can merely simulate agreement without ever arriving at the kind of commitment to a norm that entails our complicity with it. This, in fact, is the essential element in international or any other political diplomacy. It depends upon dissimulation.[21]

There is, within this, a sophisticated version of silence, which consists in speaking without saying anything: speaking without speaking out. Seamus Heaney writes of it in his poem '*from* Whatever You Say Say Nothing', where he acknowledges the ways in which a divided community – in this case, in the north of Ireland – can survive. There are a series of codes that allow understandings to pass silently – including understandings that speakers are opposed to each other: 'I live here, I live here too, I sing, / Expertly civil-tongued with civil neighbours.' Crucially, both sides or tribes agree – and maintain peaceful coexistence – precisely by saying nothing, by a speech that, even though it makes extremely pointed statements – 'They're murderers' – reduces those statements to the level of 'what everyone says'. In doing so, the statements become truisms, even banal cliché, and this, in fact, shows the power of such a 'saying nothing', for it withstands the pressures exerted politically even by the most extreme situations, including that of sectarian murder. Heaney has an appropriate term for this kind of 'spoken silence': he calls it 'the famous / Northern reticence, the tight gag of place / and times'.

Such a 'reticence' is precisely what sustained Furtwängler or Jaspers. While Jaspers fell into political silence, Furtwängler found a mode of expression through the language of music which, he claimed, was foreign to and even opposed intrinsically to, the norms of the regime. While Hitler or Goebbels claimed to hear the expression of the national *Volkstum*, Furtwängler's case is that they misheard and misunderstood, because in conducting Beethoven's symphonies, Furtwängler was speaking a completely different language, imagining an entirely different form of life and thus inhabiting a different world entirely from that devastated by Hitler and the Nazis.

* * *

---

[21]Arendt argues convincingly that it is folly to expect politicians to tell the truth. See her essays on 'Lying in Politics', in *Crises of the Republic* (Penguin, 1972), and 'Truth and Politics' in *Between Past and Future* (Penguin, 2006).

We might usefully see the full force of such reticence by setting it against another literary example of saying nothing. This second example comes from Shakespeare, and it involves Cordelia in *King Lear* expressly speaking, and uttering aloud the very 'nothing' that throws Lear into a violence in which he confuses the personal with the political, a confusion that is integral to totalitarianism. In the opening scene, Lear demands speech from Cordelia: 'What can you say to draw / a third more opulent than your sisters? Speak'. Cordelia has already told the audience, in her very first words, spoken as an aside, that she will 'Love, and be silent'. Yet silence is precisely what she disavows when she is indeed directly called upon to speak in the scene, and, in expressly uttering the word 'nothing', in expressly *saying* 'nothing', she dissents from the entire national politics of the moment, and causes extreme social and political disarray. It is the fact of her speaking out – her outspokenness – that causes the problems for the state.

Goneril and Regan have both been complicit in Lear's political manoeuvring, going along with his game or regime, speaking his language, humouring and thus flattering him and assuring him of his political power even as they plan to claim that power themselves; Cordelia is here the dissenting voice. Her dissent is not dissent in the form of opposition to a position taken by power; it is dissent from the entire language-game that establishes that power in the first place. It provokes civil unrest, her exile to France and a civil war with extreme terrorist violence (such as Gloucester's blinding or the Fool's torture and hanging[22]).

Saying 'nothing' – as opposed to 'saying nothing' – is extraordinarily powerful. More, it provokes an explosion in historical action, replacing politics (and diplomacy, Churchill's famous 'jaw-jaw') with force and war. The real power of Cordelia's dissent is not figured in her opposition to Lear. That would be a very limited dissent, in that it would remain essentially complicit with the structures of power in the regime while simply undermining the individual who holds sway (and this is the position of Goneril and Regan, ostensibly faithful to Lear while determined to occupy his position). Rather, Cordelia, in *saying* 'Nothing', stands in opposition to the entire normative structure of power in the regime itself.

---

[22] There is, of course, a debate as to whether Lear's reference to his 'poor fool' being hanged is a reference to Cordelia herself. See, for example, Tom Clayton, 'And my poor fool is hanged', *Ben Jonson Journal*, 19:1 (2012), 142–5.

One useful way of thinking about this would be to identify Cordelia more firmly with the otherwise silent condition of women in a patriarchal and masculinist society. This makes her a particular example of a feminist impulse. The key point, though, is that her feminism becomes apparent precisely as a mode of dissenting from the predominant language-game of the English court, a language-game that sustains the very masculinist power against which her 'saying "nothing"' rebels. This might be usefully construed as an account of feminism as such, considered in terms of 'political English': it brings about a new way of speaking and, with that, a new mode of judging the legitimacy of political actions or deeds. Legitimacy questions legality: the very ambiguity of 'saying nothing' and 'saying "nothing"' enables a pause in deeds, and a pause into which a genuinely political activity enters.

In *Taking Sides*, Harwood shows Major Arnold cynically intent on 'proving' that Furtwängler was, essentially, a Nazi, on the grounds that his dissent was not explicit. Furtwängler's defence is clear: 'I am no better than anybody else,' he says. 'In staying here, I believed – I thought – I walked a tightrope between exile and the gallows. You seem to be blaming me for not having allowed myself to be hanged.' Behind this lies a specific view of the dissenter: dissent has to be proved always *in extremis*, through personal sacrifice. It is as if it is only in becoming thoroughly a victim oneself that one can prove the authenticity of one's dissent. Such a view is utterly 'purist', even puritanical, and at the same time utterly self-defeating. Yet, as in Harwood's dramatic setting of this predicament, Arnold will discredit Furtwängler's stance by accusing him of hypocrisy, on the simple grounds that he did *not* become a victim: on the grounds that he survived. Furtwängler's position is, like that of Jaspers, complex: 'I tried to defend the intellectual life of my people against an evil ideology. I did not directly oppose the Party because, I told myself, this was not my job. I would have benefited no one by active resistance.'[23]

It is, in our time, a measure of the homage that we pay to making dissent completely explicit that we more or less demand that it be a matter of life and death. It is as if we can acknowledge dissent only to the extent that the exercise of free speech jeopardizes the very life of the dissenting speaker. Such an attitude is part and parcel of an entire ideology that would subscribe to the view that it is the victim of injustice who is, *ipso*

---

[23]Roncigli, 'Wilhelm Furtwängler', cites this also, directly from the actual denazification examination.

facto, just, or that if one seeks authoritative legitimation for one's views, it is better to do so from the position of utter victimization, in the shadow of the gallows. That is a position that confuses the search for legitimacy with the search for legality.

In the different context of the immediate aftermath of 9/11, Jacqueline Rose argued rightly that 'The victims of injustice … are not always, automatically, just. The state of Israel, for example, was founded on the back of a horror perpetrated against the Jewish people which was for some the worst, for others the culmination of the injustices carried out against the Jewish people over centuries. This has not made the state of Israel just towards the Palestinians.'[24]

Paradoxically, the purist stance actually devalues dissent, even as it seems to attend to its seriousness. Dissent, as the voice of criticism, always takes a stand against any and all fundamentalist ideology or fundamentalist solidarities. Here, it is worth recalling Said's other great description of the critical attitude, when he wrote that 'I take criticism so seriously as to believe that, even in the very midst of a battle in which one is unmistakably on one side against another, there should be criticism, because there must be critical consciousness if there are to be issues, problems, values, even lives to be fought for'.[25]

When the purist demands that the dissenter pays for her or his stance with her or his very life, then the purist becomes herself or himself utterly complicit with fundamentalism as such, for she or he rests the legitimacy of their stance not upon argument and doubt (Said's 'critical consciousness' or legitimacy) but upon the absolute certainty of the gallows, whose physical and violent deployment is a matter to be dealt with under the rubric of the law. Importantly, such a law does not enjoy legitimacy in the slightest and, in its deprivation of free speech, perversely embodies illegality through its enactment of an illegitimate deed.

The Manichean purist disallows political discourse and debate and disallows the play of uncertainty in a 'respectable neutrality': it disallows 'music', we might say, with all its semantic utter ambiguities. Tribalism – with its partisan claims on localized 'legality' based on simplified and single identities – trumps democracy and legitimacy in this attitude. So,

---

[24] Jacqueline Rose, '9/11 roundtable', *London Review of Books*, 23:19 (4 October 2001), available at: https://www.lrb.co.uk/v23/n19/nine-eleven-writers/11-september

[25] Edward Said, *The World, the Text, the Critic* (Faber and Faber, 1984), 28.

our pressing issue now becomes the relation between the alert critical consciousness, usually realized through speaking out, and respectable neutrality, as in the political tact that engenders silence or abstention from taking a view. This is, essentially, a question of the political manipulations of language and of silence.

* * *

In his examination of the language of the Nazis, Victor Klemperer points to the Nazi refusal of both reticence and doubt, the refusal of any kind of neutrality. His description of this draws attention to the value of a specific punctuation mark: 'it was endlessly claimed by Hitler and others during the period that all progress was thanks to the intransigent, that all inhibitions stemmed from the supporters of the question mark.' Klemperer goes on to insert his own moment of doubt here but followed by a determination of certainty: 'This [regarding the question mark] is not necessarily true, but it is certainly the case that only the intransigent have blood on their hands.'[26] The clear and present danger is that, in our contemporary predicaments, dissent is being prevented by a Manichaean politics of polarization that has learned more or less directly from the 1930s, and that demands fealty, else one will be branded not as a critical opponent but as a 'traitor' or 'enemy of the people', to be dealt with not by debate but by the spilling of blood in an act of violence.

This neo-Nazi lexicon is precisely the language used, for example, by the right-wing UK mainstream press to describe people who oppose the UK's 'decision' to leave the European Union. *The Daily Mail*, one of the UK's most widely read newspapers, described High Court judges as 'Enemies of the People' when they observed existing legal propriety, ruling that the UK Parliament must have a say – must have a voice, must speak – in order to give legitimacy to the notification to the European Union that the UK government would invoke Article 50 of the Lisbon Treaty, stating an intention to withdraw. *The Telegraph*, a more seriously high-minded right-wing UK paper, branded Conservative MPs who sided with the Labour opposition in one debate as 'Brexit mutineers', displaying their photos as if they were criminals in some

---

[26]Victor Klemperer, *The Language of the Third Reich: LTI – Lingua Tertii Imperii* (1957; trans. Martin Brady; Athlone Press, 2000), 71.

rogue's gallery, following which numbers of these politicians received numerous death-threats.[27]

These rhetorical or linguistic tactics aim to reduce the possibilities of genuine dissent, by refusing to permit the existence of a ground where critical consciousness – thinking as such with its attendant doubts and moments of reticence – can be exercised. Similar polarizations are visible in the United States, where Donald Trump's infantilist lexicon reduces and narrows everything down to the most mean-spirited and anti-intellectual, anti-thinking attitudes possible.[28] In the US case, one can still speak out, of course, but, in the Trump regime, whatever one says is immediately translated into the personalist chants of the bully in the playground, thereby losing political authority, credibility or recognition. When what one can say and what can be heard is atrophied and reduced in scope, it will follow that there will eventually be no vocabulary left in which to criticize power at all. And that is a very different mode of silence from that which affected and afflicted Jaspers or Furtwängler, say.

In some circumstances, then, silence may appear to be awkward, but it becomes evidently the lesser of two evils. However, as Hannah Arendt points out, the pragmatism – and sometimes the complicity with a specific linguistic mode, masquerading as 'diplomacy' – that enjoins the adoption of the lesser of two evils is utterly flawed, politically. First, there is the simple fact that 'those who choose the lesser evil forget very quickly that they chose evil'. Having made their choice, they become committed to it – complicit in its norms – instead of retaining doubt and preserving the possibility of establishing the good – however deferred it may be – through tactful reticence. Indeed, the subscription to the pragmatism of the 'lesser of two evils' argument is even worse than this suggests, for it is structurally intimately linked to the very regime of power from whose 'worse' evil one is allegedly distancing oneself in adopting the lesser evil. To comfort oneself by stating that one adopts the lesser of two evils is to fall into a logic that is itself 'one of the mechanisms built into

---

[27]For the *Daily Mail*, see http://www.dailymail.co.uk/news/article-3903436/Enemies-people-Fury-touch-judges-defied-17-4m-Brexit-voters-trigger-constitutional-crisis.html; for the *Telegraph*, see http://www.telegraph.co.uk/news/2017/11/14/nearly-20-tory-mps-threaten-rebel-against-brexit-date-brutal/. On the death-threats to Anna Soubry MP, for example, see http://www.bbc.co.uk/news/uk-politics-42045175. Some of the threats added a hash-tag 'Jo Cox', referring to the Labour MP who was murdered by a fascist who shouted 'Britain First' as he stabbed and shot her.

[28]See Jacobson, *Pussy*, for a satire on Trump's infantile language.

the machinery of terror and criminality'. This is so because it helps to normalize evil as the only condition available, and the 'lesser of two evils' argument is 'consciously used in conditioning the government officials as well as the population at large to the acceptance of evil as such'.[29]

This is not just of historical interest. As my examples of the language of Brexit and of Trump show, the issues here are alive and pressing for us, today. Shall we remain silent? What is the price of speaking out?

In the context of the Nazi regime, the consequences of pragmatism were disastrous. Arendt is coruscating in her analysis. 'The extermination of the Jews', she writes, 'was preceded by a very gradual sequence of anti-Jewish measures'. Nazi tactics depended on incrementalism, a phenomenon that helped to normalize things and events that would not usually be considered as acceptable politically. As Arendt writes, each such anti-Jewish measure 'was accepted with the argument that refusal to cooperate would make things worse – until a stage was reached where nothing worse could possibly have happened'.[30] This, obviously, is the case *in extremis*. However, quite apart from its own intrinsic importance, we should note that it is a model for mundane and everyday politics, in which silence – a hesitation to dissent – becomes instrumental in not just permitting but also in virtually *requiring* complicity with a politics that we might want to reject but with which we find ourselves becoming compliant and complicit. This particular mode of silence – a silence co-opted as complicity, as opposed to reticence – is clearly troubling.

The attempt, then, to justify or excuse action – or a very specific mode of silence – on these grounds looks flawed both philosophically and morally. Complicity is assured for the regime through a structure in which those who wield power (often legally but illegitimately) do not directly force individuals into collaboration or compliance; rather, they reduce the number of options available and eliminate any possibility of dissent by a gradualist approach to change. Above all, however, the gradualist approach to change in question here is *linguistic*: it relates to the gradual shifting of semantics.

Silence is culpable when it is aligned with a political regime that exercises its power through these perverse manipulations of language

---

[29]Hannah Arendt, *Responsibility and Judgment* ed. Jerome Kohn (Schocken Books, New York, 2003), 34; 36.

[30]Ibid., 36–7. The actual historical mechanics of this are laid bare in Laurence Rees, *The Holocaust* (Penguin, 2017), passim.

and, most specifically, through a reduction or diminution of the political lexicon itself, and it is part of a political process that such changes happen sometimes imperceptibly because they are so gradualist. It is always in the face of the reduction of the possibilities of linguistic change that silence becomes not political reticence but complicity with illegitimate and illegal power. In the face of this, dissent requires instead the extension of our political vocabularies, and that extension may, on occasion, include the political tact of reticence.

There is, then, a profound difference between silent complicity and silent dissent. The silence that indicates complicity is one that actually contributes to the incremental power of an established regime by accepting its norms and its language; that which denotes dissent refuses to do this and seeks instead a new language. For Furtwängler, it was music; for Heaney, it was poetry; for Jaspers, it was academic freedom. At a much lesser level than in Nazi Germany or in Troubled Ireland, silent complicity (as opposed to silent dissent) undergirds all bureaucracies that exist in everyday consensual life. Indeed, bureaucracy is utterly dependent upon such silent complicity. Writ large, it operates in contemporary politics and societies as a mode of government.

Some of our contemporary societies, with their slow but deliberate movement towards the indulgence of intolerance, find their unstated source in Nazi Germany. Victor Klemperer's examination of *The Language of the Third Reich* gives us a sense of how a language shapes a polity, and how much of the politics of Nazi Germany depended upon manipulations of the language itself. The kind of incrementalism I mention here was central to this. 'Words can be like tiny doses of arsenic', writes Klemperer, explaining that 'they are swallowed unnoticed, appear to have no effect, and then after a little time the toxic reaction sets in after all'.[31] This was how Nazi politics normalized atrocity, by the repetition of 'single words, idioms and sentence structures' that were imposed on people 'in a million repetitions and taken on board mechanically and unconsciously'.[32] Indeed, as Klemperer notes in his diary entry for 28 July 1933, 'endless repetition indeed appears to be one of the principal stylistic features' of the language and language-games of the Nazis.[33]

---

[31] Klemperer, *The Language of the Third Reich*, 15–16.
[32] Ibid., 15.
[33] Ibid., 31.

The repetition involved both semantic shifts and the evacuation of semantic content from specific words. The relevant issue here is that a word that has been emptied of meaning becomes a word that is essentially silenced. It can then be ascribed a new meaning. In our time, this kind of procedure is more immediately familiar in the example of the prevalence of the bureaucratic language of New Public Management in almost all spheres of activity. Such language permeates almost all aspects of public – and thus political – life. 'New words keep turning up, or old ones acquire new specialist meanings, or new combinations are formed which rapidly ossify into stereotypes,' wrote Klemperer.[34] He was talking of atrocity, of course, and there is a difference between Nazism and contemporary political life, no matter how debased we might consider its idiom to be. However, the structural parallels are uncanny, worrying – and they have a political consequence.

The point of the linguistic strategy in all of this – both in the atrocities and in our creeping degradation of our idiom today – is to remove substance from language, to reduce it to, at best a meaningless noise, and at worst a complete silence. Klemperer offers us the example of the word 'heroism', whose meaning shifts incrementally, such that it eventually becomes associated with the wearing of the Nazi uniform. First, the term is repeated in order to infatuate the people with the concept of heroism in its conventional senses, but then 'From the very first day of the war, right through to the demise of the Third Reich, anything and everything heroic on land, at sea and in the air wore a military uniform.'[35]

For Klemperer, the genuine meaning of the word essentially goes underground, where it is sustained by genuine heroes, 'the many brave people in the concentration camps [and] all those people who recklessly committed illegal acts'. This, figuring especially among the Aryan women 'who resisted every pressure to separate from their Jewish husbands', could be set against Nazi 'heroism' where 'there was only a superficial, distorted and poisoned heroism, witness the flashy cups and clinking of medals, witness the bloated words of indulgent adoration'.[36] Nazi 'heroism' is loud, noisy and brash, but it is also meaningless. For the reality of the semantic substance, we need to go to the clandestine realm of silence.

---

[34]Ibid., 29.
[35]Ibid., 4.
[36]Ibid., 7.

The evacuation of semantic content is perceptible in other terms explored by Klemperer. He points out that 'The Third Reich did not invent the words "fanatical" and "fanaticism"', for example; 'it just changed their value and used them more in one day than other epochs used them in years.'[37] The endless repetition of this, like the tendency to describe everything as 'historical', makes claims that are so exaggerated that they are incredible. But the point is that they are not meant to be credible; rather, they are meant simply to be repeated, to be imbibed on such a frequent basis that they become as empty as a slogan, as mindlessly mechanical as a catchphrase. Indeed, superlatives and exaggeration form a solid substratum of Nazi political language, and they do this most effectively when they can reduce discursive language to number. 'The bulletins of the Third Reich ... start off in a superlative mode from the very outset and then, the worse the situation, the more they overdo it, until everything becomes literally measureless.' The consequence is that this twists 'the fundamental quality of military language, its disciplined exactitude, into its very opposite, into fantasy and fairy-tale'.[38]

In the regime, what Klemperer diagnoses is that 'the language of a clique became the language of the people'. It did this by taking control over 'all realms of public and private life: politics, the administration of justice, the economy, the arts, the sciences, schools, sports, the family, playschools and nurseries'.[39] If we ask ourselves how such a thing is possible, the answer is only too easy to discover, in our own day. The contemporary world is one in which the reduced lexicon of commerce and money has infected every aspect of private and public life. All values in our time are 'measured', and the way that they are measured is in terms of individual wealth. What 'counts' as legitimate in our time is only what can be counted in monetary, financial or commercial terms. Thus it is that the language of the market infects justice, say, by debates about the proper tariff for crimes; markets clearly shape every aspect of the commercial economy; the arts have to justify their existence in terms of financial yield; sciences are there in order to promote GDP growth; sports and other competitions are shaped entirely by the financial success that comes with sponsorship as well as with winning competitions; even

---

[37] Ibid., 16.
[38] Ibid., 217.
[39] Ibid., 19.

our erotic relations are reconfigured in terms of investments of our time and energies; education is 'an investment' and so on.

Indeed, all the examples that I have discussed here from Klemperer's study have their contemporary counterpart. Nazi repetition, designed to narrow and reduce as much as possible the possibility of reticence and thinking, has its counterpart in the prevalence of the contemporary political slogan: 'Make America great again'; 'Take back control'; 'For the many, not the few'. In all recent military conflicts, all service personnel – regardless of any specifics – are denoted as 'heroes', and, indeed, almost any action that shows human or humane concern for others, especially in a sentimental fashion, is the action of a hero. Klemperer is relevant here again: 'The jargon of the Third Reich sentimentalizes; that is always suspicious.'[40]

Superlatives and exaggeration abound in all aspects of contemporary politicized life, reaching all the way from our university institutions that exceed excellence (a semantic impossibility but semiotic norm) through to the numerical claims that were made regarding Brexit with its £350 million per week for the NHS. This latter claim, repeatedly made by Boris Johnson, became the centrepiece of his political campaign; and, as if the exposure of this lie was not enough, he has since gone on to exaggerate it even further, to claim that Brexit will yield £438 million per week.[41] The superlative number starts to become measureless. When Klemperer points out that 'The Third Reich itself ... delighted from time to time in the rich sonority of a foreign expression', one immediately hears Boris Johnson dropping his classical allusions or jokily misusing some French or Italian.[42]

When Klemperer comes to consider Mussolini, he notes that the key to his public speech is energy, as he 'literally pumps himself up' and how, 'following brief moments of deflation, he repeatedly generates the impression of utmost energy and tautness'. But the key point is that 'you hear the passionately sermonizing, ritualistic and ecclesiastical intonation of his terse outburst, each consisting of only the shortest of sentences,

---

[40]Ibid., 35.
[41]See report at: https://www.theguardian.com/politics/2018/jan/15/leave-campaigns-350m-claim-was-too-low-says-boris-johnson (accessed 14 March 2018).
[42]Klemperer, *The Language of the Third Reich*, 9; see, for typical Boris Johnson example, the report at: https://www.thesun.co.uk/news/1889723/boris-johnson-joins-forces-with-liam-foxand-declares-support-for-hard-brexit-which-will-liberate-britain-to-champion-free-trade/ (accessed 14 March 2018).

like fragments of a liturgy to which everyone can react emotionally without the least bit of intellectual effort even if they don't understand the meaning – indeed all the more so if they don't.'[43] As with the Nazis, the point here is to prioritize emotion, at the cost of both semantic content and reasoned thinking. The pacing refuses reticence, refuses the question mark.

Combine this with technology, and you have a dangerous recipe. Radio meant that Hitler, Mussolini – and now, in our own moment, virtually any and all politicians – can address people who are not directly present in the audience. 'In addressing itself to everyone', writes Klemperer, political language 'has to make itself comprehensible to everyone and thus become more populist'. This means that the speech must address concrete issues and not intellectual abstractions: deeds, not debatable words. 'The more emotional a speech is, the less it addresses itself to the intellect, the more populist it will be.' Even more chilling is that this – entirely consistent with our own contemporary intolerance of democracies – is utterly recognizable, because 'it will cross the boundary separating populism from demagogy and mass seduction as soon as it moves from ceasing to challenge the intellect to deliberately shutting it off and stupefying it'.[44]

The attack on intellectuals as 'elitists' – partly because they do not necessarily call upon the language of 'the people' – is written right here. That attack is also, of course, an attack upon academic freedom. The intellectual will now be denied the possibility of communicating with others, including the general public. It is – at least structurally – exactly the same as the denial of communication to which Jaspers was subjected. This returns me to the kind of position outlined by Said, but now with a qualification that is of some substance and seriousness. It is true that it is a peculiar responsibility of the academic to speak out, and to speak in a dissenting voice. At the same time, it is equally true that the process of thinking that is involved in informing the free speech that is thus exercised itself takes time. It follows from this that it cannot be expected of the academic that she or he speaks out 'all the time' and on each and every occasion as it arises. Reticence is required; and reticence in turn requires silence, even if only tactful and momentary.

---

[43]Klemperer, *The Language of the Third Reich*, 50–1.
[44]Ibid., 62.

In this regard, we should note that I am making a key distinction between silence and reticence. Reticence simply indicates the simple 'avoidance of saying all one knows', as the dictionary puts it. It means that the academic, in her or his moment of reticence, is retaining the right to think, the right to remain silent, the right to retain the question mark, and the determination to avoid being the 'total citizen', for whom the entirety of life and of speech is politics. The total citizen is precisely what totalitarian regimes, such as Nazism, want; and that is why such regimes must control and narrow the semantic scope of the language. In eviscerating the language of substance, they also eviscerate the human subject and speaker of substance, and of the relative autonomy that allows them to determine the outcomes and actions shaping their own lives. From now on, that subject is nothing more or less than what our own contemporary and supposedly democratic societies call 'human resources'. As Klemperer has it, Hitler always set out physical training as the most important tribute of the individual in his regime, and 'the fear of the thinking man and the hatred of the intellect' are revealed throughout the political language of the Third Reich.[45]

* * *

Timothy Snyder refers to the structure that underpins the operations of this kind of regime as 'anticipatory obedience'. Detailing how some citizens who were not Nazis were caught up in the gradualist anti-Semitic persecutions in Austria in 1938, he notes that the 'anticipatory obedience of Austrians … taught the high Nazi leadership what was possible'. By 1941, with the German invasion of the Soviet Union, 'the SS took the initiative to devise the methods of mass killing without orders to do so. They guessed what their superiors wanted and demonstrated what was possible. It was far more than Hitler had thought.'[46]

Anticipatory obedience – another phrase for silent complicity – enables established political power itself to remain silent: the Nazi regime did not need to tell people what to do – did not need to speak or issue orders – for those people were already anticipating what they 'should' do, and were doing it, to excess. In Nazi Germany, 'it was perhaps ultimately only Goebbels himself who determined what was linguistically

---

[45]Ibid., 3.
[46]Timothy Snyder, *On Tyranny* (Bodley Head, 2017), 19–20.

permissible ... whilst the Führer gradually fell silent, partly in order to affect the pose of a silent deity'.[47] Similarly, Stalin often gave no specific orders but permitted certain hints to gain traction, and the enthusiastic cadres, keen to gain favour in the regime, exceeded what they imagined might be the most extreme actions.[48] Anticipatory obedience operates as complicity with tyrannical authoritarianism, excuses it, exceeds it and extends its workings.

In doing so, anticipatory obedience also claims to work in the service of a certain realism: a pragmatic acceptance of 'how things are'. The questions for a dissenting voice, however, are simple: who determines 'how things are'; how do they guarantee complicity with their views; and who determines how to change how things are? For us, here, what is the role of language in dissenting from whatever passes as the current reality of the world?

Václav Havel understood what is at stake in this predicament. Writing in 1979, he echoes what we saw above from Nietzsche: 'The principle involved ... is that the centre of power is identical with the centre of truth.' Next, following the logic of anti-fundamentalist criticism, the ideology from which Havel would dissent is one that 'offers a ready answer to any question whatsoever', a certainty that gave the ideology a 'certain hypnotic charm'.[49] Under these conditions, the pragmatic acceptance of 'reality' is an acceptance of what the power of the state determines as reality, hypnotizing us, magically charming us into complicity with it. The state entertains no doubt about what constitutes truth and reality, and acceptance of this precludes the possibility of exercising a critical consciousness against such fundamentalism. In exploring this, Havel turns explicitly to a specific sign: a sign that marks a supposed political commitment to a totalitarian regime.

'The manager of a fruit and vegetable shop', he writes, 'places in his window, among the onions and the carrots, the slogan: "Workers of the World, Unite!" Why does he do it?' Havel suggests that this is not an expression of the greengrocer's opinions. Rather, he puts the slogan in his window 'because it has been done that way for years,

---

[47]Klemperer, *The Language of the Third Reich*, 22.
[48]I engage this in more detail, with particular reference to the bureaucratic regime of the contemporary university, in my book *For the University* (Bloomsbury, 2011), 116ff.
[49]Václav Havel et al., *The Power of the Powerless*, ed. John Keane (Routledge, 1985; 2010), 25. The translation is by Paul Wilson.

because everyone does it, and because that is the way it has to be. If he were to refuse, there could be trouble.'[50] Here is a sign that indicates ostensible *assent* to the prevailing powers; yet it is one that does not signal any genuine expression of a statement freely and autonomously made by the greengrocer. The sign 'helps the greengrocer to conceal from himself the low foundations of his obedience, at the same time concealing the low foundations of power', writes Havel.[51] Any 'truth' in the slogan's words is simply a Nietzschean noise that permits peaceful survival.

However, it cannot be completely the case that the sign 'conceals' anything, since Havel, at least, has seen right through how the sign operates: nothing here is concealed at all. The sign really says that, for the purposes of his own sustenance, the greengrocer speaks the dominant language of the state power. This is what we usually call 'being realistic', and the greengrocer's sign is, in this, a prime example of *saying nothing* while ostensibly speaking. It 'speaks truth to power' only in the sense that it allows power to determine the conditions of what passes as true, and stands in peaceful accord with that.

The primary drive in such a social order, which Havel calls a 'post-totalitarian' order, is not directed at preserving the privileges of the ruling class; rather, it is the drive to sustain the system itself, the sustaining of 'a blind *automatism*'. Further, this operates through a manipulation of language: 'government by bureaucracy is called popular government; the working class is enslaved in the name of the working class; the complete degradation of the individual is presented as his or her ultimate liberation. … the arbitrary abuse of power is called observing the legal code' and so on.[52] To survive, individuals 'need not believe all these mystifications, but … they must at least tolerate them in silence' and, insofar as individuals do this, they 'confirm the system, make the system, *are* the system'.[53] So far, then, silent complicity – but complicated by the fact that this silent complicity is articulated in the written slogan.

Alongside the greengrocer, Havel then adds an office worker, who also displays the same slogan in the corridors of her office block. Neither of them actually reads the slogans, but 'their mutual indifference to each

---

[50]Havel et al., *The Power of the Powerless*, 27.
[51]Ibid., 28.
[52]Ibid., 30.
[53]Ibid., 31.

other's slogan is only an illusion: in reality, by exhibiting their slogans, each compels the other to accept the rules of the game and to confirm thereby the power that requires the slogans in the first place. Quite simply, each helps the other to be obedient. ... They are both victims of the system and its instruments.'[54]

Again, so far, silent complicity becomes mutual coercion in complicity, but the point is that these two characters do not read the slogan.

The ascription of complicity is complicated – and even reversed – by the fact that both the greengrocer and the office worker know exactly what is going on with their respective postings of the sign. Neither of them actually subscribes to the words on the sign, and both of them know that fact. They can therefore both 'speak' the sign while at the same time *ignoring* it: that is to say, their attitude effectively *silences the regime* even as the regime appears to be speaking through them.

What is at stake here is the establishment of a massive *décalage* or disengagement between the world of the state (or regime) and the world of everyday life: there is, if you will, a distance between official politics on the one hand and clandestine society on the other hand. For Havel, this helps us to see that one can *dissent* from the official account of reality – that given by the language and signs of the regime and state – while not necessarily being a *dissident* who actively speaks out against the state and regime. For Havel, the 'dissident attitude' arises from the simple fact that a specific individual is trying, existentially, to side-step the lies that shape a totalitarian regime. Dissent here is, effectively, the silencing of the regime by the reduction of its slogans to background – if nonetheless insistent – noise.

The dissident is trying to 'live within the truth', as Havel repeatedly phrases it. Given, however, what we know from Nietzsche, we can now be clearer about the coexistence of two regimes: the official and the clandestine. The official regime lies, and everything in official society and public life is geared towards the service and sustenance of those lies. The consequence is that the official polity becomes a bureaucracy, requiring that the material and historical facts of real life serve and consolidate the abstract and theoretical determinations that the bureaucracy suggests should be the political case. It thus becomes a self-regarding and self-serving system, with its own linguistic norms – 'Workers of the World,

---

[54]Ibid., 36.

Unite!' for example – that permits of *no other language* that would allow for there to be any doubt about its intrinsic logic.

We recognize this in our own time as the language of institutionalized 'management-speak', sometimes referred to just as 'bullshit', and replete with repetitive clichéd vocabulary: dynamic, enterprising, global, challenge, excellence, creativity, rigour, agility, professionalism, pushing envelopes, thinking outside boxes, finding opportunities in crisis, ambition, drive, passion, excitement, innovation, strategy, core strengths, vision, 360-degree feedback, aspiration, priorities, leadership, inclusion, renewal, reform and so on and on in depressing routine. Usually, as we know, in every single instance here, the word used means its opposite. Let one simple example stand for all. In March 2018, the University of Liverpool announced the 'loss' of some 220 academic posts. These people, however, were not going to be 'fired'; rather, they were involved in a 'reshaping' exercise and 'would be allowed to leave'.[55]

Our greengrocer, in Havel's example, has choices. He can mouth those words – 'Workers of the World, Unite!' – and endorse them; he can mouth those words in routine fashion, in that way endlessly rehearsing them so as to evacuate them of any semantic content and reduce them to banal and meaningless cliché; he can choose not to put the sign in his window at all; finally, he can choose to say, aloud, that he dissents from the words on the slogan and can offer a different one. This last choice makes him a dissident, and it is only the first option – endorsement – that would make him fully complicit with the regime. Rehearsing phrases until they become semantically empty cliché permits the regime to continue and protects the greengrocer from harassment. Silence – not showing or uttering the phrase at all – permits him to *dissent*, and get on with his life, but *without yet entering into open dissidence*.

This is the silence in which dissent exists for many people in everyday life, and this is the case not just in totalitarian regimes but also in any and every society that is shaped by bureaucracy – any society that is 'administered' and 'managed'. This includes many so-called democratic societies, and we now often call it just disengagement, or we describe the 'disconnect' between politics and lived realities. As one who dissents in this way – but without assuming the mantle and responsibility of the dissident, with its attendant political risks – our greengrocer can fully

---

[55] See report at: https://www.liverpoolecho.co.uk/news/liverpool-news/more-200-jobs-set-go-14442977#ICID=sharebar_twitter (accessed 22 March 2018).

participate in the unofficial and clandestine society, can be attentive to a *samizdat* culture and can thus weaken the official regime because, although he lets its words exist, he essentially silences it by refusing to take cognizance of those words, preferring those in the samizdat or clandestine culture. Like Cordelia, he can find – and make – a world elsewhere, in a different tongue. And we should remember that when Cordelia does speak out, the effect is world-shattering and devastating for official power.

Essentially, this is a political strategy of weakening the official totalitarian polity by establishing a 'second culture' whose own language will eventually supersede that of official culture and of the regime,[56] constituting thereby a 'parallel polis'. In this, 'silent dissent' simply means that whatever one says has no 'official' existence and cannot be officially recognized; yet such silence is a crucial aspect of listening to and authorizing or legitimizing the clandestine or unofficial speaker, the dissident who does speak out. Living one's life here without endorsing the regime does not indicate that one's silence makes one complicit with it. On the contrary, interestingly – in the light of the foregoing discussion of the musician Furtwängler – one of the key determinants that shaped the formation of Havel's *Charter 77* was, in fact, the defence of an underground rock band, the Plastic People of the Universe, whose members had been politically imprisoned.

Havel demanded that people be able to live in dignity, and he saw this in existential terms. The dignity in question occurs at what he calls a 'pre-political' level, or what I call 'clandestine culture'. Yet, he also holds that, in this demand for dignity, 'every free human act or expression, every attempt to live within the truth, must necessarily appear as a threat to the system and, thus, as something which is political *par excellence*'.[57] Silence can itself become the very foundation – a ground in dissent – for speaking out, dissidence. The very fact of the existence of a *silence that can be heard* poses a threat to official politics. John Cage had the same effect on the established culture of official classical music when he presented *4'33"*.

---

[56] See Havel et al., *The Power of the Powerless*, 78ff. He borrows the term 'second culture' from Václav Benda, who remains a controversial figure. A committed and even obdurate Catholic, who adopted a Manichean position with regard to politics in general, he was also a supporter of Margaret Thatcher and, even more troublingly, of Augusto Pinochet. See obituaries at: http://www.independent.co.uk/arts-entertainment/obituary-vclav-benda-1098683.html and at: https://www.theguardian.com/news/1999/jun/23/guardianobituaries2

[57] Havel et al., *Power of Powerless*, 48.

Political dignity does not make it incumbent on everyone to speak out, always and in all circumstances.

* * *

Our concluding problem in considering reticent silence as we work out the relations of dissent to complicity is this: we already have a group of 'dissenters' who have indeed formed a 'parallel polis'. These are not the oppressed poor; rather they are the already privileged and rich who more and more brazenly refuse to pay their taxes, seeing taxation – and its attendant commitment to a social order – as purely voluntary.[58] Yet the issue is that this parallel polis now operates *as* the world's governing body. They have already forced a coup d'état. They propose what Mark Fisher terms 'capitalist realism' as the only game in town. It is a game of language, and one that narrows the lexicon reducing it entirely to the language of markets and money. As Fisher writes, 'capitalist realism has successfully installed a "business ontology" in which it is *simply obvious* that everything in society, including healthcare and education, should be run as a business.'[59]

My contention is that this 'ontology' is itself dependent upon language. More specifically, it is dependent upon the *contraction* of our vocabulary such that discursive words and the question mark give way to the tyranny of abstraction and definitive number. The events of 2008 have shown that the dominance of this language has entailed disaster for many. The determination of those in power to sustain this language and to disregard any other vocabulary is a symptom of a contemporary tyranny.

There is one institution, however, that has an absolute duty to dissent from this and that exists primarily to expand the range of linguistic possibilities. That institution is the university, founded upon a principle of academic freedom, as Jaspers argued. That freedom is, or should be, the cornerstone of our professional ethics, and the tragedy of our time is that our institutions (though not all academic individuals within the institutions) have forgotten such ethics, preferring to hang a sign in

---

[58] See Fredric Jameson, 'Culture and Finance Capital', *Critical Inquiry*, 24:1 (1997), 247: 'The guiding thread of all contemporary politics seems much easier to grasp, that the rich want their taxes lowered.'

[59] Mark Fisher, *Capitalist Realism* (Zero Books, Winchester, 2009), 17. See also David Marquand, *Mammon's Kingdom* (Penguin, 2015), 96–110, on how this applies to the marketization of higher education.

their window and to endorse enthusiastically its content. That sign says that knowledge is a private matter, available like any other commodity for negotiated sale, in a market that takes acquisitive individualism and greed for granted as the fundamental principles governing all human relations; and the point of the university in such conditions is – and can only be – to serve such 'capitalist realism'.

Those within the university institution who remain silent in the face of this have forgotten their responsibility, as the critical consciousness of their society, to expand the range of human possibilities and the range of what can be thought. If we fail in this, we will find ourselves in the predicament faced by Jaspers, and the best we can hope for is to accept our political guilt. We need not fail; we must not fail.

On 28 October 1964, interviewed by Günter Gaus, Hannah Arendt revealed her deep intimacy with the German language. Gaus asks her what she misses from pre-Hitler Europe, and she replies, 'The Europe of the pre-Hitler period? I do not long for that, I can tell you. What remains? The language remains.' As she glosses this, she argues that 'It wasn't the German language that went crazy'.[60] That claim is wrong, as Klemperer's careful record shows, and the tragedy resulted from the fact that the *intentions* of the people identified with the national crazed language, and they thus became complicit with the craziness.

In the end, 'what remains' for us is, indeed, the language. Like the poets, like the musicians, we academics have a responsibility to it and to the international community who need the language to be open, exploratory, unconstrained. Dissent must speak, and it is incumbent on us, in the university, to find or invent a language that is adequate to extending the future and sustaining the species.

---

[60] Arendt, *Essays in Understanding*, 13.

SELECT BIBLIOGRAPHY

Note: Place of publication is London unless otherwise noted.

Adorno, Theodor, *The Jargon of Authenticity*, trans. Knut Tarkowski and Frederic Will (Northwestern University Press, Evanston, 1973).
Adorno, Theodor, *Notes to Literature*, vol. 1, ed. Rolf Tiedemann (trans. Shierry Weber Nicholsen; Columbia University Press, New York, 1991).
Adorno, Theodor, *Notes to Literature*, vol. 2, ed. Rolf Tiedemann (trans. Shierry Weber Nicholsen; Columbia University Press, New York, 1992).
Adorno, Theodor, *Prisms* (trans. Samuel and Shierry Weber; MIT Press, Cambridge, MA, 1983).
Ali, Tariq, *The Extreme Centre* (Verso, 2015).
Arendt, Hannah, *Between Past and Future* (Penguin, 2006).
Arendt, Hannah, *Crises of the Republic* (Harcourt, New York, 1972).
Arendt, Hannah, *Essays in Understanding, 1930–1954: Formation, Exile, and Totalitarianism*, ed. Jerome Kohn (Schocken Books, New York, 1994).
Arendt, Hannah, *Responsibility and Judgment*, ed. Jerome Kohn (Schocken Books, New York, 2003).
Ash, Timothy Garton, *Free Speech* (Atlantic Books, 2017).
Badiou, Alain, *Saint Paul: La fondation de l'universalisme* (Presses Universitaires de France, Paris, 1997).
Ball, James, *Post-Truth* (Biteback, 2017).
Barnes, Julian, *The Only Story* (Jonathan Cape, 2018).
Beckett, Samuel, *Molloy, Malone Dies, The Unnamable* (John Calder, 1959; repr. 1976).
Benyon, Huw, *Digging Deeper: Issues in the Miners' Strike* (Verso, 1985).
Blumenberg, Hans, *The Legitimacy of the Modern Age* (1966; trans. Robert M. Wallace; MIT Press, Cambridge, MA, 1983).
Braasch, John W., 'Antony Eden's (Lord Avon) Biliary Tract Saga', *Annals of Surgery*, 238:5 (November 2003), 772–5.
Brownstein, Ronald, *The Second Civil War: How Extreme Partisanship Has Paralyzed Washington and Polarized America* (Penguin, 2007).
Campbell, Gordon, *The Story of the King James Version, 1611–2011* (Oxford University Press, 2010).
Cannadine, David, *Margaret Thatcher: A Life and Legacy* (Oxford University Press, 2017).

Churchill, Winston, *A History of the English-Speaking Peoples, Vol. 1: The Birth of Britain* (Cassell and Company, 1956).
Cioran, E.M., *L'Inconvénient d'être né* (nrf, Gallimard, Paris, 1973).
Clausewitz, Carl von, *On War*, ed. Anatol Rapoport (trans. J.J. Graham; Penguin, 1982).
Collini, Stefan, *That's Offensive* (Seagull Books, Kolkata, 2011).
Collins, Philip, *When They Go Low, We Go High* (4th Estate, 2017).
Crystal, David, *English as a Global Language* (2nd edn; Cambridge University Press, 2003).
D'Ancona, Matthew, *Post-Truth* (Ebury Press, 2017).
Davidson, Donald, *Inquiries into Truth and Interpretation* (Oxford University Press, 1984).
Davis, Evan, *Post Truth* (Little, Brown, 2017).
Dickens, Charles, *Hard Times* (1854; Penguin, 1977).
Docherty, Thomas, 'Brexit: Thinking and Resistance', in Robert Eaglestone (ed.), *Brexit and Literature* (Routledge, 2018).
Docherty, Thomas, *Complicity* (Rowman & Littlefield, New York, 2016).
Docherty, Thomas, *Criticism and Modernity* (Oxford University Press, 1999).
Docherty, Thomas, *The New Treason of the Intellectuals* (Manchester University Press, 2018).
Dryden, John, *The Poems and Fables of John Dryden*, ed. James Kinsley (Oxford University Press, 1970).
English, Richard, *Armed Struggle: The History of the IRA* (Oxford University Press, 2004).
Fisher, Mark, *Capitalist Realism* (Zero Books, Winchester, 2009).
Foot, Michael, *Byron and the Bomb* (University College Cardiff Press, Cardiff, 1983).
Frye, Northrop, *The Anatomy of Criticism* (Princeton University Press, 1957).
Furedi, Frank, *What's Happened to the University?* (Routledge, 2017).
Gadamer, Hans-Georg, *Dialogue and Dialectic* (trans. P. Christopher Smith; Yale University Press, 1980).
Gadamer, Hans-Georg, *Praise of Theory* (1983; trans. Chris Dawson; Yale University Press, 1998).
Georgiadou, Maria, *Constanti Carathéodory: Mathematics and Politics in Turbulent Times* (Springer-Verlag, Berlin, Heidelberg, New York, 2004).
Gessen, Masha, 'The Autocrat's Language', *NYR Daily: New York Review of Books*, 13 May 2017.
Gessen, Masha, *The Man without a Face: The Unlikely Rise of Vladimir Putin* (Granta, 2012).
Gilbert, Martin, *Churchill: A Life* (Minerva, 1992).
Goodlad, Graham, *Thatcher* (Routledge, 2016).
Gregor, Neil, 'Beethoven, Bayreuth and the Origins of the Federal Republic of Germany', *The English Historical Review*, 126:521 (August 2011), 845.
Habermas, Jürgen, *Legitimation Crisis* (trans. Thomas McCarthy; Heinemann, 1986).

Havel, Václav et al., *The Power of the Powerless*, ed. John Keane (1985; trans. Paul Wilson; Routledge, 2010).
Heaney, Seamus, *The Government of the Tongue* (Faber and Faber, 1988).
Hegel, G.W.F., *Phenomenology of Spirit* (trans. A.V. Miller; Oxford University Press, 1999).
Hill, Christopher, *Milton and the English Revolution* (Faber and Faber, 1979).
Hutton, Christopher M., *Linguistics and the Third Reich: Mother-Tongue Fascism, Race and the Science of Language* (Routledge, 1999).
Jacobson, Howard, 'Point of View', *The Guardian: Review*, 8 April 2017.
Jacobson, Howard, *Pussy* (Jonathan Cape, 2017).
James, C.L.R., *Beyond a Boundary* (1963; repr. 5-Star, 2000).
James, C.L.R., *The C.L.R. James Reader*, ed. Anna Grimshaw (Blackwell, Oxford, 1993).
Jameson, Fredric, 'Culture and Finance Capital', *Critical Inquiry*, 24:1 (1997), 247.
Jaspers, Karl, *The Idea of the University*, ed. Karl W. Deutsch, with Preface by O.L. Zangwill (trans. H.A.T. Reiche and H.F. Vanderschmidt; Peter Owen, 1960).
Jaspers, Karl, *The Question of German Guilt* (1947; trans. E.B. Ashton; Capricorn Books, 1961).
Jenkins, Roy, *Churchill* (Macmillan, 2001).
Johnson, Samuel, *Lives of the Poets* (Oxford University Press, 1968).
Kay, John, 'Keynes Was Half Right about the Facts', *Financial Times*, 4 August 2015.
Keats, John, *Poetical Works*, ed. H.W. Garrod (Oxford University Press, 1976).
Kermode, Frank, *The Genesis of Secrecy* (Harvard University Press, Cambridge, MA, 1979).
Kermode, Frank, *The Sense of an Ending* (Oxford University Press, 1966).
Kipling, Rudyard, *Selected Poems* (Penguin, 1977).
Klemperer, Viktor, *The Language of the Third Reich: LTI – Lingua Tertii Imperii* (1957; trans. Martin Brady; Athlone Press, 2000).
Kołakowski, Leszek, *Freedom, Fame, Lying and Betrayal: Essays on Everyday Life* (trans. Agnieszka Kołakowska; Penguin, 1999).
Lasch, Christopher, *The Culture of Narcissism* (Norton, New York, 1979).
Laws, David, *Coalition* (Biteback, 2016).
Lepschy, Giulio, 'Mother Tongues and Literary Languages', *Modern Language Review*, 96:4 (2001), xlviii.
Levitsky, Steven and Daniel Ziblatt, *How Democracies Die* (Viking, 2018).
Light, Alison, *Common People* (Penguin, 2015).
Lindholm, Charles, *Culture and Authenticity* (Blackwell, Oxford, 2008).
MacCulloch, Diarmaid, 'How Good Is It?', *London Review of Books*, 33:3 (3 February 2011), 20–2.
Marquand, David, *Mammon's Kingdom* (Penguin, 2015).
McGuinness, Brian, *Wittgenstein: A Life* (Duckworth, 1988).
McLuhan, Marshall, *Understanding Media* (Routledge and Kegan Paul, 1954).

Miller, J. Hillis, *Speech Acts in Literature* (Stanford University Press, 2001).
Milne, Seumas, *The Enemy Within* (4th edn; Verso, 2014).
Milton, John, *Poems*, ed. B.A. Wright (J.M. Dent, 1976).
Monk, Ray, *Wittgenstein: The Duty of Genius* (Vintage, 1991).
Montaigne, Michel de, 'Des menteurs', in *Essais: Livre 1* (Garnier-Flammarion, Paris, 1969).
Montaigne, Michel de, 'On liars', in *Essays*, ed. J.M. Cohen (trans. J.M. Cohen; Penguin, 1958; repr. 1973).
Moore, Charles, *Margaret Thatcher: Authorized Biography, Vol. 1: Not for Turning* (Allen Lane, 2013).
Newbolt, Henry et al., *The Teaching of English in England: Being the report of the departmental committee appointed by the President of the Board of Education to inquire into the position of English in the educational system of England* (HMSO, 1921).
Nietzsche, Friedrich, *The Nietzsche Reader*, eds. Keith Ansell Pearson and Duncan Large (Blackwell, Oxford, 2006).
O'Driscoll, Dennis, *Stepping Stones: Interviews with Seamus Heaney* (Faber and Faber, 2008).
Oliver, Craig, *Unleashing Demons* (Hodder, 2017).
Orwell, George, *Collected Essays, Journalism and Letters, Vol. II: My Country Right or Left, 1940–43*, eds. Sonia Orwell and Ian Angus (Secker and Warburg, 1968).
Orwell, George, *Inside the Whale* (Penguin, 1972).
Overy, Richard, *Goering: Hitler's Iron Knight* (1984; new edn; I.B. Tauris, 2012).
Powell, Enoch, *Freedom and Reality* (B.T. Batsford, 1969).
Rees, Laurence, *The Holocaust* (Penguin, 2017).
Revol, Michel, 'De Flanby à Pépère', *Le Point*, 10 avril 2013.
Richards, Steve, 'All Shook Up', *Prospect*, 23 July 2017.
Roberts, Andrew, *A History of the English-Speaking Peoples since 1900* (Phoenix, 2007).
Rochelau, Matt, 'Trump's Cabinet Picks', *The Boston Globe*, 20 December 2016.
Roncigli, Audrey, 'Wilhelm Furtwängler, une illusion face au nazisme', *Guerres mondiales et conflits contemporains*, 227 (juillet 2007), 75–93.
Said, Edward, *Representations of the Intellectual* (Vintage, 1994).
Said, Edward, *The World, the Text, the Critic* (Faber and Faber, 1984).
Sampson, George, *English for the English* (Cambridge University Press, 1970).
Sands, Philippe, *East West Street* (Weidenfeld & Nicolson, 2016).
Sen, Amartya, *Identity and Violence* (Penguin, 2006).
Shaw, George Bernard, *Pygmalion* (1913; Penguin, 2000).
Shipman, Tim, *All Out War* (William Collins, 2017).
Snyder, Timothy, *On Tyranny* (Bodley Head, 2017).
Stonebridge, Lyndsey, *Placeless People: Writing, Rights and Refugees* (Oxford University Press, 2018).
Sugirtharajah, R.S., 'Postcolonial Notes on the King James Bible', in Hannibal Hamlin and Norman W. Jones (eds), *The King James Bible after 400 Years* (Cambridge University Press, 2010).

Swift, Jonathan, *Gulliver's Travels and Other Writings*, ed. Louis A. Landa (Oxford University Press, 1976).
Thompson, Mark, *Enough Said: What's Gone Wrong with the Language of Politics* (Bodley Head, 2016).
Westall, Claire, 'What They Knew of Nation and Empire: Kipling and C.L.R. James', in Caroline Rooney and Kaori Nagai (eds), *Kipling and Beyond* (Palgrave Macmilan, 2010), 165–84.
Westen, Drew, *Self and Society: Narcissism, Collectivism and the Development of Morals* (Cambridge University Press, 2009).
Wittgenstein, Ludwig, *Philosophical Investigations* (trans. G.E.M. Anscombe; Basil Blackwell, Oxford, 1958).
Wittgenstein, Ludwig, *Tractatus Logico-Philosophicus* (trans. C.K. Ogden; bilingual edn; Routledge, 1992).
Wodehouse, P.G., *The Luck of the Bodkins* (1935; repr. Arrow Books, 2008).
Woolf, Virginia, *Selected Essays*, ed. David Bradshaw (Oxford University Press, 2008).
Young, Hugo, *One of Us* (rev. edn; Pan Books, 1991).
Young, J.W., 'Churchill, the Russians and the Western Alliance: The Three-Power Conference at Bermuda, December 1953', *The English Historical Review*, 101:401 (October 1986), 889–912.
Zeto, Salena, 'Taking Trump Seriously, Not Literally', *Atlantic*, 23 September 2016.
Žižek, Slavoj, *Violence* (Profile Books, 2009).

INDEX

Acland, Francis 41
Adams, John 165–6
Adorno, Theodor 1–2, 4–5, 64–6, 177 n.11
Aeschylus 80
Anderson, Benedict 120
Arendt, Hannah 65, 116–17, 180, 196, 203 n.15, 213–14, 227
Aristotle 49, 159
Arnold, Matthew 86
Ash, Timothy Garton 165, 197
Attlee, Clement 166
Austin, J.L. 143–4
Aylmer, John 9–10, 94

Badiou, Alain 6, 115–16, 167
Baker, Kenneth 199–201
Ball, James 165
Barnes, Julian 45 n.22
Beckett, Samuel 109–10
Bede 90
Beesley, Ian 37
Beethoven, Ludwig van 204–6
Bell, Steve 6
Benda, Julien 196
Benda, Václav 225 n.56
Benjamin, Walter 26
Berlusconi, Silvio 6, 166–8
Bevan, Aneurin (Nye) 166, 178
Biggar, Nigel 26 n.27
Blair, Tony 95–7, 99–102, 106–7, 110–11, 184
Blumenberg, Hans 159
Brodsky, Joseph 2–3
Bush, George W. 13–14, 102, 110–11

Cable, Vince 52
Cage, John 225
Cameron, David 6, 37 n.4, 44
Campbell, Alastair 184
Campbell, Gordon 90
Carroll, Lewis 56–7, 61
Carroll, Robert 9
Carter, Jimmy 163, 164 n.30
Celan, Paul 53
Chamberlain, Neville 128
Chilcot, John 99, 101, 184
Churchill, Winston 10, 16–27, 29–30, 47–8, 70–1, 76, 81–2, 89, 166, 209
Cicero 21, 71
Cioran, E.M. 202
Clarke, Kenneth 56–7
Clausewitz, Carl von 3, 7, 171–2
Clegg, Nick 6
Clinton, Bill 181–3
Clinton, Hillary 149, 168, 170
Conway, Kellyanne 11, 163
Corbyn, Jeremy 177–9
Cox, Jo 147–8, 192, 213 n.27
Crystal, David 42–3, 47–8

Daily Mail 79–80, 85, 212–13
Daily Mirror 141
Davidson, Donald 109–10
Derrida, Jacques 106
DeVos, Betsy 30–1
Dickens, Charles 112–15, 117
Disraeli, Benjamin 20–1, 24, 166, 179
Dryden, John 186–7
Dulles, John Foster 17–18
Dylan, Bob 40

Ecclestone, Kathryn   145–6
Eden, Anthony   17
Eisenhower, Dwight   17–19, 21
Eliot, T.S.   126
Erdoğan, Recep Tayyip   57, 167, 174, 199
Evans, Richard   81 n.10

Farage, Nigel   28–31, 43, 77–8, 85, 126, 127 n.46, 134, 150, 188–9
Favreau, Jon   14
Fielding, Leslie   67–9, 77, 88
Fisher, Herbert   41–2, 89
Fisher, Mark   226
Foot, Michael   178–9
Freedman, Adam   152 n.16
Freud, Clement   166
Friedman, Milton   105
Frye, Northrop   75 n.7
Furedi, Frank   144–6
Furtwängler, Wilhelm   204–6, 208, 210, 213, 215, 225

Gadamer, Hans-Georg   65–6, 77
Gandlevsky, Sergei   61
Gardner, Bill   38
Gaus, Gunther   65, 227
Gessen, Masha   58–9, 61
Gianforte, Greg   149–51
Giddens, Anthony   106
Gingrich, Newt   148
Giuliani, Rudy   11–12
Gorbachev, Mikhail   58–9
Göring, Hermann   83–4, 180
Gove, Michael   37 n.4, 84–6
Gregor, Neil   205
Gröning, Oskar   203 n.16
Guardian   149–50

Habermas, Jürgen   100, 106
Hartley, L.P.   65
Harwood, Ronald   205–6, 210
Havel, Václav   221–5
Hayek, F.A.   105
Hayes, Dennis   145–6
Healey, Dennis   6–7

Heaney, Seamus   2–3, 43 n.17, 208, 215
Heath, Ted   46, 67, 140
Heidegger, Martin   194, 199, 201
Herbert, George   131
Hill, Christopher   93
Hindemith, Paul   5
Hitchens, Christopher   147
Hitler, Adolf   72, 74, 76–80, 82–3, 128, 130, 140, 160, 205, 208, 212, 219–21, 227
Hollande, François   79, 177
Hooper, Tom   69
Howe, Geoffrey   6–7
Hussein, Saddam   96
Hutton, Christopher M.   51
Huxley, Aldous   100

Ianucci, Armando   183–4

Jacobs, Ben   149–50
Jacobson, Howard   16, 28, 33–4
James, Clive   166
James, C.L.R.   125–6
Jameson, Fredric   226 n.58
Jaspers, Gertrud   194–5
Jaspers, Karl   194–8, 202–4, 206, 208, 210, 213, 215, 219, 226–7
Jefferson, Thomas   152, 166
Johnson, Boris   6, 46–7, 79–86, 118, 166–7, 218
Johnson, Samuel   185–6
Joyce, James   63

Kay, John   98
Keats, John   5
Kelly, Megyn   157
Kennedy, John F.   61
Kermode, Frank   98, 101–2, 114, 124
Keynes, John Maynard   98, 101
Kipling, Rudyard   124–6
Klemperer, Viktor   83, 85–6, 212, 215–20, 227
Kołakowski, Leszek   102–3
Korngold, Erik Wolfgang   5
Krieck, Ernst   195

Lenin, V.I.   90
Lepschy, Giulio   52–3
Levitsky, Steven   148–9
Light, Alison   127 n.47
Lindholm, Charles   156
Lloyd George, David   166
Love, Gary   73
Lynn, Vera   82
Lyotard, Jean-François   106

McCain, John   13
McCarthy, Joseph   17
MacCulloch, Diarmaid   91
McGahey, Mick   140
McGill, Donald   81
McLuhan, Marshall   10
Mair, Thomas   147–8, 192
Major, John   122–4, 126, 128, 189
Mao Tse-Tung   155, 160, 169
Marx, Karl   105–6
May, Theresa   44, 46, 52–7, 61, 67, 82, 85, 91
Mayer, René   18–19
Merkel, Angela   6, 167
Miliband, Ed   71 n.3
Miller, Gina   57 n.41
Miller, Jonathan   38
Milton, John   9, 90, 93–4, 197 n.9
Monk, Ray   5–6
Montaigne, Michel de   95–6, 98–9, 101, 104
Monty Python   106
Moore Suzanne   36
Mozart, Wolfgang Amadeus   76
Mueller, Robert   11
Mussolini, Benito   77, 155–6, 218–19

National Rifle Association   153–5, 157, 160, 192–3
Newbolt, Henry   69–70, 73, 78, 86–90, 123, 125, 127
Nietzsche, Friedrich   102–3, 108, 132, 207–8, 221–3
Nixon, Richard   11, 163

Obama, Barack   13–17
Observer   142
Odey, Crispin   188
Oliver, Craig   85
Orbán, Viktor   174, 191–2, 199, 207
Orwell, George   7, 14, 61–3, 66, 81, 116–17, 123, 126–31
Overy, Richard   84

Paisley, Ian   166
Parris, Matthew   84–5
Peto, Basil   41–2, 89
Plato   100
Powell, Enoch   10, 43–7, 59, 85, 120–7, 129–31, 147
Prickett, Stephen   9
Putin, Vladimir   6, 28, 58–60, 158, 174

Quiller-Couch, Arthur   89

Rafsky, Bob   181–3
Ravel, Maurice   5
Rawnsley, Andrew   184
Reagan, Ronald   105, 164, 166
Reece, Gordon   37
Rees-Mogg, Jacob   36–7, 134, 189
Richards, Steve   106–7
Roberts, Andrew   25–30, 39, 47
Rorty, Richard   106
Rose, Jacqueline   211
Rubio, Marco   60, 188

Said, Edward   201–2, 211, 219
Sampson, George   69–70, 73, 78, 123, 127
Samuelson, Paul   98, 101
Sands, Philippe   195 n.5
Sarkozy, Nicolas   6, 167, 177
Saussure, Ferdinand de   139
Scargill, Arthur   140–1
Schoenberg, Arnold   5
Sen, Amartya   168–71, 174, 183
Shakespeare, William   8–9, 49–50, 74–8, 95, 101–2, 108–9, 123, 125, 128, 165, 198, 209–10, 225

Shaw, George Bernard   87–8
Shipman, Tim   183
Simms, Brendan   82
Siwertz, Sigfrid   20–1, 23–4
Snyder, Timothy   220
Soros, George   199
Spicer, Sean   11, 163
Stalin, Joseph   17–19, 74, 160, 169, 221
Stonebridge, Lyndsey   116–17
Sugirtharajah, R.S.   92–3
Swift, Jonathan   99, 178

Telegraph   212-12
Thatcher, Margaret   6, 37–8, 46 n.25, 105, 119 n.28, 140–1, 166, 168, 172–3, 225 n.56
Thompson, Mark   16
Todd, Chuck   11
Trump, Donald   3, 6, 11–12, 14, 16, 27–31, 33–4, 47–9, 56, 58, 60–3, 66, 77, 116, 118, 137–9, 142–3, 149–50, 154, 156–7, 160, 163–4, 167–70, 174, 178–80, 183, 188, 193, 213–14
Tsvetaeva, Marina   53

Vidal, Gore   166
Virgil   43

Wagner, Richard   204–6
Weil, Simone   116
Westen, Drew   173, 181
Wittgenstein, Ludwig   4–5, 50, 207
Wittgenstein, Paul   4–5
Wodehouse, P.G.   33–4, 36, 39, 67
Woolf, Virginia   62–3, 66
Wyclif, John   93–4

Xi Jinping   174

Young, J.W.   20
Young, Toby   39–41

Zeto, Salena   143 n.4
Ziblatt, Daniel   148–9

www.ingramcontent.com/pod-product-compliance
Ingram Content Group UK Ltd.
Pitfield, Milton Keynes, MK11 3LW, UK
UKHW021900220326
469204UK00008B/99